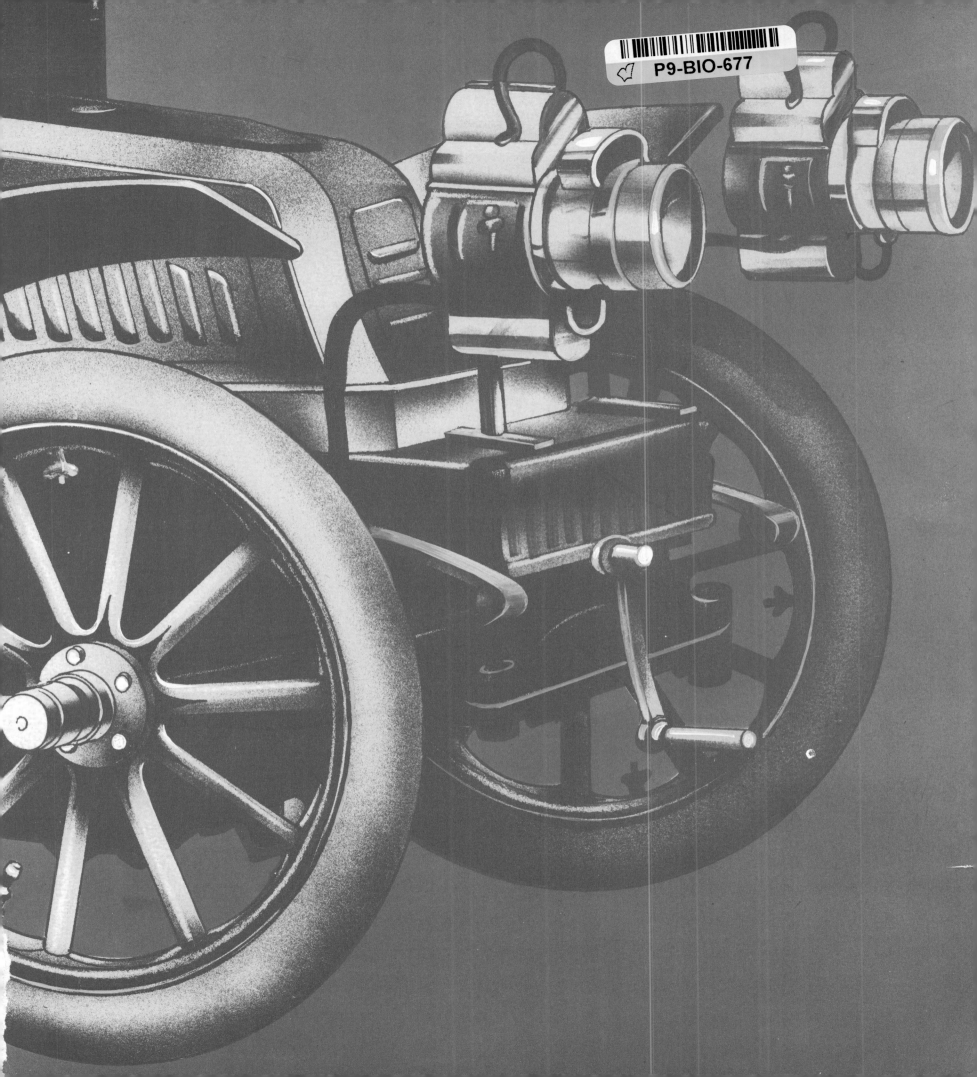

P9-BIO-677

CARS
1886-1930

CARS
1886-1930

G.N. Georgano

BEEKMAN HOUSE
New York

Copyright © 1985 by AB Nordbok, Gothenburg, Sweden.

All rights reserved.

This 1985 edition is published by Beekman House, distributed by Crown Publishers Inc.

Typeset by Concept Communications, England.

Color reproduction by Reproman, Gothenburg.

Printed in Italy.

Library of Congress Cataloging in Publication Data

Georgano, G. N.
   Cars, 1886 – 1930.

   1. Automobiles—History. I. Title.
TL15.G35   1985   629.2'222'09   85-6144
ISBN 0-517-48073-5

CARS 1886–1930 has been originated, designed, and produced by AB Nordbok, Gothenburg, Sweden, in close collaboration with the author and photographers.

Editor: Jon van Leuven.

Designer: Roland Thorbjörnsson.

Design assistant: Lena Wennström.

Chief illustrator: Syed Mumtaz Ahmad.

Artwork: Anders Engström, Munir Lotia, Lennart Molin, Holger Rosenblad, Ulf Söderqvist.

Nordbok would like to express its sincere thanks to Björn-Eric Lindh for advice. The following sources have also been of particular assistance for illustration reference material from which new artwork has been produced by the Nordbok studios: *Automotor Journal* (pages 33, 42, 48, 56, 72 bottom, 86 top); *Automobile Quarterly* (page 57); *Motorcar Journal* (pages 28, 80 top, 84 bottom); *National Motor Museum* (pages 164–165); *Profile* (pages 194–197); *The Automobile* (page 185); *The Car* (pages 20, 68 top, 181 top).

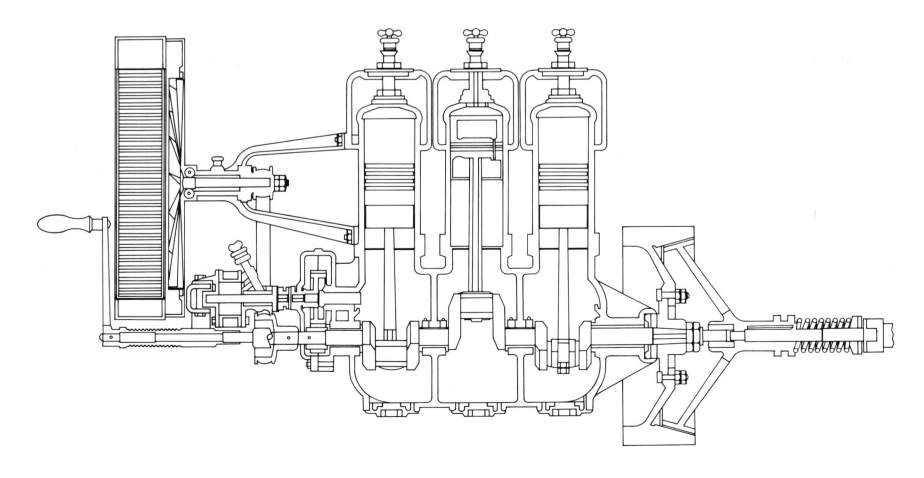

Photography

Neill Bruce: Pages 15 bottom, 52, 53, 74, 77 top and bottom right, 83, 93 top, 98, 102–103, 106, 112–117, 119, 137, 139, 144, 145, 147, 154, 158–160.

Wieslaw Fusaro: Page 168.

G.N. Georgano: Pages 18 bottom, 32 top, 34 top, 36, 41 bottom, 58 top and centre, 59 bottom, 60 top, 63, 70, 71 bottom, 75, 76 bottom, 90, 93 bottom, 97, 107 top, 111, 129, 140, 150–153, 176, 188–189, 198.

Peter Haventon: Pages 47, 81 top, 105, 121, 131, 155 bottom, 167, 169, 170, 174, 200 top.

Reinhard Lintelmann: Pages 148, 149.

Museum do Automovel Do Caramulo (Portugal): Page 18 top.

National Motor Museum (Beaulieu): Pages 15 top, 19, 24 bottom, 208, 209, 221–223.

Hans-Otto Neubauer Collection: Pages 85, 172 bottom.

Peter Roberts Collection: Pages 224, 225.

Science Museum (London): Page 71 top.

B.H. Vanderveen: page 172 top.

Nicky Wright: Pages 14, 31, 37, 41 top, 44–45, 50, 54, 62, 64, 65 right, 66, 67 bottom, 69, 72 top, 73, 77 bottom left, 80 bottom, 81 bottom, 82, 99, 100–101, 107 bottom, 109, 118, 120, 122–124, 128, 130, 132–135, 138, 141, 143, 151, 155 top, 166, 175, 177–180, 183, 184, 192–193, 199, 200 bottom, 201–205.

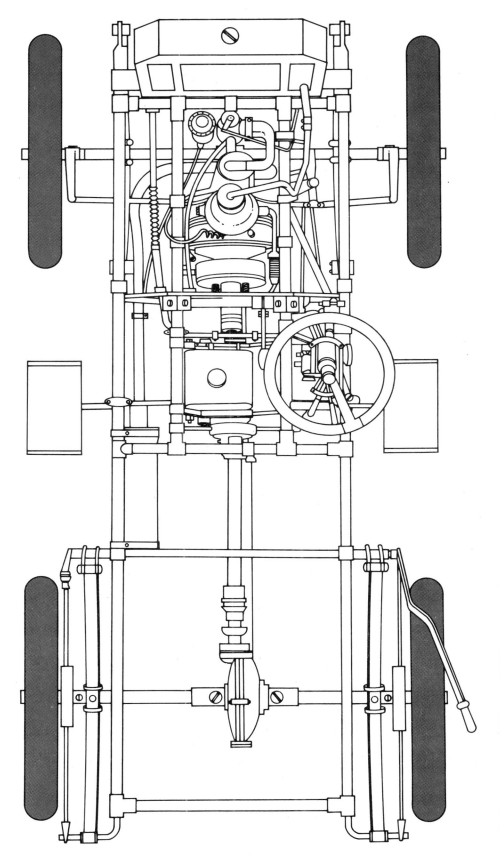

Nordbok expresses gratitude to all the owners who allowed their cars to be photographed for this book. Among them are: Philip Armour, Norman Ball, R.M.L. Biles, Peter Boyland, Sir John Briscoe, Mike Bullett, Roger Collings, Nigel Dawes, Terry Dickie, Michael Draper, Bernard Ducker, Brian Garner, Bryan Goodman, C. Hamilton-Gould, Oliver Gray, C.W.P. Hampton, B. Harding, A.R. Hartwell, George Hartwell, George Hazell, J.H. Henke, M. Jeddere-Fisher, John Lawson, Reginald Long, Tony Mitchell, John Moore, National Motor Museum, Olds Garage Ltd, J.M.A. Patterson, R. Pilkington, Peter Redman, Ron Sant, A. Simmons, R.C. Skerman, Tony Symons, Tom Threlfall, Totnes Motor Museum, Stephen Weld, Nick Whittaker.

CONTENTS

PREFACE

Unlike other books in this series, the present volume deals with the birth of one of the primary features of modern life—and with its growth from a few isolated experiments to a worldwide activity, ranging from frivolous sport to serious business. By the year 1930 in the United States, for example, the automobile industry and its tributaries of steel, rubber, and glass employed three out of ten people, while the total value of vehicles sold was more than two billion dollars. Less than fifty years earlier, not a single car had been sold to a customer, and most of the world's population had no idea that such a thing existed, or might exist. Thus, the period under consideration here tells an extraordinary story, unparalleled by any other mode of transport. Trains, ships, and aircraft also have enthusiastic followers, but they are not everyday household possessions, and an interest in their older models is necessarily by way of books and museums, rather than through personal ownership.

Owning a car has always been an intensely personal matter, and never more so than in the pioneer days, when the motorist not only drove and maintained his car, but designed and built it as well. Men like Karl Benz, Gottlieb Daimler, Henry Ford, Alexander Winton, and the Duryea brothers were as absorbed in their cars as was any Edison, Marconi, or Pasteur in experimental work. The age of those true, independent pathblazers ended in about 1896, when manufacture was already established at factories such as Benz & Co. in Mannheim, or Panhard et Levassor in Paris. Nevertheless, there was obviously an overlap, and second-generation inventors like Louis Renault were building their first prototypes by hand in the same year—1898—that the Benz factory turned out 572 cars.

The various periods in early automobile history cannot be defined to everyone's satisfaction, yet the major old-car clubs have followed a certain logic. In 1927, cars aged twenty-one years or more were allowed to participate in the first commemoration of the 1896 Emancipation Run from London to Brighton, England. In 1929, this age limit became twenty-five years, bringing the date of the youngest car to 1904, a rule which has been kept ever since. It makes sense, for by the end of 1904 car design had largely settled down to a pattern: a front-mounted vertical engine, driving through a sliding pinion gearbox to a live rear axle on smaller cars, or retaining chain drive on many heavier vehicles. The wooden frame was mostly a thing of the past, as was the automatic inlet valve. One need only look at the cars' line-up after a Brighton Run to see the great diversity of engine positions, ignitions, final drives, and so on, that prevailed in what is now called the Veteran Period. Therefore, 1904 is as good a date as any to mark the transition to the next era, which in Great Britain is commonly called the Edwardian. The latter runs from 1905 to 1918, although King Edward VII actually reigned from 1901 to 1910.

The cars described in this book were the first to attract the fascination of collectors. Their movement began in Great Britain, whose Veteran Car Club, founded in 1930, was initially open only to owners of pre-1905 cars. But in 1943, it was decided to extend the period to 1916 (later 1918), in order to save the many worthwhile cars made between these dates. Such cars became known as the Edwardians. According to current classification by the *Fédération Internationale des Véhicules Anciens* (association of veteran car clubs), pre-1905 cars are called Antiques, and 1905–18 cars are termed Veterans.

Meanwhile, another club had been formed with the object of holding competitions among the better-quality cars of the 1920s. Known as the Vintage Sports Car Club, this was started in 1934, when the youngest car for which it catered was only four years old. Still, its group of enthusiasts felt that profound changes had taken place, and that an appeal should be made to "the many discriminating motorists who believe that the motorcar of the twenties was far superior to the average product of the early thirties."

Those feelings were prompted by a very small number of cars which were close to the hearts of British enthusiasts, and which had undoubtedly declined from the hairy-chested image of the 1920s, if not faded away altogether. They included the Bentleys, the Vauxhall 30/98, the twin-camshaft Sunbeam, and the 12/50 Alvis, all destined to become staples of the V.S.C.C. Another point that endeared them to its largely young and impecunious membership was their price. A 1925 3-litre Bentley could be had for around £100 in 1935, whereas a new 3.5-litre Bentley built by Rolls-Royce would have cost the newcomer £1,100 for a chassis alone, and some £1,400 for a complete car, assuming that he wanted it.

Apart from sports cars, the year 1930 was rather insignificant in itself. However, it fell in the middle of a period—about 1926 to 1934—when enormous changes occurred in car design and manufacture. At this time, the closed body became the accepted style everywhere; in America, 90% of cars sold in 1919 were open, and 90% were closed in 1929. Front-wheel brakes and lower-pressure tyres became universal, and gear-changing became painless, with synchromesh or the Wilson pre-selector gearbox. Engines tended to move forward in the frame, giving greater passenger space, but to the detriment of the car's appearance in most cases. The Depression, which also struck in the middle of this period, accelerated the elimination of medium-size makes, although these would probably have disappeared anyway during the 1930s. One cannot imagine that even roaring prosperity would have saved Star or Swift in Britain, De Dion Bouton or Hurtu in France, Gardner or Locomobile in the United States.

The car-collecting movement soon spread to other countries, particularly in the English-speaking world. The Veteran Car Club of South Australia was formed in February 1934; the Antique Automobile Club of America, that nation's first, in November 1935; and the Horseless Carriage Club of America, on its west coast, two years later. In France, *L'Association des Propriétaires des Vieilles Voitures* began to meet in December 1935, and soon became familiarly known as *Les Teuf-Teuf*, after the noise emitted by an early single-cylinder engine.

All these early clubs were created for the sheer enjoyment of finding, restoring, and running an old car—there was no solemnity about it, and dating was sometimes a pretty haphazard affair. An exception was the Automobilhistoriska Klubben (Historic Car Club) of Sweden, founded in 1950 by two marine engineers, Curt Borgenstam and Bertil Lindblad, with an emphasis on historical research and study equal to that on preserving and running old cars. In Britain, the Veteran Car Club set up its Dating Committee in 1946, and this became the model for other clubs around the world in accurate identification and dating of old cars.

From these seeds grew the vast interest in old cars which, by now, has spread to almost every industrialized country on earth. It has become an important business for dealers, auctioneers, restorers, writers, and photographers, while the numbers of "historic" vehicles in existence must now be approaching 100,000. The definition of "historic" is necessarily elastic and, for some time, has included cars made well after 1930. Nonetheless, it was with the pioneers that the movement began. To be sure, the people who have first-hand memories of driving pre-1914 cars when they were new are a rapidly dwindling band today, and even those who drove in the 1920s are becoming fewer. But thanks to the efforts of old-car enthusiasts, a wide variety of machinery from the 1890s to 1930 can still be seen and driven with delight.

This period has also attracted historians of society, and of technology in general, with good reason. It saw the rise and development of mass production in the automobile industry, and of the tradition of car consumption which has had far-reaching influence on the way we live. Moreover, although they have become increasingly common since World War II, many of our auto-related buildings such as the motel

and the multi-level car park were already in evidence before 1930. Even the scheme of hire-purchase, or installment buying, which is now taken for granted as regards household goods, was available in America for car buyers by 1914, and was offered by Fiat—together with a cheap insurance plan, for buyers of the 509 model—from 1928 onward. Much has altered and expanded since, but the nature of motoring and its ramifications was fairly well established by 1930.

MAKING IT GO

1

The motorcar was a long time a-borning. From the first experiments of Nicholas Cugnot in 1770 to the day on which Karl Benz patented his successful petrol-engined three-wheeler, 116 years passed—longer than the century between Karl Benz and the present, when over 400 million motor vehicles ply the world's highways. There are many reasons why the gestation was so long, including bad roads and the reluctance of investors to put faith in novelties; but the most significant was a lack of adequate technology. The motorcar as it was made from the 1880s onwards arose from three separate industrial products: the carriage, the bicycle, and the stationary engine. The last two were not developed in a suitable form until the 1870s.

The influence of the stationary engine

Steam-driven stationary engines had been made ever since the end of the eighteenth century. But the first to be fired by explosive gas were made by Jean-Joseph Etienne Lenoir (1822–1900), a Frenchman who, in 1860, patented an engine similar in layout to a single-acting steam engine. In place of steam, it ran on town gas, ignited by a spark from a Ruhmkorff induction coil. Unlike later internal combustion engines, there was no compression of the gas: as the piston moved forward, the mixture was drawn down into the cylinder, to be ignited at half stroke. The resulting explosion drove the piston to the end of the stroke, and it was returned by the crank to which it was attached, while the return stroke expelled the burnt gas. The Lenoir design was quickly taken up by a company promoter named Gautier, who set up a factory for the manufacture of engines in various sizes, suitable for driving machinery or generating electricity.

The fame of Lenoir's engines spread rapidly. Before the close of 1860, *The Scientific American* commented: "The age of steam is ended—Watt and Fulton will soon be forgotten. This is the way they do such things in France." It was a highly premature dismissal of steam, which is still used for electric power generation 125 years later. Nevertheless, Lenoir's engines flourished for a while, and between 1860 and 1865 at least 143 had been sold in the Paris area alone. Some were made in England, by the Reading Iron Works for Lenoir Gas Engines of London.

In 1863, Lenoir installed the smallest of his engines in a three-wheeled carriage, with double chain drive to the rear axle. The single cylinder had a capacity of 2,543 cubic centimetres (2.5 litres, or 155 cubic inches), with what would later be called "oversquare" dimensions of 180 by 100 millimetres. Maximum power was 1.5 horsepower at a speed of 100 revolutions per minute. That September, Lenoir drove his carriage from the Rue de la Roquette in Paris to Joinville-le-Pont, a distance of about seven miles (eleven kilometres). The journey took ninety minutes each way, slower than a man could walk—although doubtless the actual running speed was higher, as there would have been some involuntary halts enroute. The inventor was not very pleased with his carriage, and the next year he turned his attention to motorboats, with great success.

This was not the end of the Lenoir carriage, though. Somehow it came to the notice of Tsar Alexander II of Russia, who decided that he would like to try the delights of internal combustion. The original carriage, or possibly a replica, was driven to the railway station at Vincennes and put on a train for St. Petersburg. Unfortunately nothing is known of its career in Russia, and there may have been no one at the Imperial Court with sufficient mechanical knowledge to make it start.

After 1865, sales of Lenoir engines began to fall off, as they proved to be rough and noisy after prolonged use. They were replaced in popularity by the engines made by Otto and Langen, of Deutz in Germany. This company, in 1873, gained a new technical director in the person of Gottlieb Daimler (1834–1900), a Swabian. He had served his apprenticeship with a gunsmith, and had then worked for various engineering firms including Armstrong-Whitworth in England. Once established at Deutz, he lost no time in appointing as chief draughtsman his old friend Wilhelm Maybach (1846–1929). The two men had known each other for years, and their wives had been school friends.

Three years after Daimler joined the firm, Nikolaus-August Otto (1832–1891) patented a four-stroke engine which had the same cycle of operation as every one of its type made until today. Neither Otto nor his lawyer partner Eugen Langen (1833–1895) had an interest in self-propelled vehicles; their ambition was to make more, and better, stationary engines. Daimler helped considerably with the former aim, raising daily production from one engine to three during his time at Deutz. However, he may have been thinking about motor vehicles as early as the mid-1870s, because he became increasingly concerned with petrol as a fuel rather than coal gas. To minimize the influence of their awkward technical director, the partners sent Daimler to manage their Russian factory in St. Petersburg, but this action only resulted in their losing him altogether. Not only did Daimler resign from Otto & Langen in 1882, but he took Maybach with him.

	Daimler	**Benz**
Engine	Vertical.	Horizontal.
cylinder size:	70 × 120 mm	90 × 150 mm
displacement:	462 cc	954 cc
power:	1.1 bhp at 600 rpm	0.75 bhp at 400 rpm
inlet valve:	Automatic poppet.	Slide valve operated by offset pin in cam-end face.
ignition:	Hot tube.	Battery and trembler coil.
Transmission		
primary drive:	Pulleys from engine to countershaft.	Belt from flywheel to differential and cross-shaft.
final drive:	Pinions on countershaft meshing with sprockets on rear wheels.	Chain to rear wheels.
Chassis		
frame:	Wood and flanged steel.	Tubular steel.
suspension:	Full elliptic springs at front and rear.	Full elliptic springs at rear, one at front.
steering:	Curved rack on front axle, and gear on vertical column.	Cog and twin racks between vertical posts of front wheel and steering column, via drag links.
brakes:	Hand-operated block brakes on rear tyres.	Transmission brakes operated by belt-controlled lever.
wheels:	Centre-lock wooden.	Centre-lock wire.

The pioneers of motorcar design, starting with no precedents to guide them, came up with contrasting ideas about how a car should look. This is well illustrated by the 1886 Daimler four-wheeler *(above)* and the 1885 Benz three-wheeler *(opposite)*. Both had, of course, solid tyres, and an engine with surface carburettor and cam-operated poppet exhaust valve. But other specifications differed widely:

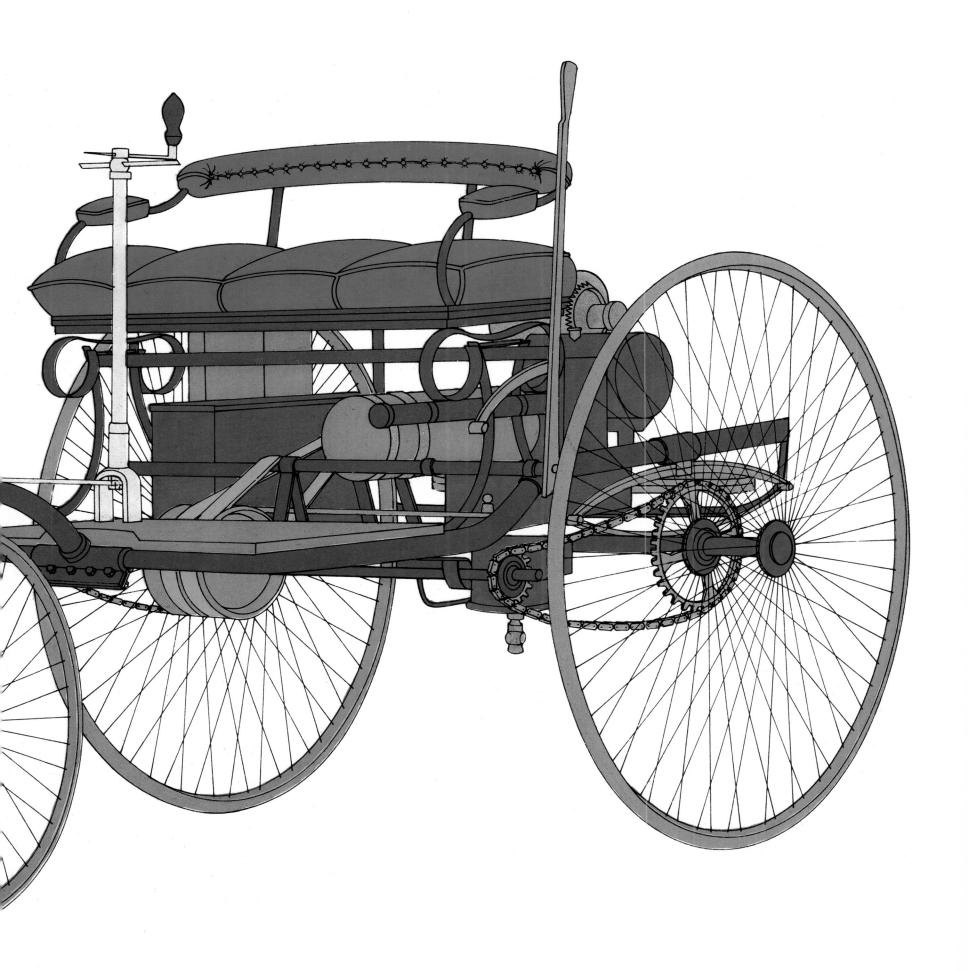

Panhard et Levassor

"The ancestor of the modern motorcar"—one of the first Panhard-Levassor cars of 1892/3. Its 4-hp Daimler-designed V-twin engine gave a top speed of 18 mph (29 km/h). The *queue de vâche* (cow's tail) steering tiller was typical of early Panhards, until replaced by a wheel in 1895. The forward lever operated the three-speed sliding pinion gearbox, and the rearward one a brake which acted on the rear tyres.

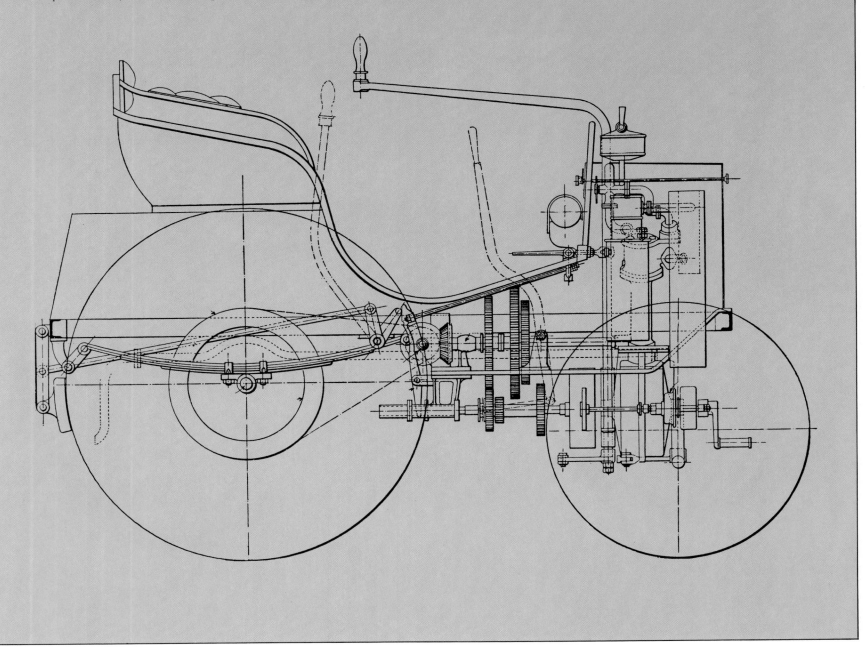

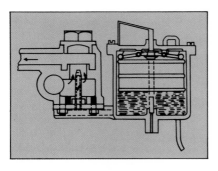

(Above) Maybach's float-feed spray carburettor, developed in 1893 while he and Daimler were working at the Hotel Herrmann in Cannstatt. There was only one jet, and Maybach claimed that, as the fuel level was kept constant by the float and needle valve, the strength of the mixture would remain constant despite varying engine speed. This did not work out in practice but, as the early engine's speed range was limited, it did not matter much.

(Below) Daimler's Phoenix engine, made from 1895 to 1902, and manufactured under licence by Panhard and Peugeot. The Maybach spray carburettor can be seen on the left, the mixture entering the combustion chamber by a vertical poppet valve, which is operated by a long pushrod from the low-mounted camshaft. Below the carburettor is the platinum tube which provides ignition. It is heated by petrol from a tank which also feeds the carburettor.

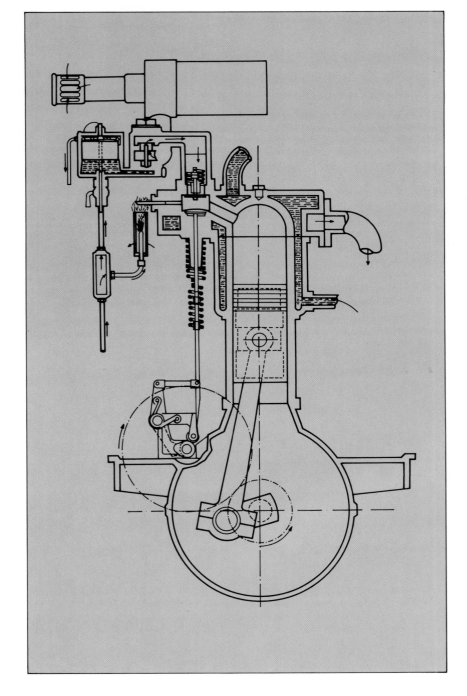

The first Daimler car

Together the two friends set up a small workshop in Cannstatt, the Daimler Motorengesellschaft. There they made stationary engines smaller in size than those of Otto & Langen, and capable of operating at higher speeds. The Otto engines ran at about 120 rpm, sufficient for the needs of a workshop or generating station, but Daimler's engines could soon attain 750 rpm, which he considered suitable for a motor-boat, railcar, or road carriage. In 1883 he was granted a patent for a high-speed, petrol-fuelled, four-stroke engine, and in 1885 he installed one of these in a crude motorized bicycle. This was more like an old "boneshaker" than the new Safety bicycles with tubular frames and wire wheels which were just coming into use in England.

The single-cylinder engine had a bore and stroke of 58 x 100 mm, giving a capacity of 264 cc, and the power developed was 0.5 brake horsepower at a speed of 700 rpm. Ignition was by the hot-tube system, in which a small platinum tube was screwed horizontally into the cylinder head, and was heated red-hot by a petrol-fed burner at its outer, closed end. The inner end was open, and therefore filled with petrol/air mixture when this was admitted to the cylinder head. When the compressed mixture reached the hottest part of the tube, it exploded. The residue of burnt gas left in the tube prevented the next charge from exploding until maximum compression had been reached, so the system was self-timing. The first Daimler vertical engine weighed about 110 pounds (50 kilograms) and stood 30 inches (76 cm) high; a gas engine developing the same power would have weighed over a ton and stood nearly seven feet (2.1 metres) high.

Daimler chose the motorcycle—which in fact had two small stabilizing wheels as well as its main wheels—because he wanted the lightest possible vehicle in which to test his tiny engines. But his next step was to motorize a proper four-wheeled carriage. He ordered a simple horse-drawn carriage from a Cannstatt coachbuilder, and mounted a larger version of his original engine in it, with bore and stroke of 70 x 120 mm and a capacity of 462 cc. This had an atmospheric inlet valve operated by suction, and a mechanical exhaust valve operated by a camshaft. The mixture was provided by a surface carburettor, in which air was passed over the surface of the petrol on its way to the cylinder, picking up enough vapour to make an explosive mixture. Ignition was by hot tube. Drive to the rear wheels was by pulleys from the engine to a countershaft, which carried gears meshing with sprockets attached to the wheels. The carriage had four seats, although the rear passengers would have had their leg-room severely restricted by the engine which projected through the floorboards, and no photograph exists showing more than one passenger in the rear.

The engine developed 1.1 horsepower at 600 rpm, and could propel the carriage at about 10 mph (16 km/h) on a level road. Daimler made his first trials with it in the later summer of 1886, but he was not particularly devoted to the motorcar, being more interested in applying his engine to as many modes of transport as possible. Over the next four years, these included boats, tramcars, and airships, and he did not complete another motorcar until 1889.

Karl Benz

Meanwhile, another German engineer had built several examples of what was, in some ways, a more advanced car than Daimler's. Karl Benz (1844–1929) was born in Mühlberg, near Karlsruhe, the son of a locomotive driver. He studied at the Karlsruhe Polytechnic before becoming a fitter at an engineering works, the Karlsruhe Maschinen-

Karl Benz' first four-wheeler was the Viktoria which he introduced in 1892. It had a large single-cylinder engine of 1,730 cc capacity, and dimensions of 130 × 130 mm, giving a relatively low output of 3 bhp at 450 rpm, no more than Daimler's twin which displaced only 1,060 cc. Later Viktorias had a larger cylinder of 1,990, 2,650 or 2,915 cc, and were fitted with four-seater bodies. But the car that really put Benz on the map was the little Velo (opposite), with 1,045-cc engine running at 500 rpm, later raised to 800 rpm and developing 3.5 bhp. The Velo weighed only 360–425 kg, compared with 650 kg for the Viktoria.

(Above) The 1897 De Dietrich was an Amédée Bollée design, made by a large engineering group famous for railway stock, in a French factory at Luneville (Lorraine) and a German one at Niederbronn (Alsace). It used a front-mounted horizontal-twin engine with two parallel cylinders. The drive was by long constant-speed belts to the gear system main-shaft at the rear, then forward by two shafts to the bevel gear of each rear wheel. This system avoided chain or belt final drive.

(Right) The engine of the 1894 Benz Velo, showing the radiator (at far left), the fuel tank next to it, the exposed crank of the horizontal single-cylinder engine, the flywheel, and the fast-and-loose-pulley transmission.

15

baugesellschaft. Like Daimler, he changed jobs quite frequently, but in 1872 he married and set up a small workshop in Mannheim, making engines with a partner, August Ritter. Their company was on a much smaller scale than Otto & Langen, and for ten years Benz was barely able to make ends meet. He became a little more prosperous in the early 1880s, and turned his company into the Gasmotorenfabrik Benz & Co. Yet he was hampered by the fact that he could only build two-stroke engines, because Otto & Langen held the patent for four-strokes. Then he discovered that his rivals' patent was invalid, as the four-stroke had been patented years earlier by the Frenchman Alphonse Beau de Rochas. This left Benz free to make four-strokes. However, instead of doing so from his original firm, he set up a new company with financial backing by two friends, Max Rose and Friedrich Esslinger. The new firm was called the Rheinische Gasmotorenfabrik Benz & Co., and concentrated on stationary engines for its bread and butter, while Benz himself turned his attention to a small engine for powering a motorcar.

During 1885 the car began to take shape. Unlike Daimler, Benz chose a purpose-built frame, a light tubular structure which—together with the wire wheels—owed more to the bicycle industry than to the carriage. The engine had one water-cooled cylinder of 954 cc, developing 0.75 bhp. This was a much lower volumetric efficiency than the Daimler engine, but the Benz had a maximum speed of 300 rpm, less than half that of the Daimler. Throughout his designing career, Karl Benz favoured slow-turning engines, which is one reason why design eventually had to be taken out of his hands. The Benz engine had several advanced features, including electric ignition by a battery and Ruhmkorff coil. On the other hand, it was less advanced than the Daimler in that, although water-cooled, it had no radiator. The water was just allowed to boil away, whereas Daimler had a sizeable tubular radiator at the rear of his car. A simple surface carburettor, which was also the fuel tank, provided the explosive mixture.

The Benz engine was mounted horizontally behind the two seats, so that the crankshaft was vertical and the large horizontal flywheel filled the whole width of the frame. The use of the largest possible flywheel was typical of stationary engine practice, and the engine was started by giving a hefty pull on the flywheel. Also inherited from the stationary engine was the flat leather belt which transmitted power to a countershaft, whence final drive was by chains to the rear wheels. The first car had no speed-change mechanism, but the belt could be moved from a free pulley on the countershaft to a fixed one, to give a clutch action. Later cars embodied a two-speed belt-and-pulley system on the countershaft. Like many early vehicles, the Benz was a three-wheeler with a single wheel at the front. At that time, the Lenkensperger or Ackermann system of keeping the front axle fixed and steering the wheels on stub axles was not unknown (Amédée Bollée had used it on a steam carriage in 1873), but was very little used. Most designers, if they used four wheels at all, employed an axle that swivelled on a centre pivot, which made for extremely heavy and dangerous steering—hence the single front wheel on many early cars, from the steam carriage of the 1860s up to Benz and beyond.

Karl Benz's three-wheeler was completed in 1885, but there is no record of when it first ran. This is a great pity, as on it hangs the question of the date of the first motorcar, which the Benz is considered to be because it was followed within a few years by replicas built for commercial sale. The first trials were doubtless very modest, due to the car's limited capabilities, and were made mostly at night in order to attract as little attention as possible from the police. On January 29, 1886, Benz took out a series of patents to cover features of his car, and later in the year he made a public appearance which was written up by the local paper, the *Neue Badische Landeszeitung*.

The first report on Benz's car was published on June 4, and the first account of a ride on the car appeared on July 3 in the same paper. This presumably did not excite the police, but unfortunately the car was not of much interest to anyone else either. A self-propelled vehicle was such a novelty that nobody really knew what to think about it, and certainly nobody would lay out hard-earned money to buy one. Benz's partners fiercely resented his obsession with what they saw as a pointless experiment, when he could have been devoting the time to the sensible business of making gas engines. The same disagreement was to arise between Henry Royce and his partners seventeen years later.

A long-distance drive

Benz had staunch allies in his family, at least, and it was his wife Bertha who made the first long-distance journey in a motorcar. Wanting to visit relatives in Pforzheim, about 50 miles (80 km) away, she was egged on by her fifteen-year-old son Eugen to take the car rather than travelling conventionally by train. Together with her younger son Richard, they set out early one morning, leaving a note for Karl to say that they were not deserting him. They made good progress as far as Heidelberg but, on the steeper hills of the Black Forest, Bertha and Eugen had to dismount, leaving thirteen-year-old Richard at the tiller.

On downhill stretches, the leather brake linings wore out, and fresh leather had to be obtained from cobblers. The resourceful Bertha lent a hatpin to clear a blocked fuel pipe, and when an ignition wire short-circuited she took off her garter to insulate the wire. Throughout their journey, they were a source of amazement, and in a Black Forest inn a fight nearly broke out between two peasants disputing as to whether the car was driven by clockwork or by a supernatural agency. Nevertheless, Pforzheim was reached before nightfall, and the family made a safe return journey five days later.

The French industry begins

It has often been said that Germany was the birthplace of the motorcar, but France was its nursery. Certainly Karl Benz himself might never have found commercial success, had he not shown a car at the Paris Exposition of 1887 and attracted the interest of a cycle-maker named Emile Roger, who had already bought a stationary engine from the Mannheim firm. Roger travelled to Mannheim to have a demonstration of the car, and promptly bought it. He later became sole concessionaire for Benz cars in France, and took out a licence to assemble them in Paris.

Frenchmen were also instrumental in making the Daimler engine into a commercial proposition. In 1887, Daimler and Maybach brought out a two-cylinder engine with the cylinders arranged in a narrow-angle V-formation. The French manufacturing rights to Daimler engines had already been acquired by a Belgian lawyer, Edouard Sarazin, who had no manufacturing premises and, therefore, agreed with his friend Emile Levassor that Daimler engines should be made in France by the latter's engineering firm, Panhard et Levassor, of Paris. When Sarazin died in 1887, his widow travelled to Cannstatt, to make sure that her husband's rights would pass to her. Gottlieb Daimler was very impressed with her business acumen and confirmed the agreement, while three years later she cemented matters still further by marrying Emile Levassor.

The first car made by Panhard et Levassor carried its Daimler V-twin engine vertically, with the crankshaft running transversely in the centre of the frame, and the four seats over it in *dos-à-dos* (back-to-back) arrangement. Transmission was by belt and pulley, and final drive by chains to the rear axle. The car was completed in 1890 and altered several times during the year, so that exact details are not known. However, it was replaced early in 1891 with a totally different design, which laid down the pattern for motorcars for years to come. For the first time, the engine was mounted at the front of the chassis, and protected from the elements by a box which the French called *un capot*, translated into English as "bonnet" and always called by Americans a "hood". The crankshaft was longitudinal—parallel to the chassis frame—and necessitated a bevel gear to turn the drive through 90° to power the rear axle. The advantage of a longitudinal engine is that, as the number of cylinders grows, they can be accommodated by increasing the length of the bonnet, whereas a transverse engine is limited to four cylinders at the most.

Just as revolutionary as the engine position was the transmission. Rather than the belts and pulleys inherited from stationary engine technology, Levassor used a sliding pinion system in which gear wheels meshed with others of different sizes to give three forward speeds. It would not be correct to call this a gearbox, as the gears were not enclosed; instead they were lubricated, in the inimitable words of the English historian Anthony Bird, "by grease, road dust and optimism in equal proportions". From the output gear shaft, the drive was taken to a bevel-geared countershaft, and thence by chains to a differential-equipped rear axle. This was soon changed so that the differential was on the countershaft, and side chains drove the rear wheels in the same manner as the Benz.

There were two brakes: a handbrake which worked contracting brakes on the rear tyres, and a foot brake operating a band brake on the countershaft. Both brakes were connected to the clutch withdrawal mechanism, so that when they were applied the engine was automatically de-clutched; this was important at a time when engines constantly ran at their maximum set speed. On the Daimler, the speed was around 750 rpm, restricted by a centrifugal governor which prevented the exhaust valves from opening when the speed was exceeded. The driver could do nothing about it until Levassor introduced a screw device on the dashboard, which allowed him to override the governor and let the engine "race". By the turn of the century, this device was pedal-operated and came to be known as the accelerator. Later still, when the governor was a thing of the past, the same name was applied to the pedal which regulated the flow of mixture into the cylinders.

The 1891 Panhard-Levassor (usually called Panhard for short, although the design was entirely Levassor's) represented "state of the art" technology in almost every way. The only way in which it might be thought old-fashioned was its use of Daimler's hot-tube ignition, but this was really no less reliable than the primitive electrical systems of the 1890s. During the year 1891, Panhard et Levassor began to make these cars for sale, at a price of 3,500 francs each. One was bought second-hand in 1893 by the Abbé Gavois, a parish priest from Rainneville, near Amiens. He was almost certainly the first motoring cleric; and what is more, he continued to use his Panhard regularly until 1921, and occasionally for a further seven years, after which it was bought back by the Panhard company.

Production of Panhards increased gradually during the 1890s, and steady improvement was made to the design. In 1894, the surface carburettor was replaced with the atomizing-spray type invented by Wilhelm Maybach. In 1895, the gears were enclosed, justifying the

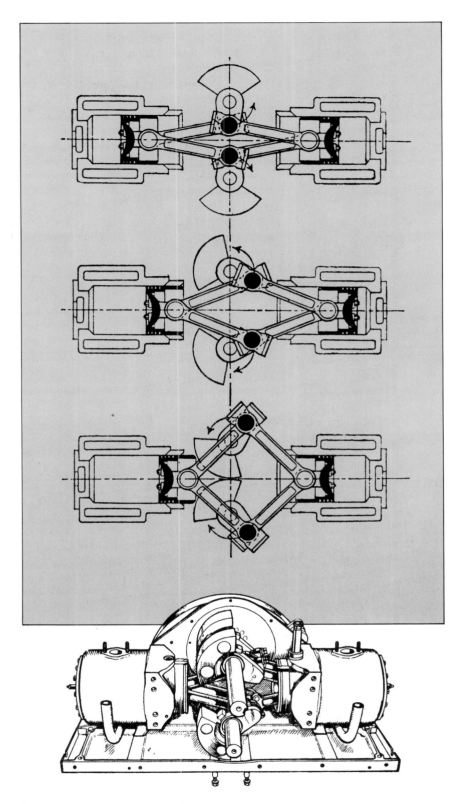

Three phases of operation in the Lanchester twin engine, vibrationless and horizontally opposed. The two superimposed crankshafts rotated in opposite directions, and were linked to the two pistons by six connecting rods. This type of engine was used on the 1897 Lanchester prototype, and on all production twins made from 1900 to 1905.

The three cars shown here, together with Benz, represent the leading European schools of thought in the late nineteenth century. Peugeot *(left)* replaced their Daimler-type engines in 1897 with a horizontal twin, designed by Gratien Michaux. This was mounted at the rear with the cylinder heads facing forward. Peugeot remained faithful to rear engines for longer than most firms: their first front-engined model was not made until 1900, and rear-engined town broughams were still available in 1905. The 1897 models had conventional radiators, instead of circulating the cooling water through the frame. The 1897 British Daimler *(opposite)* and the 1899 Panhard *(below)* followed a common theme, with front-mounted vertical twin engines and hot-tube ignition. Being two years younger, the Panhard had a steering wheel—and older Daimlers were converted to wheel steering by several British firms, including Frank Morriss of Kings Lynn, the self-styled "car repairer to King Edward VII".

Edward Butler has been unfairly
neglected by historians. His Petrol Cycle
of 1888 had Ackermann steering, a spray
carburettor, and mechanically operated
inlet valves. This drawing shows it in
original form, with rollers on which the
rear wheel could be raised from the
ground for starting.

term "gearbox" for the first time, and by this date most Panhards had four forward speeds. Transmission gave the same number of speeds in reverse, which was obtained by transferring the drive from one bevel pinion on the countershaft to another. Rather surprisingly, Levassor did not employ a radiator on his cars until 1897, preferring to rely on the cooling effect of the large water tank.

In 1895, Daimler introduced their Phoenix engine, which was an in-line twin rather than a Vee. Cylinder dimensions were 80 × 120 mm, compared with 75 × 120 mm for the V-twin, giving a capacity of 1,205 cc. Power output was 4 bhp at 750 rpm, and Levassor promptly adopted this engine in his cars. Four Phoenix-powered Panhards were entered in the 1895 Paris–Bordeaux–Paris Race, and Levassor himself was first home, after driving for 48¾ hours single-handed. He averaged

15 mph (24 km/h) over 732 miles (1,180 km), and his longest halt for oiling and adjustments was 22 minutes. Unfortunately, he could not be awarded first prize as his car had only two seats, whereas the regulations stipulated four. The prize of 31,500 francs went to Koechlin's Peugeot, which averaged 12.9 mph (20.8 km/h).

An industry emerges

Several firms were offering cars for sale by 1895, and one can begin to speak of a motor industry, although it was quite insignificant when compared with the associated industries of the bicycle or the carriage. After making about 20 three-wheelers in 1890 and 1891, Benz introduced a four-wheeler, the Viktoria, in 1892. This sold in small num-

The car that won America's first motoring race in November 1895, organized by the *Chicago Times Herald*. It was Duryea's second car, completed in 1894, and a great improvement over the first which "ran no faster than an old man could walk". The former two-stroke engine was now replaced by a four-stroke of 1,852 cc, developing 4 bhp at 700 rpm.

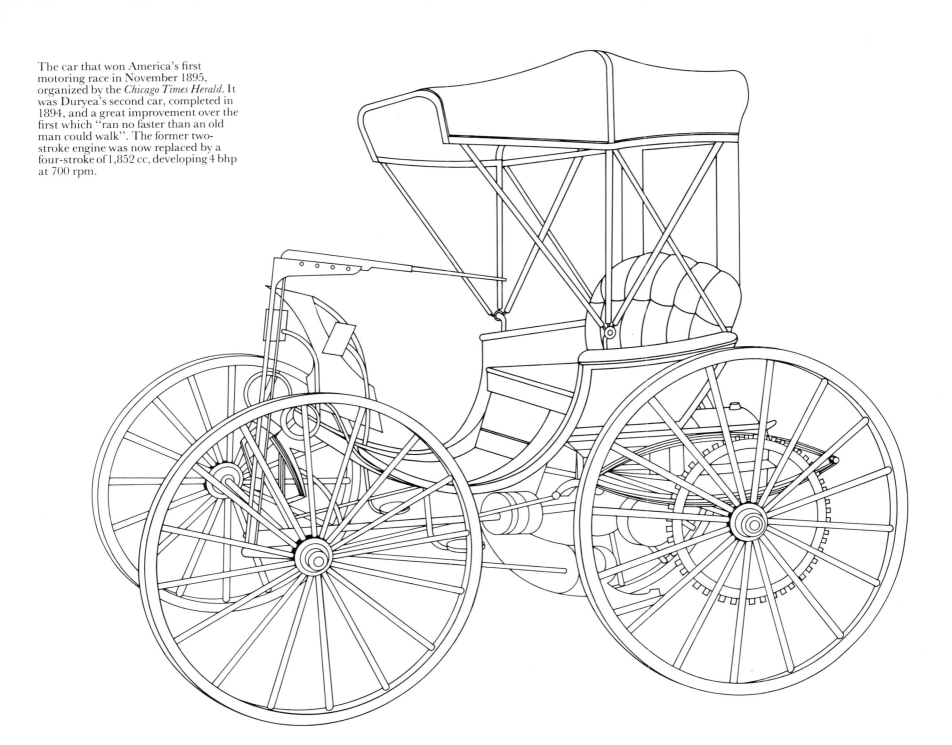

bers, but the car that really sparked off Benz' success was the Velo, a two-seater with wire wheels and a single-cylinder engine of 1,045 cc. Introduced in 1894, the Velo was much lighter and cheaper than the Viktoria, costing 2,000 marks (£500), half the price of the larger car. The Benz engine was still at the rear of the frame, and transmission was still by fixed and loose pulleys with a chain final drive. Nevertheless, the Velo sold well for several years, as it was simple to operate and maintain, and as reliable as any other car of its day. Thanks to the Velo, Benz sales increased dramatically in the middle of the decade, from 69 cars between 1887 and 1893, to 67 in 1894 and to 135 in 1895, while the 1896 figure was 181. Three years later it was 572, and throughout this period the sales of Benz cars easily exceeded their rivals. In 1896, more were sold than the combined total production of

Great Britain and the United States.

Until the mid-1890s, Benz and Panhard had only two serious rivals, Daimler in Germany and Peugeot in France. The Daimler company had rather a chequered career in its early days, as Gottlieb Daimler and Wilhelm Maybach quarrelled with their partners in 1893 and left the firm to set up an experimental workshop in an empty hotel, the Hermann in Cannstatt. Here Maybach perfected his spray carburettor, but no complete cars were ever made in the hotel—while at the Daimler factory only twelve cars were made during the three-year absence of the founders. These had in-line twin engines, but when Daimler and Maybach made peace with their partners and rejoined the firm in 1895, they brought out the improved Phoenix engine, which remained in production until 1902. The engine was at the rear, and drive was by belt and gear. The first front-engined model appeared in 1897, although the rear position was retained on cabs and trucks for at least two years longer. In 1899, Daimler revealed their first in-line four-cylinder engine, but they were beaten to the post in this important development by Panhard, who had a four in 1897.

Peugeot was another French manufacturer which was launched on its career by the V-twin Daimler engine. The company traced its origins back to the early years of the eighteenth century, and by the 1880s was making such diverse products as coffee mills, umbrella frames, whalebone corsets, saws, hammers, watch springs, and bicycles. The latter were the idea of Armand Peugeot (1849–1915), and it was he who decided that his company should become car-makers. They had made four steam cars to the design of Léon Serpollet, but in 1890 Peugeot met Gottlieb Daimler and Emile Levassor, and resolved to use Panhard-built engines of Daimler pattern. The first four engines arrived at the Peugeot factory at Valentigney in March 1890, and by the end of the year four complete cars had been made. These had tubular frames in which the cooling water circulated, and rear-mounted engines. It is said that Levassor recommended the rear, maintaining that a front-mounted engine would offend the passengers with its smell—yet within a year he was making front-engined cars himself. Peugeot did not abandon the rear engine until 1900. Production rose steadily, from four cars in 1890 and again in 1891, to 29 in 1892, 40 in 1894, and 72 in 1895. Three figures were reached in 1898 with 156 sales, and 1899 saw 300 cars sold.

Like Panhard (and unlike Benz), Peugeot entered sporting competitions as early as possible, with five cars in the 1894 Paris–Rouen Trial, and four in the 1895 Paris–Bordeaux–Paris Race. In the latter, a four-seater Peugeot was victorious, although only because Levassor's two-seater was ineligible. In the same race, the Michelin brothers entered a Peugeot with pneumatic tyres, the first to be seen in a motor race. They had endless trouble with the tyres, and had to abandon the return journey at Orléans since they had exceeded the overall time limit of 100 hours, but no blame was attached to the Peugeot car itself. Within a few years, Peugeots and practically all other cars would be running on pneumatic tyres.

The motorcar in Britain

Development of the motorcar was much slower in Britain than on the Continent. This has been explained by the Locomotives on Highways Act, which imposed a limit of 4 mph (6.5 km/h) in the country and half that speed in towns, undoubtedly with a stifling effect on cars. The only Englishman to make a petrol-engined vehicle in the 1880s was Edward Butler, who designed a single-seated three-wheeler. Its driver sat between the two front wheels, and the two-cylinder engine drove the rear wheel directly, with no intervening chains or belts. He took out his first patent "for the mechanical propulsion of cycles" in 1884, and the car was completed at the Merryweather Fire Engine works at Greenwich in 1888.

Among its advanced features were Ackermann steering (the first use of the system in a petrol-engined car), a spray carburettor (five years before Maybach), and mechanically operated inlet valves. Ignition was by magneto at first, later replaced with a coil and battery. The engine, originally a two-stroke with a capacity of 1,041 cc, was redesigned as a four-stroke, with the stroke reduced from 8 to 5 inches (200 to 125 mm) and a capacity of 650 cc. At 600 rpm, the engine developed only 5/8 hp but, even so, gave a speed of 8–12 mph (13–19 km/h). The direct drive was found to be too high, and was subsequent-

ly geared down. There was no clutch and, to start the vehicle, the rear wheel was raised from the ground onto small rollers, and the engine was started by compressed air in the manner of some stationary engines. This was eventually replaced with flywheel starting, as employed by Karl Benz.

Butler christened his machine the Petrol Cycle, the first time that the word "petrol" had been used, and six years before it was adopted as a trade name by the London oil importers of Carless, Capel and Leonard. He planned to have his tricycle manufactured by Butler's Patent Petrol Cycle Syndicate. Yet because of the legal restrictions in the case of such vehicles, he abandoned the idea in 1888, even before the machine took to the road in February 1889. It was then noted to work fairly well, but with no commercial potential it did not seem worth spending much time on, and Butler turned to making oil engines for boats and stationary use. When the speed limit was raised to 12 mph (19 km/h) in 1896, Butler revived his car, and sold the design to the British Motor Syndicate, although it was never manufactured. Edward Butler should, however, receive more honour than history has so far accorded him, for having made the first British petrol-engined vehicle, which was in several respects in advance of Continental practice.

The next British car was a light four-wheeler made by a young engineer—Frederick William Bremer—from Walthamstow, London. He had planned it as a gas-engined three-wheeler, but between 1892 when he began, and 1894 when he completed his car, he changed it to a four-wheeler powered by a rear-mounted single-cylinder engine with automatic inlet valve. Drive was by belt to a two-speed transmission, and by chain to the rear axle. Bremer had to make, or adapt, nearly all the components himself; the flywheel was a grindstone and the sparking plug was insulated by a clay pipe stem. Not as advanced as the Butler Petrol Cycle in view of its later date, the Bremer is of interest chiefly as an example of what an ingenious young man could produce with very limited resources. It ran briefly in 1895, but was soon forgotten, although resurrected for the first Motor Museum which opened in London in 1912, and again for the Royal Automobile Club's London to Brighton Run in the 1960s. Because it had never been taxed or licenced for the road, it was treated as a new car, and special permission had to be obtained to allow it to run on the roads. It can be seen today in the Walthamstow Museum.

Just as Bremer was getting his car ready, another and quite radical machine was taking shape in Birmingham. Frederick Lanchester was a brilliant engineer who worked from first principles and copied almost nothing from contemporary practice. The engine had a single horizontal cylinder with two overhanding balanced cranks, each with its own flywheel and connecting rod. The cranks revolved in opposite directions, giving a smoothness and freedom from vibration that were unknown at the time. The cylinder had a mechanically operated inlet valve, while one of the flywheels was fitted with vanes that blew cooling air over the cylinder. Transmission was by a set of epicyclic gears, as used later by Henry Ford and others, but revolutionary in 1895. Final drive was originally by chain, replaced with worm drive on the 1897 version, which also had a two-cylinder engine. The body was a full-width structure in varnished walnut, wide enough to seat three passengers on the rear seat, built upon a tubular frame. It was suspended on very long C-springs at the rear, and a single transverse cantilever spring at the front.

Lanchester, aided by his brother George, tested the car early in 1896, and found that it ran with commendable smoothness but was underpowered. They therefore built a two-cylinder engine with a capacity of 2,895 cc, giving an estimated 8 bhp and a top speed of 20

Variations on a three-wheeled theme. Although superficially similar, the Swiss Egg & Eggli *(right)* was a much milder machine than the French Léon Bollée *(below)*. Rudolf Egg chose the familiar 402-cc 3-hp single-cylinder De Dion Bouton engine, with belt final drive, to give his 190-kg vehicle a top speed of around 25 mph (40 km/h). The Léon Bollée had a 650-cc engine of Bollée's own design and manufacture, which produced 2.5 hp at a governed speed of 800 rpm, but considerably more when allowed to run up to 1,200 rpm. Its top speed was well over 30 mph (50 km/h) and, in the 1897 Paris-Trouville Race, its driver Jamin averaged 28.2 mph (45 km/h) for 107 miles (170 km). Nevertheless, the three-wheeler was a dead end at this time, and both Egg and Bollée had turned to four wheels by 1900.

The influence of Benz spread far and wide, to Australia and America. Nearer home were these two pioneers in their respective countries, the Swedish Vabis and the Italian F.I.A.T. Strictly speaking, Gustaf Erikson's four-seater of 1897 *(left)* was not a Vabis, as this name was given only to its successors. Benz-like in general appearance, it had a horizontally opposed two-cylinder engine but hot-tube ignition. The first F.I.A.T. *(below)* resembled a baby Benz, and had a 697-cc horizontal-twin engine with automatic inlet valves at the rear of its simple flitch-plate frame. The Levassor-inspired sliding gearbox gave three forward speeds, but there was no reverse until 1900, and even then it was an optional extra. All the mechanical elements were made in the factory, but the *vis-à-vis* body came from Alessio of Turin. Only eight of the original 1899 F.I.A.T. were made.

mph (32 km/h). The cylinders were horizontally opposed, and the pistons were connected to the cranks by six rods. Ever a perfectionist, Frederick Lanchester would not offer a car for sale until he was fully satisfied, so the first Lanchester did not come into the hands of the public until 1900.

Apart from Lanchester, there was little originality in the few cars made in British factories before 1900. The Coventry-built Daimlers and MMCs, made next door to each other in the Motor Mills, were generally similar to Panhards, although they had engines of German Daimler pattern. A number of more or less close imitations of the Benz Velo appeared, including the Marshall from Manchester, later to become the Belsize, and the Star from Wolverhampton and the Arnold from Paddock Wood in Kent. Only twelve Arnolds were made, but one had the distinction of possessing the world's first electric self-starter. This was a dynamotor attached to the flywheel, intended primarily for assisting the engine on steep hills or for driving the car if the engine failed. The battery turned out to be too weak to do this, but it would turn the engine over to start the car.

America enters the field

A number of pioneers had built petrol-engined cars in America by the mid-1890s. The first cars were sold to customers in 1896, by the Duryea brothers of Springfield, Massachusetts. In general, American designers did not show great originality, and the progress of the car there was as much hampered by the appalling roads outside the large towns as it was by hostile legislation in Britain. Most American cars had large wooden-spoked buggy-type wheels to cope with the roads, slow-running single-cylinder horizontal engines, and Benz-type belt-and-pulley transmissions. Two experimental cars were built in 1891, the Lambert three-wheeler from Ohio City, Ohio, and the Nadig four-wheeler from Allentown, Pennsylvania. But their builders were not publicists in any way, and their claims were completely lost in the angry bickering between the Duryea brothers and Elwood Haynes.

The Duryea car had a single-cylinder engine of 1,302 cc capacity, battery-and-coil ignition, a two-speed belt-and-pulley transmission, and chain final drive. Planning began in 1891, but it was September 1893 before the car was ready for the road. Charles Duryea said that "it ran no faster than an old man could walk . . . but it did run." The following year, a two-cylinder engine was substituted, and a speed of 10 mph (16 km/h) was attained. By June 1895, Frank Duryea reported that several orders for the car were coming in, and that some were accompanied by a request to draw on the customer's bank whatever the cost might be. The Duryea Motor Waggon Company was formed, and production began before the end of the year, with thirteen cars being sold to the public during 1896.

Meanwhile, in Kokomo, Indiana, Elwood Haynes and the Apperson brothers had built a car powered by a single-cylinder two-stroke Sintz engine, which ran for the first time on July 4, 1894. A few replicas were made by the Appersons' Riverside Machine Works, but only in 1898 was the Haynes Apperson Automobile Company founded, to establish production on a regular basis. Haynes later exhibited the 1894 car at the Smithsonian Institution in Washington as "America's First Gasoline Powered Vehicle"—a claim hotly disputed by Charles Duryea, who brought out his 1893 car and presented it to the Smithsonian, with a request that the title claimed by Haynes should be attached to his car. This was done, and probably no one at the time remembered the work of the more retiring John William Lambert and Henry Nadig. Lambert's car, in fact, was destroyed by a fire in the year it was built, and Haynes persuaded its builder not to contest his claim to be the maker of America's first car.

There may well have been other backyard builders who predated the Duryea brothers. Certainly when the *Chicago Times-Herald* proposed a 94-mile (150 km) race in November 1895, they received no fewer than 100 entries, of which at least 20 existed, though only six came to the starting line. The race was held in very snowy conditions, and just two cars finished, a Duryea and a Mueller, which was a modified Benz. Nevertheless, the race brought the car to the attention of the American public, and within three years more than a hundred cars were made for sale. By 1900, the figure was over 2,500. Most of these were powered by steam or electricity, and will be described in the following chapter.

Experiments world-wide

The making of motorcars was not confined to the countries mentioned thus far, and by 1900 the majority of industrialized lands had begun car production. Few of them showed great originality, and there was an understandable tendency to follow the lines of successful machines such as Benz and Panhard. In Belgium, for instance, the Germain made from 1898 onward was closely based on the Panhard, and was sometimes called the Panhard Belge or the Daimler Belge. The contemporary Vincke, the first Belgian car to be built for sale, was Benz-based from 1895 to 1899, joined by a Panhard-like front-engined car in 1898. The Linon and Nagant companies both entered car production by making versions of the French Gobron-Brillié opposed piston engine.

The first Swiss-built petrol-engined car was made by Fritz Henriod at Bienne in 1893. It had a single-cylinder engine with hot-tube ignition, and a two-speed gearbox with direct drive by gear wheels to the rear axle. Rudolf Egg's three-wheelers, made from 1896 to 1898, had single-cylinder engines and resembled the French Léon Bollée to some extent. The Saurer, first product of a company that later became famous for trucks, was more original in having an opposed-piston single-cylinder engine in which the explosion took place between the pistons, driving each one outward to operate its own crankshaft. This design was taken up by Koch in Paris, who made a number of cars and trucks for export to the Dutch East Indies, Persia, Tunisia, Egypt and elsewhere. The first car to run in the island of Madagascar was a Koch-Saurer. After 1900, Saurer made relatively conventional cars. More or less Benz-like cars were made in Switzerland by Rudolf Egg (after his three-wheelers), Lorenz Popp, and Johann Weber.

The Scandinavian countries produced some pioneer cars. In Sweden, Gustaf Erikson (1857–1922) built a one-cylinder paraffin engine in the autumn of 1897, to be used for a car. It did not work well, but during the next spring he placed a two-cylinder horizontally opposed four-stroke engine with hot-tube ignition in a rebuilt horse-drawn carriage, which was driven briefly in Surahammar. As this town was thought unsuitable for car manufacture, Erikson moved to Vagnfabrik AB at Södertälje in the autumn of 1898 to design cars under the name Vabis. Denmark and Norway, neither of which was to become a renowned car-making land in later years, saw the Hammel and Irgens cars respectively.

The Copenhagen-built Hammel was originally dated 1886, but is probably a few years younger. Made by A.F. Hammel and H.U. Johansen, it had a large two-cylinder engine of 2,720 cc, a single speed forward and reverse, and chain final drive. It has survived up to the present day, and came to England for the 1954 London to Brighton

Run, covering the 56-mile (90 km) route in 12.5 hours. A Norwegian inventor, Paul Henningsen Irgens (1843–1923) of Bergen, designed a taxi with four-cylinder engine as early as 1883, but it was never built. He did get a car on the road in 1898, yet this was a rather archaic design with single-cylinder engine and *dos-à-dos* seating. In the following year, he built a steam bus with three-cylinder engine, all-gear drive to the front axle, and provision for heating the interior by steam. Needless to say, only one was made, and thereafter the name of Irgens faded from the motoring scene.

Italy had no serious car production until the F.I.A.T. works were established in 1899. Even so, only eight cars were made in the initial year. The first Italian petrol-car, and one which has a claim to be the first such car in the world, was built in 1884 by Enrico Bernardi (1841–1919), Professor of Hydraulic and Agricultural Machinery at the University of Padua. In 1882, he took out a patent for a tiny single-cylinder petrol engine of 122 cc, which developed only 0.024 hp at 200 rpm. It was used to drive a sewing machine, and two years later Bernardi installed one in a tricycle for his four-year-old son in Verona. The boy moved about in his little machine, carrying sand and stones, and arousing great envy among his friends. It was never intended to be more than a toy, but nonetheless it was a self-propelled passenger vehicle. In 1892, Bernardi built a larger three-wheeler carrying two adults, and a version of this was made in small numbers by Miari e Giusti of Padua from 1896 to 1899. Another pioneer Italian car was constructed by the candle manufacturer Michele Lanza (1868–1947). His wagonette of 1895 was fairly typical of the period, with a rear-mounted two-cylinder horizontal engine, hot-tube ignition, and chain drive. It had shoe brakes working on the iron tyres of the rear wheels.

Other countries which also began their industries before the end of the nineteenth century included Austria, with the Benz-engined Präsident made in Nesselsdorf (now renamed Kovprivnice, part of Czechoslovakia). Russia had the St. Petersburg-built Yakovlev-Freze, which bore a close resemblance to a Benz. In Australia, the 1898 Pioneer built in Melbourne had a paraffin engine, iron-shod wheels, and centre-pivot steering, so it was hardly in the forefront of design.

Thus, on the eve of the twentieth century, the car was starting to become a significant phenomenon in most industrialized nations. Magazines devoted to mechanical propulsion had emerged and were flourishing in Great Britain, the United States, France, Germany, and elsewhere. France was still the home of the long-distance town-to-town race, but such events had already crossed frontiers, running from Paris to Amsterdam and back in 1898, while sprints and hill climbs as well as long-distance reliability trials were held in a number of countries. Although by no means as important as its parent industries of the bicycle and the horse-carriage, the car industry was turning into a useful employer of labour. The frail infant of 1890 had proven to be a sturdy, if often noisy, toddler. There was no doubt that it would survive.

ALTERNATIVE POWER 2

At the turn of the century, there were many people who believed that the steam car had a brighter future than the petrol-driven one. Electricity also had its keen advocates, and the electric car shared some of the advantages of the steamer. In the present chapter we shall trace the complex history and eventual fate of these options.

Steam

The light, oil-fired steamer appeared at about the same time as the petrol cars of Benz and Daimler. But coal-fired steam carriages for two or more passengers had been made spasmodically for many years before that. Josef Bozek, a teacher of engineering at the Prague Polytechnic Institute, constructed one as early as 1815. The famous builder and operator of steam buses in London, Walter Hancock, made a light four-seater phaeton in 1838, in which he regularly drove around London and, at least once, paraded in Hyde Park "attracting the favourable attention of British and foreign nobility". By the 1870s, about forty steam cars had been made in Britain alone. Yet they were all the work of isolated inventors, and none was sold to a customer.

De Dion Bouton

In 1882, a wealthy French aristocrat with a penchant for mechanical models, Count Albert de Dion (1856–1946), met two engineers, Georges Bouton and his brother-in-law Charles Trépardoux, who ran a small workshop making scientific toys. Trépardoux had long dreamed of building a steam-powered light personal carriage, but lacked the necessary funds. De Dion was a visionary, with a passionate interest in steam vehicles, although those which had inspired him were railway locomotives and ponderous traction engines. He also had a considerable private income at his disposal. It seemed the ideal partnership—and within a year the company of de Dion, Bouton and Trépardoux had been formed, experiments with marine steam generators had been started and abandoned, and a light steam car had taken to the road.

As with the petrol pioneers, the partners had no precedents or traditions of design to follow. They chose to drive the large front wheels by leather belts, and to steer by the smaller rear wheels. In order to keep the engine and boiler as compact as possible, they selected a liquid fuel, probably paraffin; after a few months of trials, the machine caught fire and was completely destroyed. Undeterred, they built another car the following year, with what was to become the accepted layout of front-wheel steering and rear-wheel drive. This could carry four passengers, and was succeeded by two still larger cars in 1885. One of these reverted to front-wheel drive and rear steering, though now using chains rather than belts to transmit the power. In 1887, Count de Dion entered his first four-seater in Europe's first motoring competition, a trial in the suburbs of Paris, organized by M. Fossier of *Le Vélocipède*, a cycling magazine. De Dion can hardly be said to have won, since his was the only car to turn up. But he did cover the route satisfactorily, and was reported to have been timed at a speed of 37 mph (60 km/h). If true, this is quite remarkable, as the first official Land Speed Record, set eleven years later, was only 39.24 mph (63 km/h).

In 1888, de Dion, Bouton and Trépardoux began to offer steam-driven tricycles for sale. These seem to have been taken up with enthusiasm by young playboys, who were part of the Count de Dion's social circle. The tricycles had boilers mounted between the front wheels, tiny two-cylinder engines beneath the riders' feet, and direct drive by a connecting rod to the rear wheel. They were made in small numbers until the 1890s, when they were joined by a large tractor which could pull either passenger- or goods-carrying trailers. This had a vertical boiler and a powerful two-cylinder engine mounted under the rear platform. Its most significant feature was its final drive, which was by non-load-bearing half-shafts with universal joints at each end. The rear axle was "dead", carrying the weight of the tractor but not transmitting power.

This system reduced the unsprung weight and, by using four steel spokes to transmit power to the wheel rim, the pressure was taken off the ordinary wooden spokes. The latter advantage was important, as the new tractors were much more powerful machines than the little tricycles and cars. The drive system came to be known as the de Dion axle, although it would be more just to call it the Bouton—or even the Trépardoux—axle. One of these tractors, attached to a horse-drawn victoria carriage minus its front wheels, took part in the Paris–Rouen Trial of 1894, finishing first at an average speed of 11.6 mph (18.7 km/h) over the journey of 78 ¾ miles (127 km). It was denied first prize, however, as two men were required to operate it, a steersman and a stoker.

De Dion Bouton continued to make steam-driven buses and trucks until 1904. But Georges Bouton's work on small, high-speed petrol engines pointed the company in a new direction. Trépardoux, a convinced steam man, distrusted this turn in the company's interests, and resigned in 1894.

Léon Serpollet

More important in the long run than the de Dion Bouton steamers were those of Léon Serpollet (1858–1907). A carpenter's son who spent his evenings working on boiler design, he perfected the flash boiler in 1885. In this, water was pumped into a multi-coiled pipe which was already heated, to be converted there in a flash into superheated steam. The result was a considerable reduction in the time needed to warm up the car before it was ready to start. As only a limited amount of water was being heated at any one moment, the danger of explosion was also reduced, although it had been greatly exaggerated anyway.

Serpollet used his boiler, or generator as he preferred to call it, in a tricycle which he built in 1887. Two years later, he had four heavier three-wheeled cars built for him by Armand Peugeot. One of these made a journey from Paris to Lyons and back in 1890, taking two weeks to cover the 790 miles (1,270 km). A few more of the three-wheelers, which could seat five passengers, were produced for Serpollet by the Parisian coachbuilder Jeantaud. But by 1892, Serpollet realized that the three-wheeler was too unstable, and turned to making four-wheeled commercial vehicles. They occupied him until 1899, when he obtained financial backing from an American living in Paris, Frank L. Gardner, who had made a fortune in Australian gold mines. A new series of Serpollet cars came into being, much more modern, with rear-mounted boilers, horizontally opposed paraffin-fired two- and four-cylinder engines located halfway between front and rear axles, and final drive by single chain to the centre of the rear axle. A hand-operated dual pump fed oil to the burner, and water to the boiler, in constant proportions. From 1904 onward, this pump was operated by a separate donkey engine.

With Frank Gardner's backing, Léon Serpollet was at last able to make a commercial success of passenger cars. Between 1900 and 1904, the work force in Gardner's large factory in the Rue Stendhal, Paris rose from about 60 to 140, and production ran at the rate of 100 or more cars per year. They ranged from light two-seaters to large, ornate touring limousines, one of which was ordered by the Shah of Persia. Serpollet was keen on sport, and in 1902 he drove a streamlined racing car, nicknamed Easter Egg, at a speed of 75.06 mph (121 km/h), setting a new Land Speed Record. He also fielded teams of racing cars in long-distance events, such as the 1903 Paris–Madrid race and the 1904 Gordon Bennett Trials, but he did not meet with great success. The steam car dwindled in popularity after about 1904 and, when Serpollet died of tuberculosis in 1907, his cars died with him. Fewer than a thousand Serpollet cars were built, but they were by far the most important of the European steam cars.

The steam car in America

It is fitting that the man who backed Léon Serpollet should have been an American, for the steam car played a much greater role in the motoring scene across the Atlantic than it ever did in Europe. This was almost entirely due to the enterprise of the Stanley twins, Francis E. (1849–1918) and Freeland O. (1849–1940), who built a reliable steam

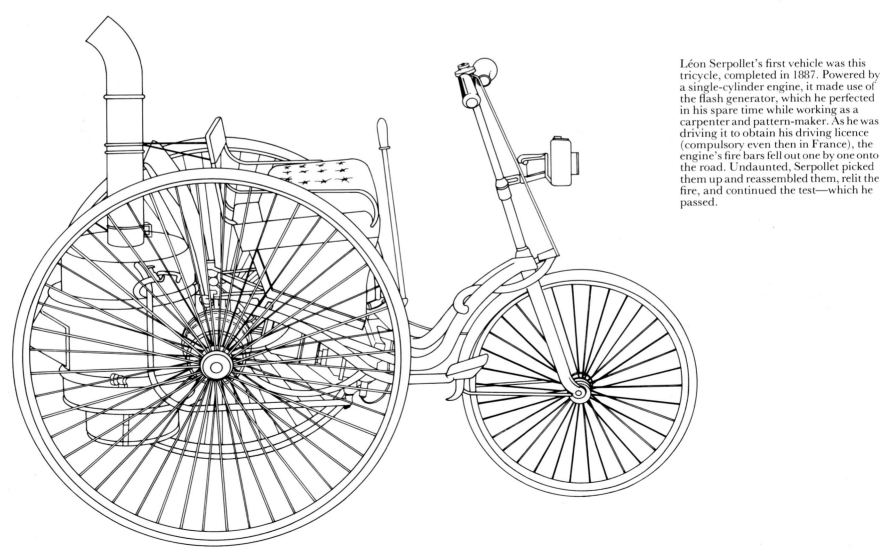

Léon Serpollet's first vehicle was this tricycle, completed in 1887. Powered by a single-cylinder engine, it made use of the flash generator, which he perfected in his spare time while working as a carpenter and pattern-maker. As he was driving it to obtain his driving licence (compulsory even then in France), the engine's fire bars fell out one by one onto the road. Undaunted, Serpollet picked them up and reassembled them, relit the fire, and continued the test—which he passed.

car at a low price. Owners of a prosperous photographic business in Newton, Massachusetts, they built their first light steam car in 1897. From autumn 1898 to autumn 1899, they made and sold 200 of these, far exceeding any other American manufacturer.

Their success attracted the attention of John Brisben Walker (1847–1931), owner of *Cosmopolitan Magazine,* and of the financier Amzi Lorenzo Barber (1843–1909). These men bought up all the patents and machinery of the Stanleys for $250,000 in the summer of 1899, and formed a new company—the Locomobile Company of America. Within a few weeks, a disagreement arose and they went their separate ways, Barber retaining Locomobile and Walker forming the Mobile Company of America. Frank Stanley joined Barber as a consulting engineer, and his brother held the same post with Walker. The two companies turned out very similar cars!

The design of the Stanley/Locomobile/Mobile was beautifully simple. A vertical two-cylinder engine was located in the centre of the frame, with a fire-tube boiler behind it working at a pressure of 180 pounds per square inch (13 kilograms per square centimetre). Behind this was a 22.5-gallon (85-litre) water tank which occupied the full width of the car. The 5-gallon (19-litre) fuel tank was placed at the front of the car, beneath the floorboards. Final drive was by a single chain from the crankshaft to the centre of the rear axle; the flexibility of the steam engine was such that no gearbox was needed. The frame was a tubular steel structure, and the body was a simple open two-seater.

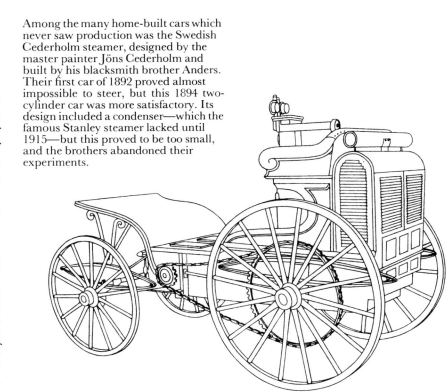

Among the many home-built cars which never saw production was the Swedish Cederholm steamer, designed by the master painter Jöns Cederholm and built by his blacksmith brother Anders. Their first car of 1892 proved almost impossible to steer, but this 1894 two-cylinder car was more satisfactory. Its design included a condenser—which the famous Stanley steamer lacked until 1915—but this proved to be too small, and the brothers abandoned their experiments.

One of several Serpollet cars to have streamlined bodies, this is the "Easter Egg", with which its builder covered a flying kilometre in 29.8 seconds, equivalent to a speed of 120.8 km/h (75.1 mph), at Nice in April 1902. This made Serpollet the fastest car driver in the world, beating the previous record by 14.9 km/h (9.3 mph).

(Left) The Locomobile was a typical light steamer made in America at the turn of the century, the same design being built also under the name Mobile. This 3.5-hp two-seater of 1899 was known as a Spindle Seat Runabout, and had a top speed of around 25 mph (40 km/h). The fuel tank was mounted under the floorboards, while the water tank occupied the full width of the rear part of the body, the boiler being dovetailed into it. The single chain drive went to the centre of the rear axle *(opposite top)*. To avoid infringing the Locomobile patents, the Stanley brothers geared their horizontal two-cylinder engine directly to the rear axle.

The whole car weighed about 700 pounds (317 kg), and top speed was 25 mph (40 km/h).

Running a steam car

Such a car had several important advantages over the internal combustion engine. It was virtually silent except for a hiss when accelerating, and free from the vibration which was a curse of cars powered by "nasty explosion engines". Best of all, there was no gearbox, so that the grinding and groaning associated with unskilled use of a sliding pinion transmission was unknown to the owner of a steam car. Nevertheless, skills of a different kind were needed, as well as patience. The starting procedure for a steamer was complicated and time-consuming, taking anything up to 45 minutes. The basic steps can be summarized as follows:

1. Check that the boiler and water tank are full.
2. Pump the fuel by hand up to minimum working pressure.
3. Heat the pilot burner, either by burning petrol in a cup, by alcohol wick, or by acetylene torch.
4. Allow the pilot to burn until the vapourizer is hot, then open the main burner valve carefully and check for correct operation.
5. While the water is heating, oil all moving parts.
6. When pressure reaches about 200 lb/in² (14 kg/cm²), get into the car and throw the reverse lever to its full forward and backward position. Open the throttle slightly, then close it at once, repeating until the engine starts. Work the reverse lever back and forth with the throttle open only a crack, so that the car "see-saws" gently. This will work the water out of the engine and warm up the cylinders, until the entering steam ceases to condense. *This process*

must not be hurried. An attempt to cut it short is likely to result in damage to the engine. As long as water is present, the engine will run jerkily. When it runs smoothly, the car is ready to run.

Once the car was running, a careful watch had to be kept on the pressure. Otherwise the engine would literally "run out of steam" on a hill, and a ten-minute pause would be necessary before the ascent could be completed.

In the early days, when all cars were capricious and needed skilful handling, this complexity could be forgiven. But as the petrol car became easier to drive and to maintain, the steamer did not, and the lengthy starting procedure in particular came to be regarded as an unacceptable chore. Another serious drawback was that, although the 5-gallon (19-litre) fuel tank was good for about 80 miles (130 km), the 22.5-gallon (85-litre) water tank needed to be refilled every 20 miles (30 km) or so. A journey of any length involved planning the watering halts, either at friendly houses, shops, or wayside streams.

Nevertheless, the steam car boom, albeit short-lived, was a remarkable phenomenon. Locomobile outsold all petrol-engine makes of car in 1899 and 1900, second only to the Columbia Electric in the American sales league. For the next two years they topped the league, selling about 1,500 cars in 1901, and 2,750 in 1902. Mobile had ten factory branches and 58 agencies from coast to coast. The steamer's centre of popularity in manufacture and sales, however, was New England. Of 84 makes of steam car which flourished in the United States, mostly between 1899 and 1905, no fewer than 38 were made in the states of Massachusetts, New Hampshire, New York, and Maine. These included most of the leading makers such as Locomobile, Mobile, and Stanley. In 1902, only 909 new passenger cars were registered in the

The Stanley twins tried to keep prices down through simplicity of design. They never adopted the flash boiler, and did not feature a condenser until 1915. Their 1904 folding-front four-seater *(page 31 bottom)* sold for $750, and in 1906 they introduced a series of Roadsters which were some of America's first sports cars. These were made in three sizes: the Model EX (18-inch boiler, 10-hp engine), Model H (23-inch, 20-hp), and Model K (26-inch, 30-hp). The H, and its 1910 successor the Model 10 *(above)*, were known as Gentleman's Speedy Roadsters. It was capable of 68 mph (109 km/h), and F. E. Stanley was once stopped by the police when doing 87 mph (140 km/h) in his special Model K. The Stanley engine, driving directly on the rear axle, was little changed after twenty years, and a postwar example is illustrated here *(right)*.

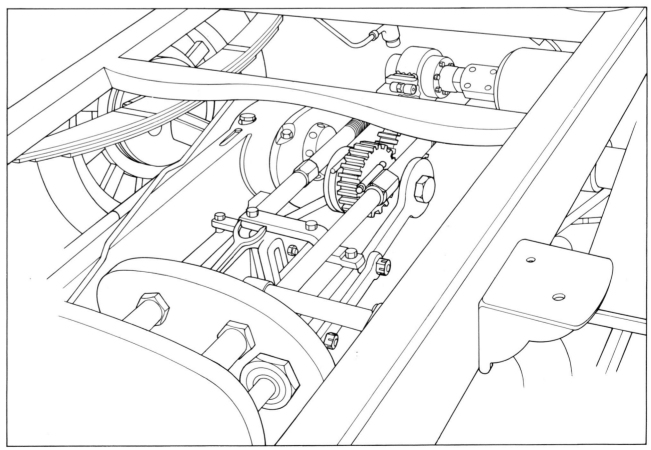

Almost from the start, the White was a more sophisticated machine than the Stanley. This 1905 chassis of the 15-hp car has a flash steam generator surmounted by flues below the driver's seat, a water feed controllable by the driver, and a clutch which allowed the engine to run and operate the pumps while the car was stationary. Previously, the pumps had to be hand-operated except when the car was moving. The front-mounted condenser gave the White the appearance of a petrol car.

With a side-entrance tonneau body, the 1905 White cost $2,000, nearly twice the price of the equivalent Stanley steamer.

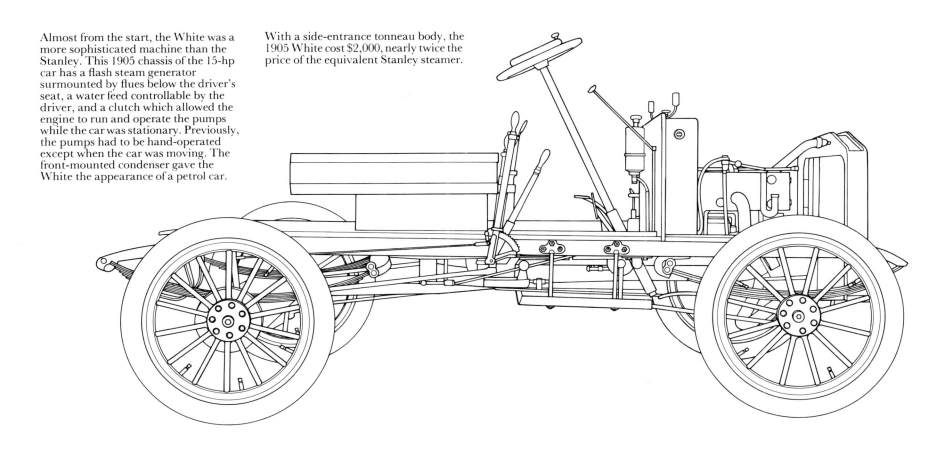

State of New York, and 485 of them were steam-powered.

On the whole, the little steamers were pretty much the same in design, following the Locomobile pattern. But when the Stanley brothers set up on their own again, they had to make alterations in order not to infringe their own patents, which now belonged to Messrs. Barber and Walker. The main change they introduced was to mount the engine horizontally and gear it directly to the rear axle. They kept this layout for the next 25 years, being by far the longest-lived steam car manufacturers. The Stanleys also adopted a front-mounted boiler. Other variations on the basic design included the flash generator used by White of Cleveland, Ohio; shaft drive in the Century from Syracuse, New York; four-wheel drive by chains, as well as four-wheel steering, on the Cotta from Lanark, Illinois; a V-twin engine in the Crouch from New Brighton, Pennsylvania; and a three-cylinder engine and shaft drive on the Boston-built Eclipse. The Hood Electronic Safety Steam Vehicle from Danvers, Massachusetts, had a four-cylinder engine with magnetic inlet valves operated by three batteries guaranteed for more than six months' use—yet alas, the makers themselves lasted for little more than twelve months. The Kidder of New Haven, Connecticut, employed two horizontal cylinders, one on each side of the boiler, driving the rear axle directly.

Most of the smaller manufacturers assembled their cars from bought-out components, bringing short-lived prosperity to a variety of component makers. This explains the general uniformity of design. The J.W. Skene Cycle and Automobile Company of Lewiston, Maine, was unusual in claiming that every part of their car was made on the premises except for the tyres. Perhaps the fact that they also made bicycles helped.

The decline of steam

The steam-car boom was very short-lived indeed. By the end of 1903, 43 firms had come and gone—including the leaders in the field, Locomobile and Mobile. The former switched to internal combustion cars, which they made with great success up to 1929, while Mobile simply faded away after building 6,000 cars in five years. Possibly their mistake lay in making too many models: 20 in 1902, and 15 in 1903, ranging in price from $550 for a runabout to $3,000 for an enclosed limousine. A few makers struggled on for five or six years, but the only important survivors were Stanley and White.

White abandoned the light two-seater buggy, and went in for larger five-seater tourers priced at up to $4,700. Their refinements included a clutch which allowed the engine to run free at any speed when the car was stopped, and a "flow regulator which provided constant steam pressure at a constant temperature under all conditions". For several years, White steamers sold well, and in 1907 they opened a new factory on a 30-acre (12-hectare) site outside Cleveland, to cope with the rush of orders. In fact, 1906—when they sold 1,534 cars—was their best year, although they stayed in four figures until 1910. In that year, they followed Locomobile in opting for the internal combustion engine, later concentrating on commercial vehicles which are still made today.

Stanley continued to make cheaper cars, such as the $850 Model FX Runabout, as well as more expensive models including sporting cars that had a very fair turn of speed. The delightfully named Gentleman's Speedy Roadster was capable of 68 mph (109 km/h) in 1906. Indeed, the unofficial Land Speed Record was held by a special Stanley which achieved 127.66 (205 km/h) at Ormond Beach, Florida, in January 1906. Unfortunately, prices tended to rise as the Stanleys

The steam car was a rarity by the 1920s, although Stanley struggled on until 1924 and several other makes sputtered briefly across the scene. The 1920 Stanley Model 735 four-passenger coupé *(right)* cost around $3,800, and fewer than a thousand Stanleys found buyers that year. Like the Stanley, the Canadian-built Brooks *(below)* had a boiler under the bonnet, and a horizontal two-cylinder engine driving the rear axle directly. Its 21-gallon (80-litre) copper water tank, mounted behind the rear axle, gave a range of 450–500 miles (725–800 km), while the 15-gallon (57-litre) fuel tank was good for 250–300 miles (400–480 km). This was a reversal of the situation in the early days, when water consumption was the enemy that kept the range down. Thanks to an efficient condenser, water loss was now much lower. The 1925 fabric-bodied sedan was Brooks' only style, but its cost of $3,885 was later reduced by a thousand dollars.

tried to keep up with the growing ease of operation of the petrol car, and this inevitably hit their sales. As we have noted, in 1902 steam cars easily outsold petrol ones in New York, and the margin was probably even greater in the Stanleys' home state of Massachusetts, but it was not to last.

R.W. Stanley, the son of "F.E.", remarked that one evening in 1904 his father returned home and announced that he had just learned something which made him feel very unhappy. The list of cars registered in Massachusetts revealed that, for the first time, there were more petrol-engined cars registered than steamers. By 1916, just 779 Stanleys were registered in Massachusetts, compared with 30,871 Fords and 25 other makes of petrol car whose numbers exceeded those of the Stanley. At that time, no other steamers were being made in the United States. The cheapest Stanley now cost $2,750, which put it in the upper price bracket—yet despite their advertising, it was a much more complex machine to manage. A petrol car in the Stanley's bracket would almost certainly have had a self-starter, while the owner of a 1916 Stanley had to follow the same "firing up" routine listed earlier in this chapter. Thus, there was a distinctly hollow ring about the Stanley ad:

> The Stanley uses no clutches, gearshifts, flywheels, carburettors, magnetoes, spark plugs, distributors, self starters, or any of the marvellously ingenious complications with which inventors have had to overcome the difficulties inherent in the explosive engine. That is why 90 per cent of Stanley owners drive their cars without the assistance of trained chauffeurs.

Many people would have retorted that, if you didn't need a trained chauffeur, you had to be a trained engineer in order to operate a Stanley properly. And anyway, more than 90 per cent of Americans generally drove without the aid of a chauffeur.

During the 1920s, Stanley sales dwindled still further, and owners became a tiny group of "enthusiasts"—ever keener as their numbers grew rarer, but quite insignificant in the motor industry as a whole. In 1922, Americans bought more than 2 ¼ million cars, of which only 600 were Stanleys. By then, an enclosed brougham cost $3,950, more than a Cadillac V-8. The last Stanleys, complete with such up-to-date features as hydraulic front-wheel brakes and balloon tyres, were made in 1925.

Curiously, there was a sudden surge of interest in the steam car in 1922/23, and—apart from Stanley—eight firms announced their intention to make steamers. Some were mere stock promotion schemes, but the Canadian-made Brooks was a serious contender on the market, and about 180 of these were sold beween 1923 and 1926. The cream of the steam cars was the Doble, made in very small numbers in Emeryville, California. One of the most expensive cars on the American market, it had a flash boiler and a four-cylinder horizontal engine located ahead of the rear axle. A really efficient condenser consumed practically all of the steam generated, which gave the car an excellent range of 1,500 miles (2,413 km) on a 24-gallon (90-litre) tank, compared with 30–40 miles (48–65 km) for an earlier steamer. Instead of a pilot light, there was an electric ignition system which enabled the car to move off in about 40 seconds, compared with as many minutes for a Stanley.

With a light body, a Doble could reach 108 mph (174 km/h), and accelerate to 40 mph (64 km/h) in eight seconds. Most of the 45 Dobles made carried custom coachwork by Walter Murphy of Pasadena, with price tags from $8,800 to $11,200. The number of people who were both wealthy and sufficiently adventurous to go in for steam in the mid-1920s was very small, although the young millionaire Howard Hughes had two. After the last Doble was completed in 1931, no more steam cars were made commercially. Still, amateur engineers continued toying with the idea up to the 1960s.

Electricity

Like the steamer, the electric car was silent and free from gear-changing. But it was slow, unsuited to climbing hills, and generally limited to a range of some 50 miles (80 km) between battery charges. The first electric cars were made in 1888 and 1890, by Magnus Volk in England and William Morrison in America. Volk sold a dogcart to the Sultan of Turkey—the first British export of a passenger car—and Morrison made twelve vehicles between 1890 and 1895. The first serious manufacturers of electric cars, however, were Henry Morris and Pedro Salom of Philadelphia. They built an experimental car in 1894 and, the following year, began production of their Electrobats.

Initially each of these cars carried its own name, as did ships and railway locomotives: the Fish Wagon, Crawford Wagon, the Skeleton Bat, and so on. Yet after they had made a dozen or so, they ran out of names, and the 1896 models were called simply Electrobats. Most had front-wheel drive and some rear-wheel steering, the front wheels being considerably larger. Each wheel contained its own electric motor, and the cars had a range of 25 miles (40 km) per battery charge at a steady 20 mph (32 km/h). The bulk of Morris and Salom's production was devoted to hansom cabs which were operated in New York, Boston, and other cities. In 1897, their Electric Carriage and Wagon Company was bought by Isaac L. Rice, who incorporated it in his Electric Vehicle Company of Elizabethport, New Jersey. This later became part of Colonel Albert A. Pope's empire, which had been founded on the manufacture of bicycles and, by 1900, included petrol, steam, and electric cars. A wide range of Columbia electric vehicles was made by Pope's firm in its extensive factory at Hartford, Connecticut, from the little Town and Country Runabout at $950 to a Town Brougham at $3,500.

Although Columbia was the main maker of electric cars—in 1899 and 1900 they led the country in car production—they were not alone. In the early years of the century, there were several respected names such as Baker of Cleveland, Riker of Elizabethport, and Woods of Chicago. In 1907, these were joined by the Detroit Electric, which became the best-known and longest-lived of all. Open cars were made by Detroit and other manufacturers, but from about 1910 onward the usual electric car was a fully closed brougham, sometimes nicknamed a mobile china cabinet because of its tall, angular lines and large area of glass all round. A typical electric brougham had a 40-cell battery, a 4-hp motor geared to the rear axle, and five or six speeds controlled by lever or pedal. The pedal operated in the opposite way to the accelerator of a petrol car: when it was fully depressed the brakes came on, and as it was progressively released the speed rose.

The years 1910 to 1915 represented the peak period for making and using electric cars. They appealed particularly to women, for whom the absence of a self-starter put most petrol cars out of the question unless there was a helpful male around. But with an electric brougham, Madame could go shopping and pay social calls, protected from the weather and with the greatest ease of driving. What she could not do was to travel more than about 50 miles (80 km) per day, or to venture onto country roads. But then the normal electric-car owner was a city dweller who kept her daily journeys to within the city limits. If she wanted to go further afield, she rode in her husband's petrol car or,

These two electric cars were typical of their respective periods. In 1901, when the Baker two-seater *(opposite)* was made, most cars—whether electric or not—were open, and this runabout differed little in appearance or amenities from petrol or steam cars. The 1915

Detroit Electric *(below)* has a fully enclosed brougham body, like most of its kind. Electric cars were not cheap: Detroit's prices ran from $2,550 to $3,000 in 1914, and a Borland-Grannis limousine cost $5,500.

more likely, they both took a train. The electric car became more popular in America than in Europe because roads outside the cities were so bad, and because wealth tended to be concentrated in the cities rather than spread over every town and village. There were, of course, the very rich, such as the Rockefellers and Vanderbilts who had country estates. Yet the average successful businessman had only a town house, from which his wife could drive her electric car to the shops. His British equivalent bought a manor house in the country, where an electric car was much less practical.

The importance of the electric car to the well-off, urban American woman is clearly shown in a photograph of the cars assembled outside the Detroit Athletic Club in about 1914, when the members invited their wives to inspect the premises. Of about 35 cars visible in the picture, all but three are electrics. This happy state of affairs did not last long, and within six or seven years the electric car was on the wane. The introduction of the self-starter had something to do with this, but people's expectations were rising as well. A top speed of 20 mph (32 km/h) and a limited range were acceptable in 1914, but no longer so in 1920 when improved roads made out-of-town journeys more feasible.

The "lady image", which electric cars had always had, became an "old lady image" in the 1920s. They were still favoured by those who had used them when younger, but whose daughters now went for a Dodge or Chevrolet coupé or, if more sporting, a Jordan Playboy. In 1921, only 18,184 electric cars were registered in America, out of more than nine million. There were more Peerlesses or Auburns, neither of these being particularly well-known makes, than all the electrics put together. Ten years later, the number of electrics was so insignificant tht it did not feature in statistics. The Detroit was theoretically available until 1942, although 1938 seems to have seen the last known delivery. By then, they had lost the china-closet look, as they used the sheet metal of the current Dodge cars. This, sadly, did not help sales.

In Europe the electric car was always in a minority, and one would never have seen clusters of electric coupés outside the London or Paris equivalent of the Detroit Athletic Club. In London, the Electromobile Company manufactured town cars, and also hired them out at a charge of £325 per year to cover maintenance and all expenses except the chauffeur's wages. Since this was equivalent to more than £6,000 in today's money, it is hardly surprising that there were few takers. One or two French manufacturers explored the petrol-electric avenue, a compromise in which a petrol engine drove a dynamo that generated power for one—or sometimes two—electric motors. This combined the electric car's freedom from gear-changing with the petrol car's greater range, but it was not an efficient use of power, and lasted only a few years. The system was more popular in commercial vehicles, such as the British Tilling-Stevens buses of the 1920s.

Virtually no electric passengers cars were made in Europe after 1914. Still, commercial applications continued to appear, and today Britain produces more electric milk-floats and other light vehicles than any other country in the world.

THE BATTLE OF
THE CYLINDERS

3

Returning to the mainstream of motorcar development, we may recall from Chapter 1 that the *systéme Benz* lasted throughout the 1890s on the Mannheim-built cars and their imitators. But by 1900, it was clear that the forefront of design was moving away from Benz in practically every respect. The rear-mounted horizontal engine driving through a belt-and-pulley arrangement grew less popular, on the larger cars at any rate. What now took strong root was a front-mounted vertical engine driving through a sliding pinion gearbox and chains. The best-known proponent of this system was the Panhard et Levassor. Yet in the summer of 1900 rumours began to come out of Germany about a new car which would instantly make all its competitors seem old-fashioned. In July, Paul Meyan—editor of the influential French magazine *La France Automobile*—warned that "French factories would do well to get busy extremely quickly, in order that Daimler should not set the fashion in France."

The birth of the Mercedes

The newcomer arose through one man's dissatisfaction with the existing Daimler cars. Emil Jellinek, Pro-Consul of the Austro-Hungarian Empire in Nice, was no ordinary customer, though. He acted as an unofficial salesman for the cars amongst the wealthy and fashionable set who congregated on the French Riviera during the winter months. By 1900 he had sold 34 cars, but he encountered increasing resistance because the most powerful four-cylinder Daimler Phoenix was too short and high for safety. In March, Wilhelm Bauer was killed in one, when it ran wide at the first corner of the La Turbie hill-climb at Nice, and crashed into some rocks. This was the last competition appearance of the old-style Daimler.

Even before that, however, Jellinek had been to Cannstatt and requested a more up-to-date, safer design, promising substantial orders if he liked what was offered. Paul Daimler had already designed a light car with two-cylinder engine, crankcase and gearbox cast as a single unit, and a foot-accelerator. Wilhelm Maybach improved on this, and added a honeycomb radiator, much more efficient than the old gilled-tube type, which needed a separate water tank since the tubes could not hold enough. The honeycomb consisted of a vertical tank pierced by more than 5,000 small square-section air tubes, with a thin film of water separating each tube from its neighbour. This allowed a large engine to be adequately cooled by a relatively small amount of water, requiring no separate tank.

Other advanced features of the new car were adopted on the new car. A pressed steel frame replaced the customary armoured wood. A gate-type gear-change enabled the driver to select each speed at will, instead of having to proceed through every gear when going from top to neutral. Maybach added, to these features, mechanically operated inlet valves and a much lower, longer frame, giving the car a completely fresh appearance. The radiator was raised so as to be fully framed by the bonnet, rather than being slung bween the front ends of the chassis frame.

Jellinek was very pleased with the new design. As early as April 1900, before any cars had been finished, he placed an order for 36. Feeling that the Daimler name was somewhat discredited in France, he called the new car a Mercedes, after his eldest daughter. At first, this name was to be used only in Jellinek's own territory of France, Belgium, Austro-Hungary, and the United States. But it was soon adopted everywhere, and the alternative name of New Daimler never became established. However, the company remained the Daimler Motoren Gesellschaft, and subsequently Daimler-Benz AG, until the present day.

The first Mercedes engine had a capacity of 5.9 litres and was known as the 35-hp. In 1902, it was increased to 6.8 litres and 40 hp, to be joined later in 1902 by the most famous of all early Mercedes, the 9.2-litre 60-hp. This had overhead inlet valves and, with a light body, could reach 75 mph (120 km/h). The chassis was therefore ideally suited to touring or racing. It could carry a heavy limousine body—of which the extreme was represented by Jellinek's own car, resembling a small bus with twin rear wheels—or a stark two-seater that could, and did, compete in the major races. In modern terms, the Mercedes 60 combined in one car the functions of a Rolls-Royce Phantom VI and a Formula One racer. Its sporting ability was demonstrated when the team of 90-hp racing cars entered for the prestigious Gordon Bennett race was destroyed in a factory fire. Rather than withdrawing the team, the company hastily called back three cars from their private owners, stripped and prepared them for racing, and sent them over to Ireland. The car driven by the Belgian, Camille Jenatzy, won the event, with another Mercedes 60 in fifth place.

The success of the Mercedes 60 put the German company at the frontier of fashion and design. By 1904, it was *the* car to own if you could afford it, and to copy if you were an ambitious manufacturer. Suddenly the Panhard seemed archaic with its gilled-tube radiator and armoured-wood frame, and lost forever the preeminent position which it had held for ten years. Well-known makers who took up the

Mercedes theme included Berliet and Rochet-Schneider in France, Martini in Switzerland, Ariel and Star in England, and Fiat in Italy. The last was particularly close in appearance as well as design, and led one magazine, *The Car Illustrated*, to describe the 1905 models as "Italian editions of the Mercedes". Supporters of this idea pointed to the fact that British owners of Mercedes who were touring Italy took their cars to the Fiat works for servicing. But this was simply a tribute to the good workmanship of the Fiat service engineers. In any case, there were precious few other garages for them to go to.

The coming of the Six (and more)

While the Mercedes 60 and its imitators had four-cylinder engines, there was a limit to the size of each cylinder, if any degree of smooth running and silence was to be achieved. Just as the four-cylinder engine had replaced the twin-cylinder for larger cars, so the logical extension of the four was the in-line six. The Dutch firm of Spyker was the first to put a six-cylinder engine in a car, an experimental machine completed in 1902. This had an 8.7-litre T-head engine which developed about 40 hp, although later publicity called it a 60-hp. It was also a pioneer in having four-wheel drive and braking, but it was in no way a production car. There were plans to enter it in the 1903 Paris–Madrid Race, yet components frequently broke when tested, and it was not reliable enough to withstand several hundred miles of racing.

The first company to offer a six for commercial sale was D. Napier & Sons, of Acton in West London, who launched an 18-hp car with an engine of 4,852 cc in October 1903. Like the 60-hp Mercedes, it had overhead inlet valves. At a price of £1,050 for the chassis, it was by no means cheap, and few of the initial Napier sixes were made. Still, it launched the company as the pioneer manufacturer of six-cylinder

cars. Napier's director, S.F. Edge, lost no opportunity of championing the six, from the end of 1903 until his separation from the company eight years later. In countless advertisements and letters to the press, he set out to demonstrate, as historian Anthony Bird has written, "that the four-cylinder engine was all wrong, the six was right and the Napier sixes were righter than all the others."

In theory, the six did have a great advantage over the four. Its overlapping power impulses gave much better low-speed torque, which should reduce the need for gear-changing. As this was the *bête noire* of most drivers, Edge had a strong argument. But severe problems soon showed up with the six, due to crankshaft vibration. The crankshaft was obviously longer than in a four-cylinder engine and, in order to save weight, it was lighter in construction. This meant that it tended to turn on its axis, "winding and unwinding like the elastic of a toy aeroplane" (the inimitable Anthony Bird again). Although exaggerated, the twisting effect often led to fracture of the crankshaft and to total destruction of the engine.

Torsional vibration plagued not only the six-cylinder Napiers, but also the 30/40-hp Rolls-Royce and the early six-cylinder British Daimlers. The latter were so troublesome that the company had a stock of cars on their hands which were unsaleable, leading them to call in Frederick Lanchester. His solution was to employ a secondary flywheel at the front of the crankshaft, the Lanchester Torsional Vibration Damper. In fact—because it was used first on Daimler cars, long before the Daimler/Lanchester merger in 1931—Lanchester's invention was generally called the Daimler crankshaft damper, or the Warner Crankshaft Damper in America where the patent rights were bought by the Warner Company. Henry Royce solved the problem in a similar way, also using crankpins and journals of twice the diameter of those in the 30/40-hp engine.

The 1899 Daimler Phoenix (opposite) foreshadowed the first Mercedes, notably in its use of a gate gear-change and pressed steel frame. The radiator was mounted low down, between the front wheels and below the coal-scuttle bonnet. A raising of the radiator, so as to be framed by the bonnet, was what gave the Mercedes its more modern appearance.

The 60-hp Mercedes (right), made from 1902 to 1905, was the car that brought the new marque into the limelight, combining power with flexibility as well as quality of workmanship. It was produced in America by the Daimler Manufacturing Company, of Long Island City, an affiliate of the famous piano makers William Steinway, and it set a pattern that was imitated by numerous designers on both sides of the Atlantic. Among these "crypto-Mercedes" cars was the 40-hp Berliet (below), from the best-known automobile factory in Lyon (which still makes trucks today, although now under Renault ownership and carrying Renault badges). The 6.3-litre Berliet shared the Mercedes' mechanically operated overhead inlet valves, honeycomb radiator, and pressed steel frame.

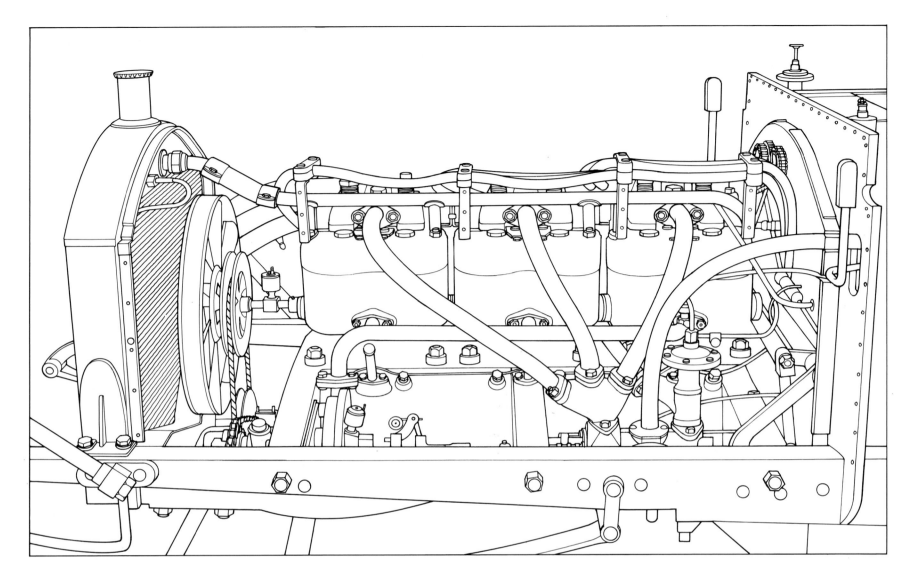

Even prior to the adoption of the vibration damper, there was a rush to take up the six-cylinder engine from about 1906 onwards. Mercedes and Fiat built their first six in 1907, and other well-known firms who followed the trend included Darracq, Delaunay-Belleville, Lancia, Renault, and Sunbeam. There were also many sixes from smaller firms, some being final flings before a slide into bankruptcy, such as the 30-hp James & Browne Vertex or the 35/45-hp MMC. Doubtless their undamped crankshafts hastened their end. Proprietary engine makers like White & Poppe in Britain and Mutel in France offered sixes, helping to swell the numbers on the market.

In 1908/9, no fewer than 62 makes of six-cylinder car were on the British market alone, and the worldwide figure must have approached 80. Many of these were made in very small quantities, though, and from 1910 onwards the fashion waned. The best sixes such as Daimler, Lanchester, Napier, and Rolls-Royce were continued, but Fiat abandoned their enormous 50/60-hp after only 116 had been made. With a capacity of more than 11 litres, it was the largest road-going Fiat ever built, and counted among its owners the German Kaiser and the great English car connoisseur Lionel de Rothschild. However, it was renowned for its crankshaft vibration, which was described by one owner as "tooth-shaking", and its smaller sisters were not much better. In 1911 Fiat gave up sixes altogether.

Another famous manufacturer to burn his fingers with the six was Henry Ford. After founding his company with the low-priced two-cylinder Models A, C, and F, he was persuaded by his partner Alexander Malcolmson to enter a higher-priced market with the six-cylinder 6.6-litre Model K, which sold for $2,500. It made no profit for Henry, and an increase to $2,800 only stiffened the sales resistance. Nonetheless, in 1906 the new $500 four-cylinder Model N was selling well, and Henry took advantage of this to unload Model K's on his dealers. If they wanted the Model N, they had to take one Model K with every ten of the popular small cars. Even so, it took more than two years to dispose of the 584 Model K's produced. This experience made Henry so wary of six-cylinder cars that Ford did not create another until 1941—and then it was a cheap model, not a luxury car.

The V-8

If six cylinders promised greater smoothness than fours, the logical next step was to eight. The two most widely used ways of arranging eight cylinders both appeared in France in 1903. The 7.2-litre straight-eight C.G.V. employed two of the company's four-cylinder engines, and was thought to be so flexible that it dispensed with a gearbox altogether. However, it never went into production, nor did it compete in a race—unlike the first V-8 car, the 3.6-litre Ader. Clément Ader has gone down in history as a pioneer of the telephone in France, and

(Opposite) Napier's first six-cylinder engine was not particularly successful, but it set a trend that was followed by numerous other designers, and characterized Napiers until the end of the company's car-making life in 1924. Announced in February 1904, this 4.9-litre unit was rated as an 18-hp, but developed around 30 hp at 900 rpm. Visible here are the mechanically operated overhead inlet valves, actuated by long exposed pushrods. The combination of overhead inlet with side exhaust valves was a Mercedes feature, copied by many makers.

(Above) In the days when transmissions required frequent maintenance, it was an advantage to have a body which could be hinged out of the way, without the complication of removing floor-boards. This system was popular on some American cars and, if they were mid-engined, the power unit was accessible as well. Among American makes which offered tilting bodies were Gale and Model.

also for his attempts to fly in a steam-powered aeroplane in the 1890s! But he also made a number of cars powered by V-formation engines. He began with a 904-cc V-twin, and joined two of these together to form a V-4. When he wanted a more powerful car to compete in the 1903 Paris–Madrid Race, he combined two V-4's to make the world's first road-going V-8 engine. Not more than three or four were made, and they were never offered for sale.

Compared with the six, the V-8 was slow to catch on. Rolls-Royce made three of their "Legalimit" in 1905, but it was the least successful car that the company ever made, and the only model of which there are no survivors. Darracq took the World Land Speed Record in December 1905 with a 22.5-litre V-8. The following year, the French Antoinette company brought out a V-8 engine "suitable for use in motorcars or aeroplanes". However, virtually no V-8 cars were made for sale until De Dion Bouton launched their 6.1-litre Model CJ at the 1910 Turin Show. It had a twin-barrel carburettor, for each bank of cylinders, and dual magnetic ignition. The CJ was followed by several other De Dion-made V-8's, the smallest being the 3-litre EC, and the largest the 14.8-litre EZ with twin rear tyres which may never have been more than a prototype. These engines took the company into the luxury car market for the first time, but they did not sell very well. Although smooth, the engines developed inadequate power in relation to their size, and the company lacked the resources to improve them.

By 1911, when this Barker-bodied Silver Ghost landaulette was made, Rolls-Royce were already advertising themselves as "The Best Car in the World", and were well on the way to deserving the title. Their cars were certainly smoother than Napiers and more lively than Daimlers, their chief British rivals. The original four-speed gearbox with overdrive top gear had been replaced in 1909 by a three-speed box, and the engine was so flexible that speeds of 3 to 65 mph (5–105 km/h) were possible on the direct-drive top gear. Combined with a remarkable lightness of steering and clutch, this made the Edwardian Silver Ghost one of the most enjoyable cars to drive.

No other European manufacturers followed De Dion Bouton, and it was left to Cadillac to make the first commercially successful V-8 engined car. Designed by Wilfred Leland, this developed 70 bhp from its 5.1 litres, a much greater volumetric efficiency than any of the De Dions, and it sold at a modest $2,700 for a five-passenger tourer. Introduced in October 1914 as a 1915 model, the Cadillac V-8 was an immediate triumph, and boosted the company's sales from 7,818 to 20,404 cars in its first year of production. Other manufacturers were not slow to follow the V-8 fashion, aided by the entry of the proprietary engine makers into the field. These included Herschell-Spillman, Ferro, Northway, and Perkins (of Detroit and unrelated to the British diesel-engine makers). Northway was owned by General Motors, and in fact built Cadillac V-8's, so it is somewhat surprising that they also supplied engines to Cole of Indianapolis and to Jackson of Jackson, Michigan. By 1918, at least twenty American car makers were offering V-8 power to their customers, from the well-known Cadillac and Oldsmobile, through small quality firms like Cunningham and Daniels, to the obscure and seldom-heard-of Murray, Vernon, and Yale.

The V-12

Hard on the heels of Cadillac's V-8 came the world's first commercially built V-12, the Packard Twin Six, which was launched in the spring of 1915. It developed 88 bhp from 6.9 litres, and featured coil ignition, aluminium pistons, and full-pressure lubrication. For such an advanced car, it was remarkably cheap: prices started at $2,750, hardly more than the cheapest Cadillac, although for an Imperial Limousine one had to fork out $4,800. From 1916 to 1920, the Twin Six was Packard's only model, and by the time manufacture ended in 1923 they had sold 35,000, more than the total production of Rolls-Royces from 1904 to 1939. As with the V-8, the Twin Six brought forth imitations. National of Indianapolis made their own engine; but when Weidely Motors Company, of the same city, announced a proprietary V-12 in 1916, the way was open for all sorts of small firms to add the prestige of a twelve to their range. However, none of them had much success, and by 1921 the short-lived V-12 vogue was over, to be revived ten years later by such well-known firms as Cadillac, Lincoln, and Pierce-Arrow.

On the other side of the Atlantic, the multi-cylinder trend took much longer to become established. The V-8 and V-12 flowered in America while Europe was tearing itself to pieces in war. When the conflict was over, Lancia built a prototype narrow-angle (22°) V-12 engine. Fiat actually produced a handful of their Super-Fiat 6.8-litre 60° V-12, but it only lasted in the catalogue for one season (1921–22). In Britain, the Wolverhampton truck makers, Guy, offered a 4-litre V-8 from 1920 to 1924, selling about 150 of these; and another truck firm, British Ensign, promised a V-12 which never appeared. It was not until 1926 that a production V-12 came from a European factory, the sleeve-valve Double Six Daimler.

Technical developments

The emergence of bigger engines went hand in hand, often as a cause or effect, with many other specific inventions and refinements in the earliest luxury cars of the twentieth century. These ranged from improving the generation of power to increasing the general road-worthiness of the car for an ever more discerning public.

Valves and carburettors

When Wilhelm Maybach introduced mechanically operated inlet valves, he greatly raised the potential of the petrol engine. The automatic inlet valve had opened by suction when the piston dropped, and was closed by a spring. If the spring was too strong, the valve would not open in time; and if it was too weak, the valve would bounce on the seat and eventually break. Automatic valves tended to work best at a constant engine speed of not more than 1,500 rpm, which was fine for the gas-engine derived unit of the Benz type, but very restrictive for the more ambitious designer. A mechanically operated inlet valve permitted unlimited development of engine speeds, although this did not happen quickly.

The general arrangement of the valves was to have the inlets on one side of the engine and the exhausts on the other side, each worked positively by cam and tappet, and closed by springs. This layout, known as the T-head, required two camshafts, one for each set of valves. It was to avoid this complication that the L-head arrangement, with all the valves on one side of the engine, became the norm from about 1906 onwards. The L-head was not suited to high performance, as the combustion-chamber shape was not very efficient. So the next step was to mount the valves in the cylinder head, preferably inclined at an angle. This was first seen on the Belgian Pipe in 1904, but it did not become widespread until the 1920s.

A popular alternative to the conventional poppet valve was the sleeve valve, invented by an American, Charles Yale Knight (1868-1940). Here, two concentric sleeves within the cylinder moved up and down, uncovering inlet and exhaust ports as they did so. They were operated by short connecting rods from an eccentric shaft which performed the duties of a camshaft. As the connecting rods operated positively both up and down, there was no need for springs as with the poppet valve. The sleeves had a much longer life than poppet valves, which at that time needed grinding or replacing every few thousand miles (km). The engine was also much quieter, since there were no camshafts operating on tappets to cause the mechanical clatter associated with contemporary poppet-valve engines. Against this, one had to set the greater cost, because of the precision required for manufacture of the sleeves, and also because of the $100 royalty taken by Knight for each engine made. The sleeve-valve system used more oil, and if the sleeves became even slightly deformed—their working clearances were about 3/1,000 inch (0.08 mm)—they allowed oil into the combustion chamber, resulting in a heavy smokescreen from the exhaust. They were so delicate that they had to be stored on their ends, as laying them on their sides could cause deformation.

Despite these drawbacks, the Knight engine became very popular with makers of the more expensive cars. The first to take it up was Daimler in Britain, who made sleeve-valve engines exclusively from 1909 to 1933. They were followed by Minerva in Belgium (1909-1939), Panhard in France (most of whose models were sleeve-valve from 1911 to 1939), and Mercedes in Germany who made a mixed range of sleeve- and poppet-valve engines from 1909 to 1924. In America, Willys took up the design in 1914 and made the Willys-Knight until 1932, besides the associated Falcon-Knight and Stearns-Knight. Famous manufacturers who joined the Knight supporters in the 1920s included Voisin, Mors, and Peugeot; altogether about thirty firms used Knight engines. Other systems were tried, such as the Burt McCollum single sleeve valve that was favoured by the Scottish Argyll, the cuff valve (a smaller sleeve), and the rotary valve. Renault patented, but apparently never made, an extraordinary engine with overhead poppet inlet valve and sleeve exhaust.

This Lanchester double landaulette of 1910 is typical of the idiosyncratic designs by "Doctor Fred" in the Edwardian period. It has virtually no bonnet, the engine being located between driver and front passenger, but the long wheelbase gave an unusually comfortable ride. By 1910, all Lanchesters were supplied with steering wheels, though the lever was theoretically available until 1911.

As well as the mechanically operated inlet valve, Maybach made a vital contribution to car development with his spray carburettor. This was a great improvement over the Benz system, in which the air was simply passed over the surface of the petrol in the tank, channelled by baffle-plates or perforated pipes to aid the production of an inflammable mixture. Maybach employed a float feed and a spray which mixed petrol with air. This was later refined by Krebs, of Panhard et Levassor, who devised an extra air inlet under the driver's control, so that the ratio of air and petrol could be varied while the car was in motion. Attempts to make this an automatic function were not always successful and, for a number of years, skill with the hand control was necessary if good results were to be obtained. Until about 1906, most manufacturers made their own carburettors, after which proprietary firms such as Solex took over. Rolls-Royce, characteristically, continued to make their own until 1936. Another individual design was the Lanchester wick carburettor, in which air passed over numerous cotton wicks whose lower ends were immersed in petrol. This gave better fuel economy than contemporary spray carburettors, and was less hampered by dirt or dust. It was standard wear for all Lanchester cars up to 1914.

Ignition

Although the hot-tube ignition system described in Chapter 1 was used until about 1900, Karl Benz had employed electric ignition by battery and coil on his first car of 1886, and this became widespread. It incorporated a trembler coil—an induction coil depending on an electromagnetic vibrator to break the primary circuit and induce a high-tension current in the secondary winding. It worked well enough at low speeds and with single-cylinder engines, but a problem was the dependence on a battery, which needed to be regularly charged. Another contact piece and trembler coil had to be added for each extra

Clement Ader was one of the pioneers of the Vee engine, making a V-twin in 1900, a V-4 in 1903, and a V-8 later in this same year. Another early designer of Vee engines was Emile Mors, who made a V-4 as early as 1895. This is Ader's 16-hp V-4 of 1904, with mechanically operated inlet valves actuated by a camshaft in the neck of the Vee.

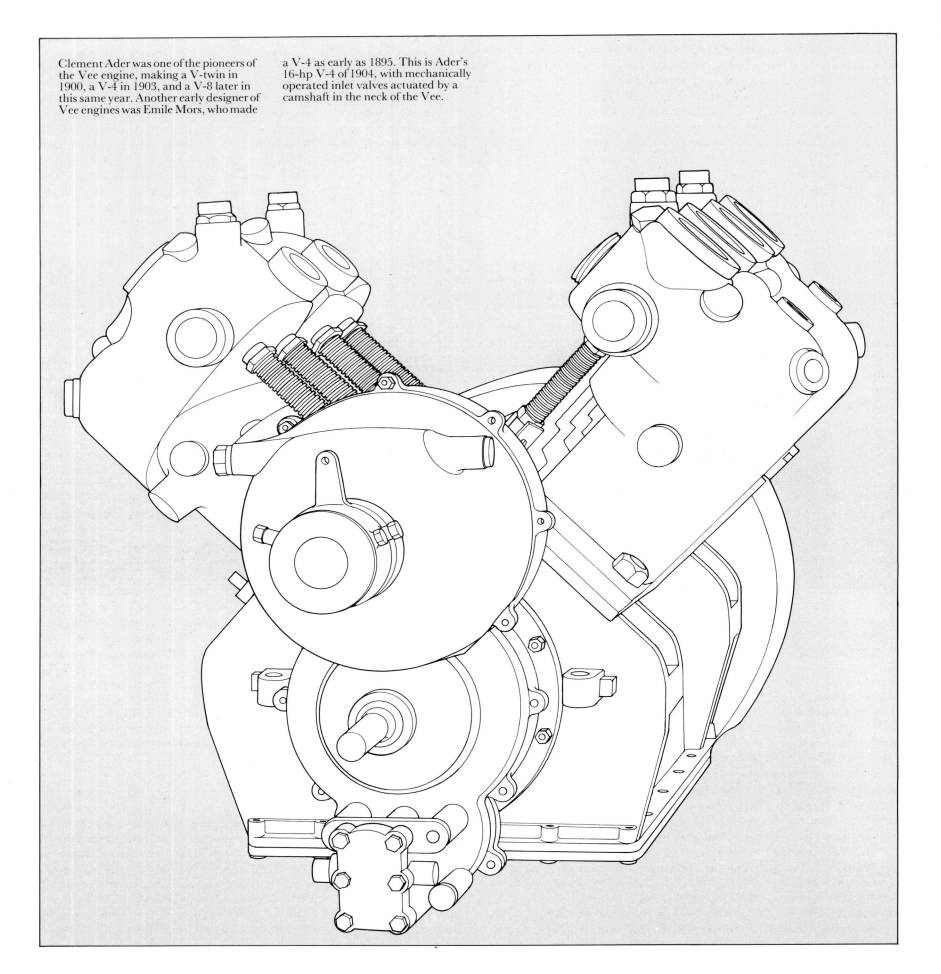

cylinder and, since the tremblers did not necessarily have the same rate of vibration, the sparks delivered to the cylinders varied in strength and timing, which was clearly unsatisfactory. The solution was the high-tension distributor, which supplied all the sparking plugs from a single coil. This was developed by Napier, Renault, and Winton in America, around 1904. Georges Bouton devised a non-trembling coil with a mechanical make-and-break operated by a cam, which was the ancestor of the modern coil ignition system.

To avoid dependence on a battery, the magneto was devised by Frederick Simms in England, and perfected by Robert Bosch in Germany. It was a permanent-magnet dynamo which generated current when turned by the engine. As the voltage was too low to jump the gap in the sparking plug, movable contact pieces in the combustion chamber were operated by a cam-and-tappet mechanism. This low-tension magneto ignition was introduced by Bosch on the 1899 Daimler Phoenix, and soon taken up by Benz, Mors and Turcat-Méry in France, Nesselsdorf in Austria, and many other companies. Lanchester, individualistic as always, had employed his own form of magneto—which was part of the flywheel—from 1897.

In 1903, Bosch took a major step forward with the high-tension magneto. It had a high-tension coil wound on the same armature, and a distributor. This generated enough voltage to be used with an ordinary sparking plug, thus doing away with the complex moving points inside the cylinders. The high-tension magneto soon became widely used, and it largely replaced the coil until the 1920s. A very hefty swing on the starting handle was needed to persuade the magneto to give a spark, so the coil was retained for starting purposes on large engines.

Lighting and starting

The only form of lighting available on the earliest cars was the candle lamp, inherited from the horse-drawn carriage. It was barely adequate to render the car or carriage visible by others, but was quite useless as illumination to show the driver where he was going. By 1900, the acetylene headlamp had made an appearance, with oil lamps serving as side and rear lights. Acetylene gas was generated by dripping water onto calcium carbide; this was sometimes done in the lamp itself, but more often a generator was carried on the running-board. Between 1900 and 1910, acetylene lamps grew to enormous proportions, contributing in no small way to the "Mr. Toad" character of the large Edwardian tourer. They gave a good clear light and, to avoid dazzling other motorists and passersby, one of the leading lamp makers—Bleriot of Paris—devised a blue glass screen, which could be swung between the gas burner and the mirror that magnified the flame. This screen was operated from the dashboard by a lever-and-cable system.

Electric lighting was slow to come to the motorcar, although widely used in houses since the 1880s. This was because it was difficult to make an efficient dynamo that was small enough to be driven by a car's engine, and also because small bulbs were very unreliable. The invention in 1910 of the tungsten filament bulb solved the latter problem, while the small dynamo appeared at about the same time. At first, electric lighting sets were sold as extras, but in 1912 Cadillac offered a combined lighting and starting system. The starter motor was adopted from those made by the Dayton Engineering Laboratories Company for operating cash registers. This company, under the abbreviated name Delco, soon became the leading suppliers of electrical equipment to the American motor industry.

Various starting systems had been tried before the advent of the electric motor, none of them very satisfactory. Fiat employed a compressed-air starter on their largest models, as did Delaunay-Belleville.

A small compressor, driven by the engine, pumped air at 180 pounds per square inch (13 kg/cm²) into a cylinder on the side of the frame, whence it was released into the engine cylinders. The starter fitted to the Czar of Russia's 70-hp limousine could also be used to inflate the tyres, jack up the wheels, or blow a whistle. The American Presto Lite Company offered a variation of this, in which acetylene gas—otherwise used for the headlamps—was released into the cylinders. According to the makers, this had no ill effects on the engine, and indeed helped to keep the cylinders free from carbon. Other systems of starting from the driver's seat involved clockwork springs or complicated gearing. None had the reliability or simplicity of the electric motor, and within a few years all makers of large cars had followed the lead set by Cadillac. The smaller European cars continued to rely on hand-cranking until the 1920s.

Transmission and final drive

The sliding-pinion gearbox invented by Emile Levassor continued with little basic change throughout the pre-1914 period, and even beyond that until Cadillac introduced synchromesh in 1928. Maybach's selective gear change on the 1901 Mercedes improved control of the car, and was widely copied on both sides of the Atlantic. The first American make to adopt it was Packard in 1902, but some firms, such as Maxwell-Briscoe, were still using the progressive gear-change in 1908. On the original Panhard system, all the four speeds were indirect and involved gear-wheels; but Louis Renault, on his first car of 1898, used a direct top gear, in which the power was transmitted straight through the gearbox without altering the ratio.

This Renault system later became widespread. In most cases, direct gear was top speed. Yet Rolls-Royce made third gear their direct one, so that top was a geared-up overdrive for use on long, level stretches of road. The latter was used on the Light Twenty, Thirty, and Silver Ghosts up to 1909. The fourth speed was then dropped, because of the lay public's obsession with hill-climbing. They asked: "Will the Rolls-Royce climb a one-in-ten hill in top gear as the Napier will?" The answer, of course, was no, as the Rolls' overdrive top gear was a higher ratio than the Napier's direct top, and it was in vain that the salesman pointed out that Rolls' third gear was equivalent to Napier's top. So Rolls-Royce went over to a three-speed gearbox. When they adopted four gears again in 1913, the additional speed was an extra low gear.

The general anxiety about climbing hills in top gear was due to the fear of gear-changing which bedevilled early motorists, both owner-drivers and professional chauffeurs. The skill needed to match the engine speed to the gearbox speed was beyond many drivers, so that "the prolonged side-grubbing of teeth" (as contemporary journalists called it) was widespread. In order to avoid this, designers came up with various solutions, of which the epicyclic gearbox—known in America as the planetary transmission—was the most common. It involved a train of planet gear-wheels acting on a sun wheel. A contracting brake, acting on the drum containing the gear train, was in effect a separate clutch; one lever both selected the gear and tightened the brake, to bring the gear into action. This did away with the clutch pedal as such, although a separate pedal was required for each speed, which did not matter very much since the average epicyclic system had only two forward speeds. The epicyclic gearbox was more popular in America than in Europe, the most famous example being on the Ford Model T. Lanchester used a refined form, in which three speeds were obtained by a pre-selector system. The latter prevailed on the big Forty until 1929, while the smaller Lanchesters used conventional gearboxes from 1923 onward.

Other easy gear-changing systems were tried from time to time, but

America took the lead in making commercially successful V-8 and V-12 engines. Because of the large domestic market, the price of these complex power units could be kept down to a reasonable level. Wilfred Leland's 1915 Cadillac Model 51 *(opposite)* had a 90-degree V-8 engine with overhead valves, and was the first Cadillac to feature left-hand drive. Six body styles were available, from $2,700 to $3,350. Jesse Vincent's 1915 Twin Six Packard *(below)* was even better value, with a five-passenger tourer costing only $2,750. Not only was it America's first production V-12, but its engine *(right)* was the first in the industry to employ aluminium pistons. Detachable cylinder heads came in with the 1916 models, which cost $450 more. Twin Six Packards were very popular in Latin America, and led to agencies being set up in cities like Buenos Aires and Rio de Janeiro.

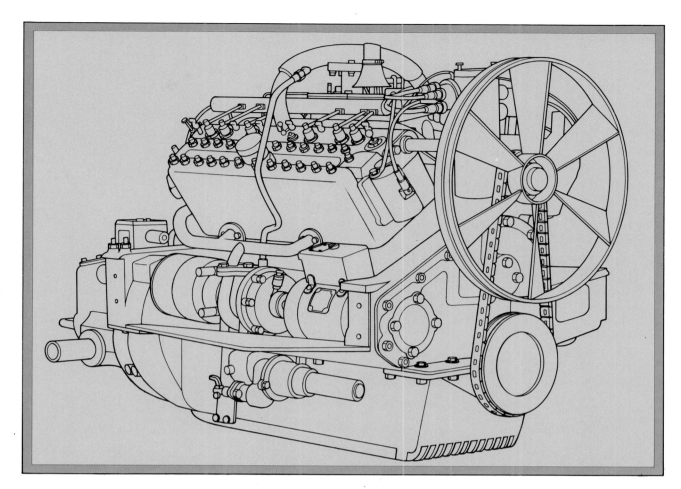

The Italian motorcar industry, with a very limited domestic market, tended to concentrate on large expensive cars for export, particularly to France, Great Britain, and the United States. The Züst company, from Brescia, offered a 50-60 hp chain-driven monster which they called the *Tipo America* as late as 1911, at a price of $5,000 in New York. But they also went in for more up-to-date designs such as the 4.7-litre 25/35-hp Tipo S.305 *(page 52)*. It had an L-head monobloc four-cylinder engine, compensated rod-operated brakes on the rear wheels, and one of the first examples of the pear-shaped radiator that was to become so common on Italian cars after World War I. This sporting tourer has optional Riley wire wheels. Similar in many ways to the Züst was Lancia's 1913 Theta *(page 53)*, with the same type of engine, and unit four-speed gearbox. Lancia shared with Hispano-Suiza the distinction of having the first standardized electric starters in Europe. The pedal-operated Rushmore starter was standardized on the Theta from 1914 onward. So confident were the makers in their starter that the crank-handle was relegated to the tool kit. Thetas could be had with wire or artillery wheels, and were made from late 1913 to 1918. A much larger car then the Züst or Lancia was Fiat's Tipo 55 of 1914 *(left)*: with 9 litres, it developed 75 bhp at 1,500 rpm. This is in fact an American-built example, the native Italian version being the Tipo 5. Fiat's factory at Poughkeepsie, New York, operated from 1910 to 1918, and built only the larger models.

they mostly failed because of complexity and expense. They included the Lentz hydraulic transmission, offered by Charron in 1913; the Owen Magnetic, in which power was transmitted magnetically across an air gap; and the petrol electric (see Chapter 2), used on the French Krieger and the German Mercedes-Mixte. A system popular among light-car makers was the friction-disc transmission, which will be described in the next chapter.

Chain drive from a countershaft to the rear wheels was pioneered by Emile Levassor on the 1891 Panhard, and became the accepted system for the more powerful car. The alternative of a propeller shaft, driving to a differential on the rear axle, was introduced by Louis Renault on his first light car of 1898. He never employed chains, even when his cars grew in size. But in general, the system of shaft and live axle was thought suitable only for light cars. This was doubtless reinforced by the widespread imitation of the chain-drive Mercedes. However, Napier in England, and Itala in Italy, were making 60-hp cars with shaft drive by 1905, and gradually that system took over throughout the world. Mercedes adopted it on their smaller models from 1908, although the big 37/90PS four-cylinder sports car retained chain drive until 1914. The disadvantage of chains was that they were noisy, particularly when worn, and they were exposed to all the mud or dust thrown up from the unsurfaced roads of the time. The recommended method of cleaning chains was to remove them from the car and boil them in Russian tallow!

Frames and wheels

We have already observed that the motorcar was born of the horse-drawn carriage and the bicycle. This was no more clearly displayed than in the construction of the chassis frame. Karl Benz employed a tubular steel frame of typical bicycle practice, while Gottlieb Daimler's 1886 motorized carriage had a wooden frame reinforced with steel under the part which carried the engine. The Panhard of the 1890s had a wooden frame strengthened with metal flitch plates, and this "armoured wood" system became widespread up to the first few years of the twentieth century. The 1899 Daimler Phoenix had an all-steel frame of channel section, which gradually took over from the armoured wood.

Together with tubular steel, armoured wood remained the province of the light car and cyclecar. Some of the latter still had wooden frames in the early 1920s. Among these were the British Whitehead and the German Slaby-Beringer, which had a wooden integral body/chassis unit. An exception among larger cars was the American Franklin, retaining its wooden frame until 1927. Most steel chassis had rolled or pressed cross-members rivetted to them. But Darracq, from 1903 onward, was unusual in using a whole chassis pressed from one piece of steel except for the rear cross-member. The Dutch Spyker had an undershield of light pressed steel which ran the full length of the chassis, protecting all the working parts from dust and dirt. This earned the cars the name "the Dustless Spyker".

Wheels, like frames, were descended directly from the carriage or the bicycle. Indeed, the wire wheels used by Karl Benz on his Velo of 1893–99 were supplied by the well-known cycle makers, Adler, who later produced cars of their own. Benz used both types of wheel, for his large Viktoria (1893–99) had wooden spoked wheels of the carriage type. Generally speaking, the larger cars had wooden wheels until about 1907, when the Rudge-Whitworth detachable wire wheel came into use. This was an inestimable blessing to the motorist, for it did away with the dreaded task of prising a punctured tyre from the rim of a fixed wheel. When punctures were frequent, this was the motorist's

Two alternative valve layouts are exemplified by the T-head Cottereau *(top)* and the L-head De Dion Bouton *(bottom)*, both dating from 1904. In Europe, the T-head had been generally abandoned by 1910, but it persisted on some larger American cars into the 1920s, and was retained by Locomobile on their "48" model until 1929.

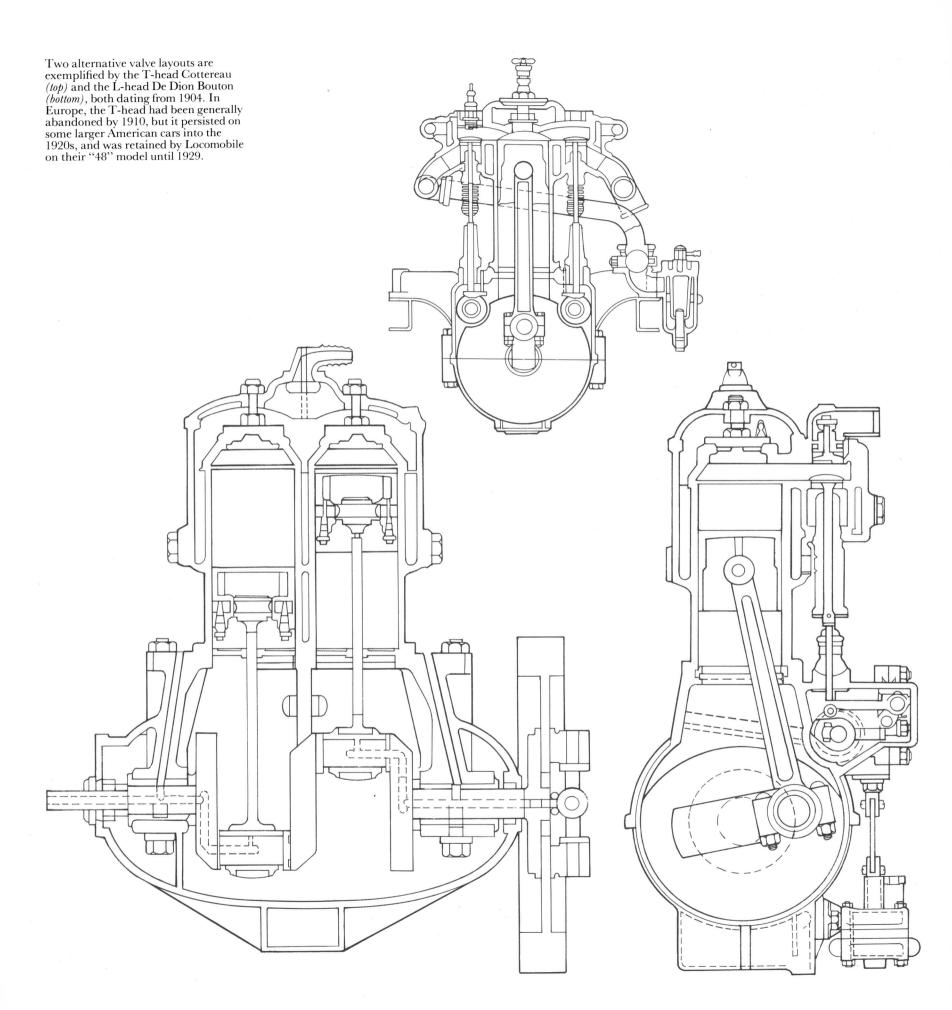

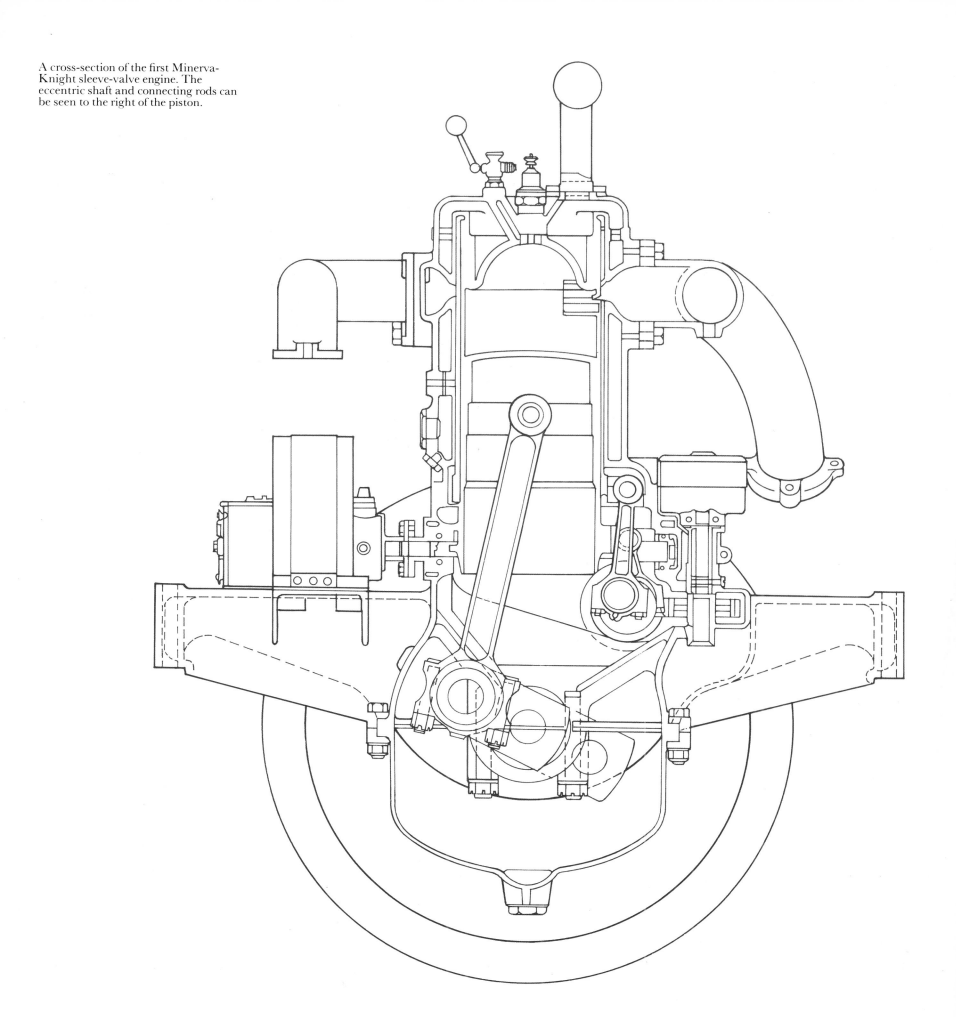

A cross-section of the first Minerva-Knight sleeve-valve engine. The eccentric shaft and connecting rods can be seen to the right of the piston.

biggest bugbear, and the cause of far more involuntary halts than was mechanical failure.

The Rudge-Whitworth wheel was handsome as well as easy to handle, and soon became standard wear for the better-quality car in Britain and Europe. Other makers such as Riley also began to supply wire wheels to many manufacturers. In America, the fixed wooden wheel survived much longer, often with detachable rims, and even the detachable wheels tended to have wooden or thick metal (artillery) spokes rather than wire. Since wire spokes were more difficult to keep clean, perhaps the relative rarity of the paid driver in America acted against their adoption. Wire wheels were seldom standard on American cars, but a number of manufacturers offered them as a higher-priced option. Exceptions included Chevrolet, whose 1915 Amesbury Special and Royal Mail Roadster both had wire wheels, and Jeffery who offered them from 1914.

Brakes

The brakes on the earliest cars followed horse-carriage practice, in being shoes which acted directly on the rear tyres. They were of limited value, particularly in wet weather when they gave very little grip, and were suitable only with solid rubber tyres. The next step was the contracting handbrake, acting on the rear wheels. This, on early Panhards and other makes, was a single band which had a self-wrapping action when the car was moving forward, but tended to unwrap in reverse and to be virtually useless. To counteract that problem, the cars were fitted with a sprag—a strong, pointed iron bar which could be dropped onto the ground, so that the point stuck into the road surface and stopped the car if it began to roll backward.

After about 1900, the better-quality cars were fitted with internal expanding drum brakes, which were usually hand-operated. The foot brake, acting on the transmission shaft, was often still of the contracting-band type. Overheating of brakes was a great problem, and some cars such as Mercedes and the Italian Milano had a water-drip system to cool the transmission brake. Other makers, including Delaunay-Belleville and Gobron-Brillié, employed two independent foot-brake systems, each with its own pedal, acting on different parts of the transmission. By using them alternately, the likelihood of overheating was reduced. However, drivers soon found that the transmission brake imposed a great strain on the propeller shaft and universal joints, so they tended to rely on the handbrake acting upon the rear wheels. The logical solution, general today, did not occur to designers for some time: making the footbrake act on the wheels. Several American and German companies adopted it from about 1910 onward, yet many French and British cars retained the pedal transmission brake into the 1920s.

In 1909, the Scottish Arrol-Johnston company offered a four-wheel braking system. Here, the foot brake operated internal expanding brakes on the front wheels, and the handbrake looked after the rear wheels. A similar idea was adopted by another Scottish firm, Argyll, and by Isotta-Fraschini in Italy two years later. The drawback was that the brakes were uncoupled, requiring simultaneous action if they were to work properly. Braking the front wheels before the rear wheels was particularly hazardous, and the potential advantage of the system did not outweigh the risks, especially when low speed and sparse traffic made emergency stops fairly rare. Arrol-Johnston abandoned the system after two years, but Argyll made their brakes "diagonally compensated" in 1913—the foot brake operated on the offside front and nearside rear wheels, while the handbrake worked on the other two. Nonetheless, widespread use of four-wheel brakes did not arrive until the 1920s.

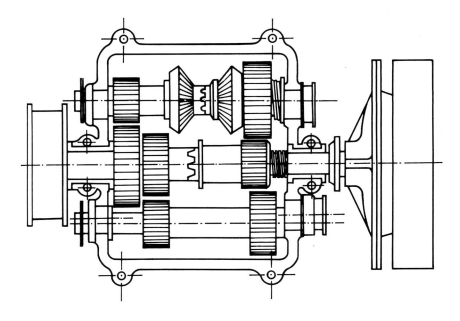

(Opposite top) Acetylene headlamp on a 1902 7-hp Panhard.

(Opposite centre) Oil was retained for side and rear lamps until the second decade of the twentieth century, and even longer on taxicabs and commercial vehicles. This is a side lamp on a 1904 De Dion Bouton.

(Opposite bottom) Louis Renault's gear-box of 1898 was the first to employ a direct-drive top gear. He obtained this by coupling together the two halves of the main centre shaft with a jaw clutch, and leaving the lay shafts out of mesh. When a different gear was needed, one or another of the lay shafts was swung sideways into mesh with the main shaft. To provide reverse, the bevel gears meshed with a third bevel, not shown here.

(Right) Planetary transmission as used on its most celebrated exponent, the Model T Ford.

(Below) Double chain drive, the accepted method of transmission for powerful cars up to about 1908, is seen here on a 1904 30-hp Mercedes.

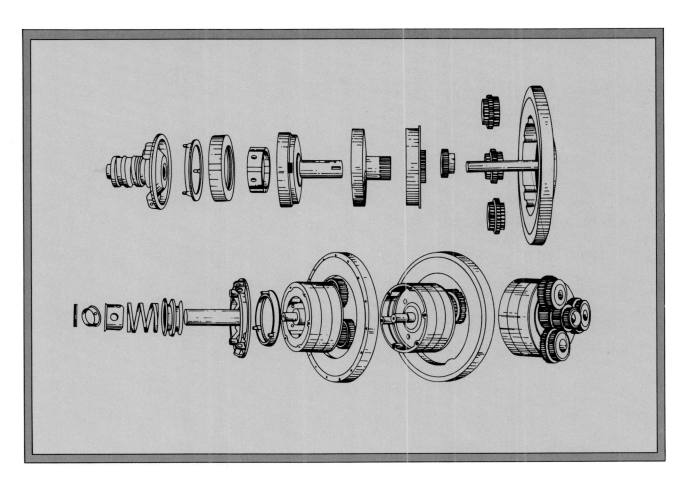

Horse-carriage practice is clearly displayed by the shoe brake on the rear wheel of an 1899 Panhard wagonette *(above)*. This was already an outmoded system by that time, and contemporaries such as Daimler (German and English), Peugeot, and Renault were offering contracting band brakes—or better still, internal expanding drum brakes. Shown here is Renault's example *(below)*.

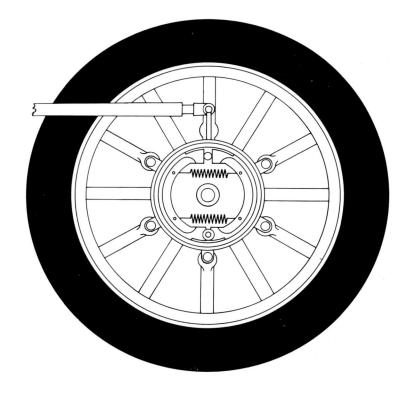

THE MODEST MAN'S MOTOR

4

Practically every history of motoring describes the early car as "a rich man's toy", or "the plaything of the wealthy". Yet in fact, reasonably priced light cars were on the market from the beginning of the century. *The Autocar*'s guide to cars available in Britain in February 1904 listed no fewer than 38 models costing less than £200, of which the cheapest, a single-cylinder 3.5-hp New Orleans, went for only £80. Not that this was within reach of the average working man, for whom £2.50 was a very good weekly wage. But then, a new car was not a familiar part of the British working-class household until well after the Second World War. However, many middle-class families with an annual income of around £400–500 could afford to buy and run a light car, which was easier to maintain, and took up less space, than did a pony and trap.

The first professional men to take up the car, for obvious reasons, were doctors. By 1905, the motor magazines were full of articles on "motors for medical men" and the advantages they offered. Once a doctor had become a confirmed motorist, he was likely to influence many of his patients, so these professionals acted as valuable salesmen for the light car.

Among the most popular early small cars were De Dion Bouton and Renault. De Dion had made petrol-engine tricycles since 1895, and launched their first petrol car in 1899. It could seat four passengers in the *vis-à-vis* layout, in which the front passengers faced back toward the driver and the passenger at his side. It was ideal for conversation, assuming that voices could be heard over the noise of the engine, but the driver did not have very good forward vision. Actually, the rear-facing seats were not regularly used, as four passengers severely reduced the performance of the car. The single-cylinder engine was mounted under the driver's seat, and drove the rear wheels via a simple gear-change with a separate clutch for each of the two speeds, operated by a wheel on the steering column. An anti-clockwise turn operated the low-speed clutch to move the car away from rest, while a turn in the opposite direction released the low-speed clutch and actuated the high-speed one.

In 1903, the engine was moved to the front, under a bonnet, and the *vis-à-vis* layout was abandoned. The new model was called the Populaire, and popular it was, selling about 200 units per month. Two engines were offered, a 6-hp which usually powered a two-seater, and an 8-hp which was often seen with a four-seater tonneau body, although it was powerful enough to propel a closed limousine, landaulette, or delivery van. The single-cylinder De Dion Bouton was made until 1912, and total production must have been in the region of 20,000 cars. Many have survived, and there are 132 registered with the Veteran Car Club of Great Britain alone. They are the most popular cars on the annual London to Brighton Run.

As well as making cars, De Dion sold their engines to other manufacturers, and thus had a widespread effect around the world. About a hundred firms in France, Germany, Italy, Britain, and the United States entered the market with De Dion-powered cars. And if many were obscure, there were also famous names among them, such as Delage, Renault, Peerless, and Pierce-Arrow.

Large cars may have settled down to the Mercedes pattern, but there was less conformity at the other end of the scale. While Louis Renault used shaft drive from the start, chain or belt transmission persisted on light cars for much longer. In particular, much greater divergence existed across the Atlantic, with the American car following a quite different pattern from those in Europe. Peerless and Pierce-Arrow used a De Dion engine whose single cylinder displaced 402 cc and turned at 1,500 rpm. Much more typical was the Oldsmobile Curved Dash. This had a far larger cylinder with a capacity of 1,565 cc which turned at the Benz-like speed of 500 rpm. Transmission was by a two-speed epicyclic gearbox and final drive by single chain to the centre of the rear axle. Top speed was 20 mph (32 km/h), and at this rate the slow-turning engine was said to produce "one chug per telegraph pole". The suspension was unusual, consisting of two springs which ran the length of the wooden frame, reinforcing it and curving downward at each end to provide springing for the axles.

The Curved Dash Oldsmobile was the first quantity-produced car in the world. In 1901, despite a disastrous fire at the beginning of the year, 400 were turned out. The 1902 figure of 2,500 was double that of all the cars then registered in the State of New York. Successive increases brought the total made in five years to nearly 19,000. Although nothing like Ford's moving assembly line of ten years later, the Oldsmobile factory made tentative steps toward mass production, in that the cars were wheeled along for components to be added sequentially by groups of workmen. This was in contrast to the normal practice, where the car was stationary and the men brought their components to it.

Many other American car makers followed the Oldsmobile pattern, though with more conventional suspension of semi-elliptic springs at the front and rear. Among the better-known names were the Cadillac Model A and the Rambler, while the Ford Model A was very similar to the Cadillac in appearance but had a two-cylinder engine. Other

De Dion Bouton was the leading early maker of light cars, or voiturettes (a term coined by Léon Bollée for his 1895 three-wheeler, but soon taken up by manufacturers and journalists for any light car). Their *vis-à-vis* from 1900 *(above)* had a 402-cc 3.5-hp engine under the driver's seat. The wheel for changing gear can be seen on the steering column. The De Dion axle *(left)* has the two driving shafts separate from the fixed axle. In 1903, the engine was moved to the front, and the cars assumed a more up-to-date appearance. The company's 6-hp Populaire from 1904 *(opposite)* sold in England for £200, and found many customers. This example has an extra "spyder" seat behind the driver and passenger, a forerunner of the dickey seat.

variations on the theme included the Knox with air-cooled engine, the two-stroke Elmore, and the Union which replaced the usual epicyclic system by friction drive. This involved two discs rotating at right angles to each other, and a shaft enabling the driven disc to be moved across the face of the driving one. The driven disc gave a low gear when near the centre, and an ever higher gear as it was moved toward the perimeter, whereas it gave reverse when moved across the centre. Here was a simple solution to the problem of providing painless gear-changing, but suitable only for transmitting relatively low power. The discs, faced with cork or fibre, needed frequent replacement as flat spots soon developed in them. Nevertheless, friction drive was widely used in light cars and cyclecars up to 1914, and persisted on the British G.W.K. until 1931.

The American light cars, or runabouts as they were usually called, perhaps seemed primitive by European standards. Yet they were well adapted to the frontier conditions which prevailed outside the big cities. They were simple to maintain, and easy to drive for people whose previous experience was limited to a horse and buggy. By about 1906, fashion dictated that a respectable car should have a bonnet, even if the engine still lived under the seat. Thus, makes such as Oldsmobile, Cadillac, and Rambler sprouted little bonnets, and eventually moved the engine forward to fill them. To satisfy those who hankered after the old type of runabout, and who were indifferent to appearance and fashion, a new breed of car sprang up in America. This was the high-wheeler motor buggy, and it resembled the horse-drawn variety more than any other type of car. Its heyday was from

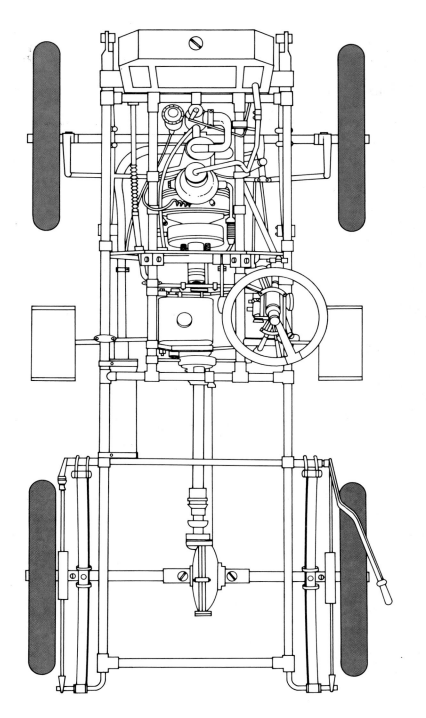

Among the many light cars struggling for sales on the British market in the early years of the century was the Humberette, here of 1903 *(opposite)*. This 5-hp model was the first successful car from a well-known cycle maker, and followed the De Dion Bouton formula of a water-cooled single-cylinder engine mounted at the front of a tubular frame *(left)*, with shaft drive to the rear wheels, retailing at £125. Another such light car was the two-cylinder Alldays & Onions *(above)*, made by a Birmingham engineering firm whose history dated back to 1650. For all of £175, the buyer got a four-seater, though with a rather cramped rear-entrance tonneau.

about 1907 to 1912 but, to the uninitiated, it could have been made before the turn of the century, with its solid tyres, horizontally opposed engine under the seat, and carriage-type body.

More than 75 manufacturers made these high-wheelers. The best-known included the Holsman, which had a rope final drive; the I.H.C., made by the famous Chicago farm-machinery company, International Harvester; and the Sears. The latter was sold through mail order by the leading firm in this field, Sears Roebuck of Chicago. It was fairly typical in having a 10/12-hp horizontally opposed twin engine, friction-disc transmission, and double chain drive. Top speed was 25 mph (40 km/h), which prompted the makers to advertise that "The Sears will do everything that a $5,000 car will do except travel faster than 25 mph." Prices were very reasonable, ranging from $325 for a basic two-passenger buggy to $485 for a "cosy coupé". Sears sold about 3,500 high-wheelers between 1908 and 1912. After that, demand for these cars practically disappeared, no doubt killed by the Ford Model T (see Chapter 7), which coped with poor roads just as well, gave greater speed and comfort, and cost no more. Unlike the Oldsmobile, Cadillac, and Ford, the high-wheelers were not sold in Britain, though some went to Sweden, and they were also exported to South Africa and India.

The two-cylinder light car

De Dion made their first two-cylinder engine in 1903, and soon this layout took over from the single-cylinder for most light cars. One of the

Two ways of catering to the large market for the American runabout. The 1903 Curved Dash Oldsmobile *(above)* was well-made, simple to operate, and good value at $600. Its large single cylinder turned at only 500 rpm, giving a top speed of 20 mph (32 km/h). Similar in many ways was the 9-hp Model B Cadillac, shown here from 1905 *(opposite)*, although its dummy bonnet— introduced the previous year—gave it a more modern appearance. Both cars had horizontal single-cylinder engines mounted in the middle of the frame, as well as two-speed planetary trans-missions and single-chain final drive. The Cadillac's tonneau body was detachable, and cost an additional $100.

Cadillac

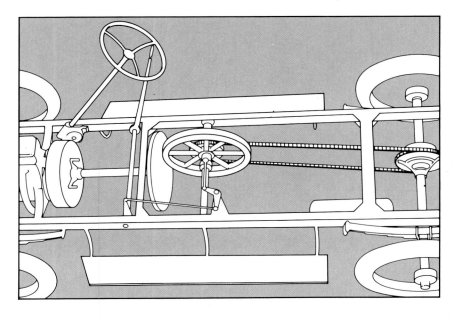

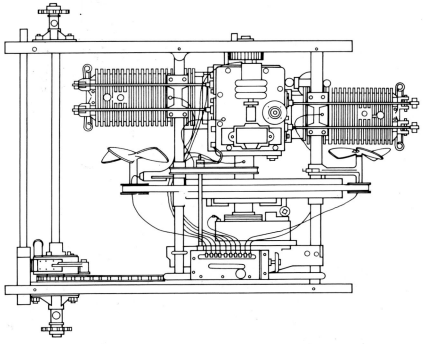

best-known twins was the Renault, made from 1905 to 1914 under various designations, of which the AX (1908–1912) was made in the largest numbers. Its two cylinders were cast in one block and mounted vertically under the familiar "coal scuttle" bonnet, with the radiator behind the engine. It was otherwise conventional, with side valves in an L-head, high-tension magneto ignition, shaft drive, and semi-elliptic springs all round. Its reliability and the comparative smoothness of the engine made it very popular, and it was the most important car to contribute to the rise of Renault to the position of leading French car manufacturer by 1914. Although intended as a two-seater, the AX and its successors frequently had to carry four passengers, and the engine was used in the famous Renault taxicab. By 1909, this was the best-known make of taxi in Paris and London. It won undying fame when General Gallièni commandeered 600 taxis from the streets of Paris to transport troops to the Battle of the Marne in September 1914.

Other manufacturers followed Renault's lead, and soon there were a number of reliable two-cylinder light cars on the market, including Darracq, De Dion Bouton and Peugeot in France; Alldays, Humber, and Swift in Britain; and Adler and Opel in Germany. A short-lived fashion for in-line three-cylinder engines lasted from about 1904 to 1907, and included Rolls-Royce, Panhard, and Vauxhall among its followers. But on the whole, the light-car makers favoured in-line twins until about 1910, when four-cylinder engines, often monoblocs, became popular for cars in the class of 10–14 hp. The German Stoewer company was among the first in the world to make a monobloc four, in 1907, and they were emulated by their compatriots Adler, NSU, and Opel.

Bugatti, which was German until 1918 as a consequence of the German occupation of the province of Alsace, made the beautiful little Type 13, with a 1,327-cc four-cylinder engine and overhead camshaft, from 1910. Even smaller, at 855 cc, was the Bugatti-designed Bébé Peugeot. The Swiss Martini had overhead inlet and side exhaust valves, and the German Wanderer had full overhead valves, but most other light fours relied on side valves in an L-head. German makes led the way, although Fiat launched their 1.8-litre Tipo Zero in 1912, which marked the company's successful entry into the light-car field. In Britain, William Morris turned from cycle to car manufacture with the 1913 Oxford two-seater, powered by a 1,018-cc White & Poppe side-valve engine, while his competitors included A.C., Calthorpe, Singer, and Standard. These were all reasonably refined and comfortable small cars, with top speed of around 45 mph (70 km/h) and priced at £150 to £200.

The Cyclecar

For those who could not afford the conventional light car, there was a race of hybrid vehicles called cyclecars. Their ancestry dated back to the tricars and quadricycles made at the turn of the century. The first tricars appeared in 1902, with two wheels at the front, between which the passenger rode in a wicker-work seat. But from the handlebars backward, they were identical to motorcycles, with a saddle for the rider, a fuel tank below the bar, and a fairly large engine, usually a V-twin, driving the rear wheel by belt or chain. They were popularized in England by Century, Humber, and Phoenix in particular. Among the many other firms making tricars were two which later became famous for their cars, Lagonda and Riley.

Although the earliest tricars used motorcycle components, it was soon found that a more substantial frame was desirable, together with a clutch and two-speed epicyclic gear. Gradually they became more car-like, with a seat replacing the saddle, and the handlebars giving

(Top) Friction drive was a beautifully simple solution to the problem of gear changing, so long as the power transmitted was not too great, but the driven discs needed frequent replacement. The G.W.K. company of Datchet, and later of Maidenhead, was the most loyal user of friction drive. In America, the system was employed by Union, Lambert, Metz, and the Cartercar of which this is a 1910 example.

The Chicago-based Holsman Automobile Co. was the pioneer maker of high-wheelers, and it was their success between 1902 and 1906 that led numerous other companies to get in on the act. Most of the other principal makers of high-wheelers were located in Chicago, with a few in St. Louis, so they were inevitably dubbed a "midwestern" type of automobile. Certainly, very few

were seen on the East Coast, and few were exported to Europe, although some went to India and Australia. Shown here are a 1908 Kiblinger *(opposite)* and the works of the 1911 I.H.C. *(above)*. The latter, with a horizontally opposed two-cylinder engine, planetary transmission, and single chain drive, was made as an Auto Buggy with two rows of seats for passengers, or as an Auto Wagon light truck. The Holsman's own transmission was distinctly unusual: forward drive was taken by ropes from a countershaft to large pulleys bolted on the rear wheels, but reverse was obtained by moving the countershaft rearwards until wheels on each end acted directly upon the rear tyres. In later models, the rope was replaced by wire rope, and deeper grooves were made in the countershaft wheels so that they acted on the rear wheels' rims rather than tyres.

Popular two-cylinder light cars of the Edwardian period included the 1907 De Dion Bouton Model AV *(opposite)* and the 1911 Renault AX *(left)*. Both were produced in fairly large numbers, for taxicab work as well as private cars. The 10-hp Renault cost £380 or £410 according to chassis size. By contrast, Henry Royce's beautifully made 10-hp Rolls-Royce of 1904 *(above)* sold only 16 units before its builders decided to move on to larger machinery. Yet at £395 for the chassis, it was not particularly expensive.

The light four-cylinder car was a considerably larger machine in America than in Europe, where 1.5 litres were regarded as the top limit for a light car. The 1910 Buick Model 10 *(left)* had an engine displacing 2.7 litres—and over-head valves, like most Buicks from their start in 1903 until the present day. The Model 10, one of the most successful early Buicks, and described as "the car that made Buick", had a two-speed planetary transmission and cost $1,050 to $1,150 according to body style. The 1911 Regal *(opposite)* had a 3.2-litre engine and conventional three-speed gearbox, but its unusual chassis was inverted so that the frame members passed beneath the axles.

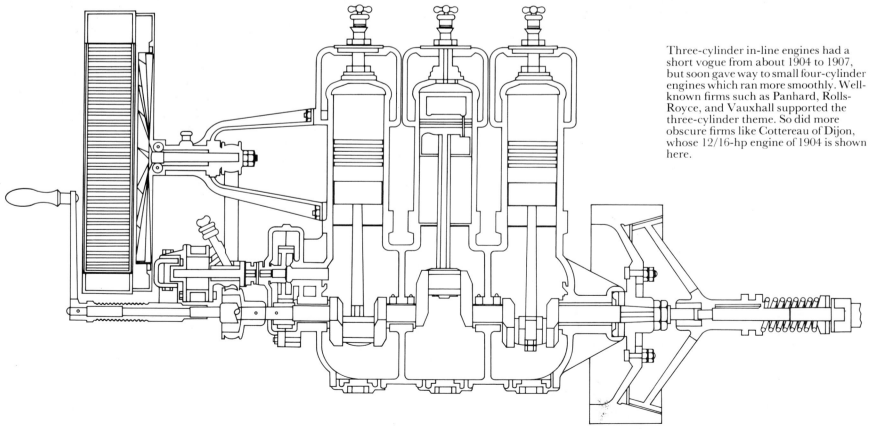

Three-cylinder in-line engines had a short vogue from about 1904 to 1907, but soon gave way to small four-cylinder engines which ran more smoothly. Well-known firms such as Panhard, Rolls-Royce, and Vauxhall supported the three-cylinder theme. So did more obscure firms like Cottereau of Dijon, whose 12/16-hp engine of 1904 is shown here.

A typical British light car of the immediate prewar era was the 1914 Morris Oxford (*opposite*). An assembled car, it used an engine by White & Poppe, axles and steering by E. G. Wrigley, wheels from Sankey, lamps from Powell & Hanmer, and bodies from Raworth. At £175 for a two-seater, it was good value, and Morris sold 393 in his first year, raised to 909 in 1914 when other, more expensive bodies were available as well. Most Humber components were made by the factory, which was one of the best-established in Britain, and one of the dozen largest car manufacturers in Europe. The 1,593-cc Humber Ten of 1914 (*right*) was the smallest four-cylinder model, and cost £250 for a four-seater tourer.

way to a steering wheel. The 1905 Riley Tricars of 6 hp and 9 hp had both these features, as well as a watercooled V-twin engine with a radiator. The trouble was that these car-like features made them just as heavy and expensive as a light two-seater car. The latter was clearly more acceptable to the public, with its side-by-side seating. One feels that the front-seat passenger in a tricar (usually the driver's wife or girlfriend) was never very happy, being exposed to wind and dust, not to mention being in the "firing line" for any accident in which the man's lack of skill might land them. After 1907, the last season for the tricars, their makers either produced proper cars—as did Riley and Phoenix—or abandoned the field altogether. Those who could not afford a car contented themselves with a motorcycle and sidecar.

The lure of the ultra-light car persisted, however, and in 1910 appeared the first example of a new breed, which was christened the cyclecar. This used mainly motorcycle components such as engines, gearboxes, and belt or chain final drive, combined with simple wooden frames, fibreboard bodies, and cable-and-bobbin steering. The first examples, born within a few months of each other, were the British G.N.—made by H.R. Godfrey and Archie Frazer-Nash—and the French Bédélia, made by Henri Bourbeau and Robert Devaux. All were very young, Godfrey and Frazer-Nash being 23 and 21 respectively, while the two Frenchmen were both 18. The whole cyclecar movement was infused with an air of naive enthusiasm and youthful optimism. It is significant that hardly any major manufacturer of either cars or motorcycles took up the cyclecar.

The G.N. in its original form had an air-cooled V-twin J.A.P. engine, but production models used a Peugeot-based V-twin with Godfrey and Nash's own design of inlet-over-exhaust-valve cylinder head. Transmission was by belts, and the cars had an ash frame. They

went into production in 1911 at the rate of two per week, and sold steadily until 1916 when the war forced them to stop. In 1919, they resumed manufacture on a larger scale, with a new model featuring a steel frame and chain drive.

The Bédélia also employed a V-twin engine and wooden frame. Its narrow body seated two in tandem, with the driver at the rear, steering through a complicated system of wires and bobbins to a centre-pivot front axle. But the passenger could not just sit back and admire the scenery, as he had the task of varying the tension of the belts with a lever, and—on early models—of shifting the belts from the low-speed pulley to the high. The editor of the British magazine *Motor Cycling*, W.G. McMinnies, saw an early Bédélia in Paris in 1910, and was so impressed that he persuaded Arthur Armstrong, head of Temple Press, that a magazine specially devoted to these new devices was needed. This appeared, in November 1912, as *The Cyclecar*. The first issue (148 pages, price one penny) sold 100,000 copies, and described 35 models from the Rollo Monocar at 70 guineas (£73.50) to the Singer Ten at £185, which was a proper light car rather than a cyclecar. The definition of the cyclecar was never very precise, but generally covered any car with less than four cylinders, and with a transmission system other than the normal sliding-pinion gearbox and shaft drive. Three-wheelers were included, and among these was the first of the Morgans, a make which specialized in three-wheelers up to the mid-1930s.

The variety in cyclecar design was remarkable, but perhaps not unexpected in a field that had no established precedents and did not envisage long production runs. In the spring of 1913, there were 107 models on the British market, of which five were monocars (single-seaters), 32 were chain-driven two-seaters, 30 were belt-driven two-seaters, and 40 were shaft-driven two-seaters. The latter figure, how-

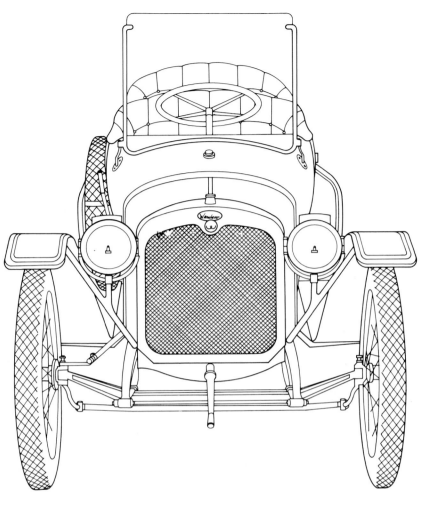

(Left) A cross between a light car and a cyclecar was the Wanderer "Puppchen" (doll), made at Schonau in Saxony from 1912—as shown here—to 1914. Aspects of the light car included its four-cylinder engine, conventional three-speed gearbox, shaft drive, and live rear axle, but its tandem seating recalled the cyclecar. It sold well, and descendants with side-by-side seating were made until 1922.

The heyday of the tricar was between 1902 and 1907, and this 9-hp V-twin Riley of 1904 *(below)* shows the breed in transition. The saddle has been replaced by a seat, and the handlebars by a steering wheel, while a car-type radiator can be seen just behind the passenger's seat. At £136, such vehicles were cheaper than almost any four-wheelers. Yet the lack of weather protection, and the unsociability of the seating arrangements, were serious deterrents to sales.

(Opposite) Cyclecars spanned the Atlantic. The 1914 G. N. *(top)* was the most successful British example of its kind, offering a sporting performance, economy, and reasonable reliability. The McIntyre Imp *(bottom left)* was made by a high-wheeler manufacturer in Auburn, Indiana, and had a hefty V-twin engine, friction transmission, and final drive by a long belt running more than half the length of the car. The 1919 A.V. Monocar *(bottom right)* was about as simple a design as one could get. Derived from a prewar concept by John Carden, it had a rear-mounted V-twin J.A.P. engine, and a pencil-thin body made of plywood, mahogany, or compressed paper.

ever, included some of which would be considered light cars, such as the Calthorpe Minor and the Morris Oxford. The engines were nearly all proprietary brands, by firms like J.A.P., Precision, and Fafnir, and were single-cylinder or vertical twin or V-twin. Flat-twin engines, by such firms as Douglas and BMW, were taken up by some makers in the early postwar years.

Some cyclecars were offered in kit form, and indeed there was an uncanny resemblance between the cyclecar scene and the world of the "kit car" today. Firms sprang up in large numbers, some only to collapse after twelve months or less, others merging and changing their names with confusing frequency. It was a hectic world, operating with very little capital, and few of the entrepreneurs made much money out of their activities. Nevertheless, their optimism was boundless, and cyclecar enthusiasm knew no frontiers. In France, the Bédélia had many imitators.

In Spain, which had a quite small native motor industry, the cyclecar movement grew out of "downcar" racing. This was initially performed with unpowered vehicles, which resembled toboggans and careered down the steep hills of Barcelona. It was described as "an agreeable sport, full of emotions and easy to practice". Pulling them back up to the summit was not so much fun, though, and the contestants fitted motorcycle engines as an aid. From there, it was only a small step to racing up hills under power, and soon some of these powered vehicles were offered for sale. Makers such as David, Ideal, and Diaz y Grillo became well-known competition machines, and had many sporting successes in the years 1914 to 1922—after which the cyclecar movement died in Spain as it did in most other countries.

The cyclecar in America

It would not have been surprising if the cyclecar had never appeared in America, with such vast distances and poor country roads. Yet a meteoric movement occurred there too. At least three magazines catered for enthusiasts: *Cyclecar Age*, *The American Cyclecar*, and *Cyclecar and Motorette*. In January 1914, the American Cyclecar Manufacturers Association was formed, and optimism outdid that of Europe. "We believe that the 1,125,000 horse-drawn buggies that were sold in 1913 will all be supplanted with two-passenger light cars", trumpeted cyclecar maker Charles Coey. The nation's first female cyclecar dealer, 21-year-old Anna Sheeley of Passaic, New Jersey, said ". . . there is no limit apparently to the number of cars I can sell." Cars, maybe, but not cyclecars—for by the end of 1915 the boom had collapsed, taking the magazines and the manufacturers' association with it.

Americans were not to adopt the small car for another fifty years, and the regular price reductions of the Model T Ford were fatal to the cyclecar. In 1913, a Ford two-seater cost $550, compared to $350 or $400 for a cyclecar, which was a reasonable difference. But two years later, the Ford was down to $440, and the cyclecars were priced the same as before. Who wouldn't pay an extra $40 for a full-sized car with a four-cylinder engine, able to cope with rough roads, and with an established reputation and widespread servicing facilities? While the cyclecar staggered on in Europe until the mid-1920s, in America it was extinct by the time the nation entered the war in 1917.

COACHBUILDING

5

I t is often said that the earliest cars were horseless carriages. A truer view would be that the real pioneers were engines on wheels, with no carriage work to speak of at all. This certainly applied to the 1886 Benz three-wheeler and the 1889 Daimler "Stahlradwagen", even if Gottlieb Daimler's first car of 1886 was an adapted horse carriage. Not until the mid-1890s, when manufacturers started to offer a range of bodies, did the characteristic horse-drawn styles begin to be transferred to the motorcar. At first, they were all open bodies, as the engines were low-powered, and no manufacturer in his senses would load them with the additional weight of a closed body.

The simple open two-seater was sometimes called a Phaeton or, if fitted with a hood, a Victoria. Sometimes an extra seat would be provided behind, known as a Spider or Spyder—and the name was revived in the 1950s for an open sports car. It was not long before motorists demanded four seats, and these were provided in a variety of ways. The conventional touring car with side doors for the rear passengers was not possible until about 1902, as wheelbases were too short, and the widely-used driving chains to the rear wheels would have made access to the rear seats difficult. The solution was to install rear-facing seats for two passengers, either in the *vis-à-vis* position ahead of the driver, as on the Benz Viktoria or the De Dion Bouton voiturette, or back-to-back (*dos-à-dos*) as on Daimler, Panhard, and other heavy cars.

The third alternative was to mate the phaeton with the body known in horse-drawn circles as a Governess Cart or Tub Cart. This had a rear door between the two seats, and the resulting four-seater car became known as a rear-entrance Tonneau, from the French for "tub" or "cask". A less familiar style was the Siamese Phaeton, in which the rear seat was a bench identical to the front one. But this involved clambering over the front seats, unless one half could be swung open to allow access to the rear. Another solution was the Brake, with longitudinal seats on which the passengers faced each other. This could seat at least four, in addition to the driver and the passenger beside him. But it was generally considered more suitable for transporting servants or weekend guests from the station than for the owner's use. It might be used for carrying a shooting party, though—and hence the name Shooting Brake, which applied until replaced by the Estate Car in quite recent times. In America the breed is still known as a Station Wagon.

As with so many other improvements in the motorcar, it was Mercedes who initially made a chassis long enough to mount a side-entrance four-seater body. One of the first was that built by the Parisian coachbuilder Rothschild et Cie., to the order of King Leopold

of the Belgians. The story goes that the King and his celebrated mistress Cléo de Mérode were discussing the style of the new car with a representative of Rothschild, when the lady put two elegantly curved easy chairs together and suggested that this style should be reproduced in the car. Certainly this body, which was fitted to the King's Mercedes, was known as the Roi-des-Belges for a number of years—or alternately as the Tulip Phaeton, since its opulent curves had a tulip-like appearance. Simple side-entrance four-seaters were known as Double Phaetons, but this term was soon replaced by Tourer (Touring in America), which prevailed until the virtual disappearance of the type in the mid-1930s.

The closed car

The first closed bodies emerged in France towards the end of the nineteenth century, on Mors and Panhard chassis. Some of the latter resembled small buses, with rear entrances and side-facing seats. The driver was perched above the engine, with a horizontal steering wheel in his hand, so that as much as possible of the wheelbase could be utilized for passenger-carrying. In 1900, Louis Renault offered an enclosed coupé body on his little single-cylinder chassis. Made for him by the well-known Parisian firm of Labourdette, it had a very curious look, being higher than it was long. But it was the first car in which driver and passenger were completely protected from the elements, by a windscreen and side windows as well as a roof. It was not imitated straightaway, but was the ancestor of the Doctor's Coupés which were made on many light-car chassis from about 1906 onwards.

Because of its weight and ungainly form, the closed car took some time to become established. A surprising amount of the extra weight was accounted for by the glass, especially that of the windscreen. With the low bonnets and high roofs prevailing at the time, this could be as much as 3.5 feet (1.1 m) high and 4 feet (1.2 m) broad. The earliest closed cars seldom had a windscreen for the driver, who was a paid chauffeur, but were completely enclosed in the tonneau area. Access to this might be by rear door, or by a door beside the driver's seat. When the chassis of cars were lengthened to allow a side-entrance tonneau, the way was open for more elaborate and spacious bodies.

One of the most sumptuous examples was built in 1902 for the Shah of Persia, on a Gardner Serpollet chassis. The interior was arranged as a divan, and among the lavish accessories were a table that could be raised from the side panel, a clock, thermometer, and loaded revolver! Similarly, a "touring saloon" on a 25-hp MMC chassis, exhibited at the 1903 Paris Salon, was fitted with four luxurious revolving arm-

Scotland was a country of large landed estates, and both these natives of the country were designed to cope with rough roads and heavy loads. The 1901 Albion *(left)* was the more conventional, with a rear-mounted horizontal two-cylinder engine, three-speed gearbox, and single chain drive. Its body is a somewhat rustic rear-entrance tonneau. The 1902 Arrol-Johnston *(below)* had a curious opposed-piston engine, in which each cylinder had two pistons with the combustion chamber between them. Here, the body was of the *dos-à-dos* style, with two additional seats ahead of the driver. This design, old-fashioned when it was introduced, was still being made in 1905, by which time it was truly archaic.

(Opposite top) A typical rear-entrance tonneau body on a 1903 two-cylinder Scania chassis. Later in the year, the Maskinfabriks AB Scania of Malmö brought out a new model, also a rear-entrance tonneau, but with a more modern Mercedes-type bonnet. One of these early Scanias was bought by Crown Prince Gustaf of Sweden, who used it for many years.

(Opposite bottom) Rear-entrance tonneau on a 1903 20-hp Winton. Note the single chain drive to the centre of the rear axle, unusual on such a powerful car as the 4.5-litre Winton. Most cars of this size had double chain drive.

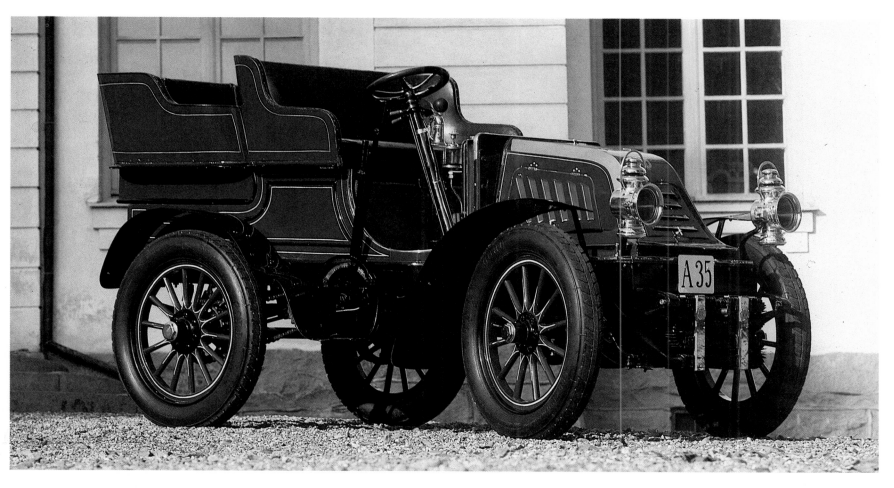

chairs, a ceiling of white Lincrusta, and curtains of dark green velvet with silver embroidery. Fittings here included a clock, thermometer, barometer, and what was described as an "engine room telegraph" for communication with the driver. This unfortunate character was completely unprotected, having neither a windscreen, doors, nor a roof.

These were the extremes of pomp, and were doubtless thought very ostentatious by most motorists. Nevertheless, by 1905 or so, the closed body had reached a high standard of comfort. The closed car became popular in France several years earlier than in England, where fresh-air enthusiasts held sway. The spirit of Charles Kingsley—

'Tis the hard grey weather

Breeds hard Englishmen—

was very much alive among English motorists, and not until 1926 were more closed cars sold on the United Kingdom market than open ones. In 1902, Sir Max Pemberton, novelist and author of *The Amateur Motorist*, wrote: "The pleasures of motoring are the pleasures of the open air. An open motorcar enables you to see the country as you can never see it in a train, on a bicycle, or afoot. The splendid exhilaration of speed in the open air has, above all else, established the motorcar in the affections of the people. If we are to lose this, if we are to box ourselves up in stuffy limousines, then, I say, we are better off in any train, even the meanest..."

An alternative to the stuffy limousine that became popular everywhere was the landaulette. This car, though closed, had the rear part of the roof made of leather, and able to be folded down. There were three kinds: the Single Landaulette in which only the rear quarter of the body folded, the Double in which part of the roof opened as well, and the Three Quarter distinguished by a window between the folding head and the door. The style was seen on quite small chassis, not to

mention on Rolls-Royces and Napiers, and was much liked for taxi-cabs. Before World War I, practically every taxi in the world was a landaulette, and they were still being made on Austin chassis for the London cab trade until 1939. They were, of course, ideal for the parade in the park, whether it was Hyde Park or the Bois de Boulogne, not only giving the occupants a good view and fresh air, but also allowing them to be seen in all their finery by the populace. And in those days, nobody worried about assassination or kidnapping.

A fine example of a Roi-des-Belges tourer body in the style of Henri Binder appears here on a 1904 25-hp C.G.V. chassis *(opposite)*. By 1913, the opulent curves of the Roi-des-Belges had given way to straight-through lines, typified in the 30/35-hp Napier *(above)*. With a bonnet line raised still further, this kind of touring body lasted right through the 1920s.

Wood gives way to metal

The structure of car-body work changed considerably between 1900 and 1914. The traditional material was wood, an ash frame with panels of mahogany ¼ inch (0.5 cm) thick. However, the voluptuous curves dictated by the Roi-des-Belges design were very difficult to reproduce in wood. So aluminium was used, starting with the French coachbuilder Rothschild and spreading to many other firms in the years after 1900. At first, single-curvature panels, as used on cheaper cars, continued to be made of wood, which was cheaper than alumin-ium and avoided the problems involved in joining the metal to the wooden framing. But by 1912, wooden panelling had largely been abandoned, being replaced by sheet iron on cheaper cars.

An interesting style that retained wood was the Skiff, a boat-shaped open four-seater, with a copper-riveted mahogany hull. Its nautical trim was sometimes extended to portholes for bonnet ventilators (an idea revived by Buick in 1949), rowlocks instead of door-handles, and halyards and cleats to hold down the hood. The first of these was built in 1912 by 24-year-old Jean-Henri Labourdette, on a Panhard chassis, for the Chevalier René de Knyff, managing director of Panhard et Levassor, and a well-known pioneer racing driver. He stipulated that the body should have no doors, which prompted young Labourdette

(Right) Louis Renault's extraordinary "pillbox coupé" of 1900. The body was built by the famous Parisian *carrossier* Henri Labourdette, on a standard Type B Renault chassis powered by a 2.75-hp De Dion Bouton engine. This was probably a one-off, but another coupé was built on the slightly longer Type C Renault chassis later in 1900.

The rear-entrance principle was applied to closed cars as well as open ones, although relatively rarely in the first years of the twentieth century. This limousine on a 10-hp Mors chassis of 1901 *(below)* was made by a small country coachbuilder, W. T. Edwards of Ashford, Kent. It featured an electric interior light, though the headlamps are acetylene models. The enclosed top could be removed by simply taking out four screws, to convert the car into a wagonette for summer use. More permanent is the curvaceous enclosed body on a 1904 28/32PS Mercedes *(opposite)*, built by Neuss of Berlin for Kaiser Wilhelm II.

Mercedes

to ask how one was to get in.

"By climbing," replied de Knyff.

"And the ladies?"

"Oh, they will climb too—then at last one will see their legs and get a good laugh."

The appearance of the stylish de Knyff promenading in his Panhard Skiff brought forth a rash of imitators at the 1913 Paris Salon. Labourdette built several replicas on Abadal, Peugeot, and Rolls-Royce chassis, while another coachbuilder who entered the field was Alin et Liautard.

The vintage tourer

The Skiff was a rare style, made almost exclusively in France. But the ordinary tourer body was becoming more modern and integrated. The low bonnet and radiator of the early Edwardian era were raised, so that the high scuttle between bonnet and body gradually faded. Doors to the front seats as well as the rear were introduced around 1906, and the compound curves of the Roi-des-Belges gave way to a straight line from the windscreen to the rear. For a long time, the back-rests of the front seats stood proud of this line, and the line was not totally smoothed until the late 1920s, by which time the open-tourer body was on its way out.

On the more expensive cars, the rear seats had their own windscreen. And by the 1920s, this led to the dual-cowl phaeton, a very stylish machine in which the rear seats had not only a separate windscreen,

but also a cowl or scuttle which separated them from those in front. Sometimes, instruments such as the speedometer would be duplicated for the benefit of the rear-seat passengers. The dual-cowl phaeton was a speciality of Le Baron Inc. in New York, who built it on chassis as grand as the Duesenberg Model J, and as humble as the Ford Model A. Other American coachbuilders to go in for the dual-cowl phaeton included Murphy of Pasadena, and La Grande (Union City Body Co.) of Union City, Indiana.

The extreme form of dual-cowl phaeton was found in the Scaphandrier, by the Parisian coachbuilders Kellner. Mostly seen on the enormous Renault 45 chassis, the Scaphandrier (French for diver) had a tiny cockpit with its own screen, and a roof for the rear-seat passengers. This claustrophobic box was the only closed part of the car—the chauffeur and front-seat passenger, if there was one, being unprotected save for a windscreen. Labourdette also built in this style, calling it the Cab Skiff, on Hispano-Suiza and Panhard chassis.

Closed cars and new techniques

The upper end of the coachbuilding trade continued in the 1920s much as it had done before the war, in methods although not in style (see Chapter 9). For cheaper cars, however, there were two major developments, the all-steel body and the fabric body. Coupled with these new materials, and to a large extent dependent on them both, was the worldwide movement toward closed bodies.

De Dietrich voiture de route

Wolseley landaulette

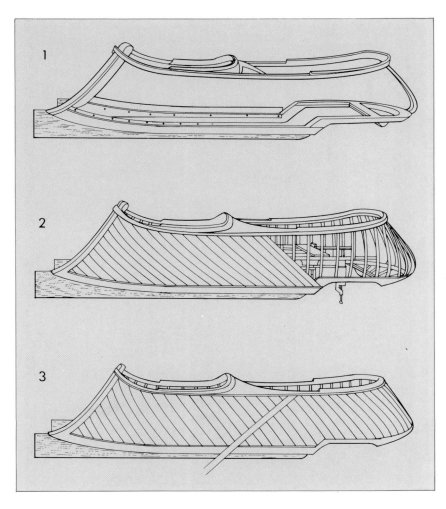

(*Opposite top*) Once it became possible, with longer wheelbases, to have more elaborate coachwork, the coachbuilders really went to town. This 40-hp De Dietrich *Voiture de Route*, shown at the Paris Salon in December 1904, featured a table for four passengers as in a railway carriage. The interior could be converted at night to accommodate a double bed.

(*Opposite bottom*) A three-quarter landaulette body on a 16/20-hp Wolseley of 1913. The lower part of the window frame between the rear door and the folding hood is just visible. The driver's compartment is typical of the chauffeur-driven car of the period, with no side windows, and with a windscreen whose upper half opened.

(*Above*) Three stages in the construction of a triple-planked skiff body: (*1*) the basic ash frame, (*2*) the ribs in place with part of the sheet mahogany covering, and (*3*) the second layer of mahogany placed at right angles to the first. The curved rear ribs and sheets needed very skilled craftsmanship, as they had to be steam-heated and curved by hand.

Apart from the two-seater Doctor's Coupé, the owner-driver's closed car was virtually nonexistent before 1911. In that year, the obscure Speedwell Motor Car Co. of Dayton, Ohio, introduced a two-door closed car which they called a sedan, the first known use of this word. Two years later, Hudson, Kissel, and Studebaker brought out their own sedans, followed by Franklin, Ford, and Dodge. These were all two-door models, of the type called a center-door: it gave access to the front and rear seats, but not very conveniently to either. On some, the driver had a door next to his seat, with the central door on the other side. None of these was terribly practical and, when Hudson brought out the Essex Coach in 1922 with two doors in the conventional position, the center-door sedan faded from the scene. Four-door sedans were slower to catch on in the low-price field because of their cost.

The Essex Coach was a significant car for several reasons. The Essex line had been created by Hudson in 1919, with a low-priced four-cylinder car designed to compete in the Ford and Chevrolet market, thus rescuing Hudson from financial difficulties. It was a great success, lifting the make from tenth to seventh place in the American sales league—and ultimately to third, in 1925. The first Essexes were open tourers but, when the Coach appeared in 1922, it offered four seats in closed comfort, with sensibly placed doors, for only $100 more than the open tourer. This was revolutionary at a time when most manufacturers charged a hefty premium for their sedans, and Hudson made no profit on the early Essex Coaches. However, sales increased so much that the break-even point was soon reached and then exceeded. By the summer of 1922, sales of closed Hudson and Essex cars were 55% of their total, pointing the way for other manufacturers, who would soon also make more closed cars than open ones.

While the Essex Coach brought about a revolution in style, it was not particularly advanced in either chassis or body. The latter was still a composite structure, with pressed steel panels over a wooden frame. Another major American manufacturer, Dodge, broke new ground by offering an all-steel touring body in 1916. This was made for them by the Budd Company of Philadelphia, and was followed by an all-steel four-door sedan in 1919. Ford built its own first all-steel body in 1923, but Chevrolet and other General Motors products were slower to go over to steel. These did not finally abandon the composite body until 1937, despite the much-vaunted Turret Top on the 1934 La Salle, which was simply a one-piece steel roof over a composite frame.

Actually, many of the "all-steel" bodies in the 1920s still contained some wood, for roof framing and for inserts to attach the upholstery. Traditional body building was a difficult and often unpleasant job, and labour problems in the industry were one reason for manufacturers to go over to steel. Another factor was the growing shortage of good-quality hardwood, and the consequent increase in price. A particular group who rejoiced at the change were the furniture makers, who were generally outbid for supplies of wood by the richer motor industry.

The steel body comes to Europe

The pressed-steel body is only viable if made in large numbers. And at the beginning of the 1920s, no European manufacturer was making cars in sufficient numbers to justify the giant presses, which cost upwards of £12,000 each. The first to think this a worthwhile investment was André Citroën, who installed machinery made in France by the American-owned Bliss company, paying royalties to Budd of Philadelphia which held the patents. Even so, the 1925 Citroën 11.4-hp four-door saloon cost only £100 more than the tourer. William Morris followed Citroën two years later, although he bought his

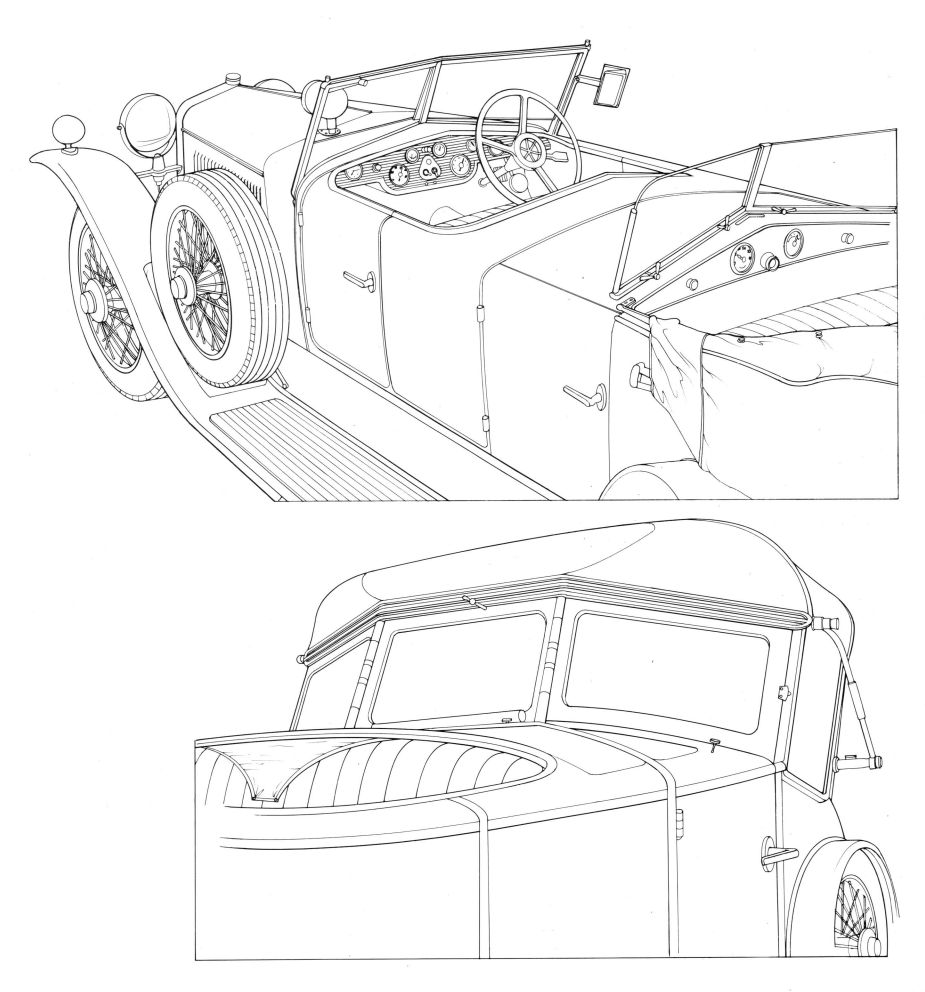

Three examples of the dual cowl phaeton: one by Bligh Brothers of Canterbury on a H6B Hispano-Suiza of 1924 *(opposite top)*, a Scaphandrier by Kellner on a 45-hp Renault of 1925 *(opposite bottom)*, and a cab-skiff by Labourdette on a 1925 Hispano-Suiza *(below)*. The portion of the decking above the rear door was spring-loaded to open upward, giving easy access to the rear seats when the rear doors were opened.

bodies from Pressed Steel in Cowley, who obtained their presses from the United States.

Budd had a financial interest in Pressed Steel, as they also had in their German subsidiary, Ambi-Budd of Berlin. German manufacturers who used Ambi-Budd bodies included Adler, Audi, BMW, Ford, NAG, and Wanderer. Ford in Britain were also customers of Pressed Steel—but they soon turned to Briggs, itself an American company, who built a big body plant to serve Ford's new Dagenham factory. Fiat joined the pressed-steel brigade in 1929 with their none-too-popular Tipo 514, yet followed it with the highly successful 508 Balilla (1932–37). As one would expect from such a self-sufficient company, who even generated their own electricity, Fiat made their own body pressings.

The fabric body

As car speeds increased faster than the road surfaces improved, a serious problem arose. Chassis frames flexed, placing a strain on the bodywork. The French *carrossier* Jacques Kellner lamented that "bodies are strained and pounded unless they are specially reinforced to assist the chassis in taking the stress." Reinforcing was really no solution, as it simply added to the weight.

At the 1921 Paris Salon, there appeared a new type of closed body construction, patented by Charles T. Weymann. This involved a fabric covering, over a jointed timber frame in which none of the wooden members touched each other, being joined by thin metal plates or wire tensioners. Thus, the frame was able to flex slightly with chassis movement, and without any of the drumming or squeaking that was associated with conventional closed bodies. Although not cheap by comparison with mass-produced pressed-steel bodies, the Weymann cost less than the traditional steel or aluminium panels on a wooden frame, commonly used in France. Not only was the panel-beater dispensed with, but also the painter, for the fabric was already colour-impregnated when it left the factory. This "colour" was traditionally black, although some French coachbuilders ordered fabric with basket-weave or tartan patterns. Weymann, whose father was American, had the fabric made by the Zapon company in Stamford, Connecticut, and later in France by the Société Française Zapon. The bodies were padded under the fabric, with horsehair if they were expensive, and with cotton waste if they were not.

Weymann bodies soon became so popular that a British subsidiary, Weymann Motor Bodies (1925) Ltd., was set up at Addlestone, Surrey. They worked on a variety of chassis, from Rolls-Royce, Daimler, and Hispano-Suiza to the 5CV Citroën, also selling patents for body-making to Jowett and Rover. E.C. Gordon England built Weymann-type fabric bodies on Austin Sevens. Weymann licences were sold to thirty French coachbuilders and fifteen manufacturers, to six coachbuilders in Italy, four in Germany, two in Belgium, and one each in Austria, Czechoslovakia, and Hungary. In addition, Weymann had his own factories in Paris and Addlestone, and in 1926 he opened one in Indianapolis. His bodies were taken up by Stutz, itself of Indianapolis, but otherwise most American manufacturers shunned the Weymann body. A very limited number was ordered by Marmon and Peerless, and about thirteen Model J Duesenbergs received Weymann bodies.

The Weymann system natually brought forth imitators, and by no means every fabric body in the 1920s was a Weymann. To save construction costs and royalty payments, some body-makers did away with the flexible joints, simply putting a fabric covering on an ordinary ash frame. This did away with one of the Weymann's greatest advantages—freedom from squeaking. Clyno, on their cut-price Nine

Three generations of the dickey-seat. The first, on a 1904 De Dion Bouton *(page 63)*, was more often called a spyder seat, a term derived from the light horse-drawn vehicle whose rear seat might be occupied by a footman. The 1914 Rover *(top)* can hold two people in its dickey seat, but weather protection is pretty limited. By 1930, the Model A Ford *(bottom)* offered a really snug dickey, or "rumble seat" as its American makers would have called it. When not in use, the seat back folded down to give a clean line to the rear of the body.

Two cars which brought closed-car motoring to the American public were the 1917 Dodge centre-door sedan *(above)* and the 1922 Essex Coach *(below)*. Wire wheels were standard on Dodge sedans, and gave the boxy-looking cars some distinction. All-steel sedans did not join the Dodge range until 1919, and then they had the more practical four-door layout. The Essex was exceptionally good value at $1,295, and it sold 36,222 units in 1922, despite its Plain Jane appearance.

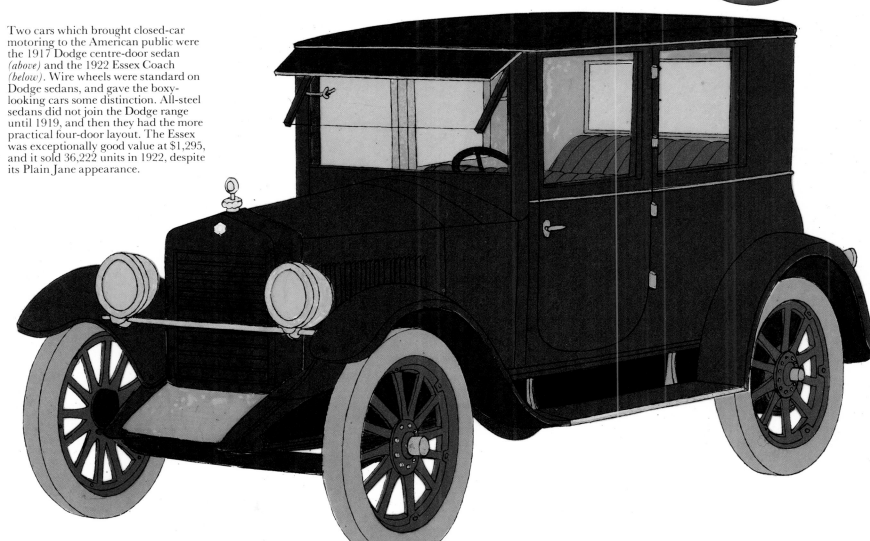

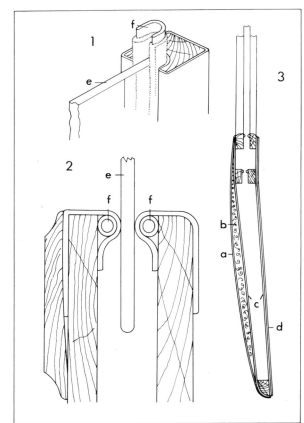

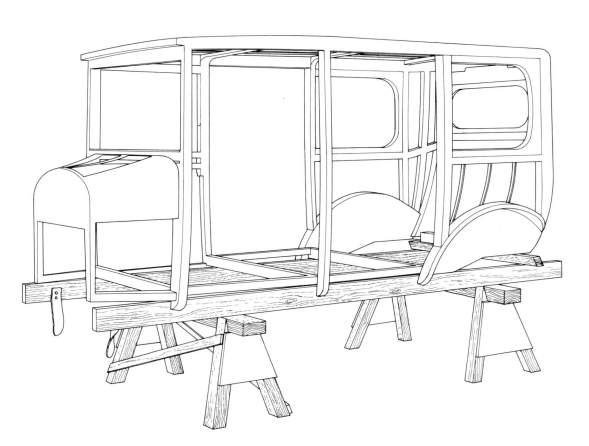

Triumph offered two types of fabric
saloon in 1929: a Weymann type at
£172, and the Gordon England *(below)*
with a more streamlined shape at £200.
Unlike that of Weymann, Gordon
England construction was rigid, but was
mounted to the chassis by rubber blocks
which absorbed most of the stress. In
1928, the Weymann body had cost £5
less than the coachbuilt Triumph
saloon, but its price was the same in
1929.

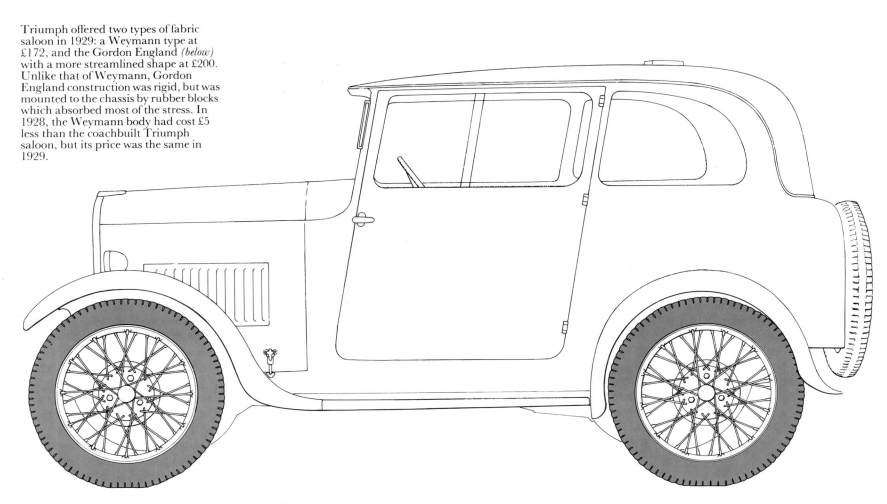

(*Opposite top*) Among the British firms who took out licences to manufacture the Weymann body was Rover. This is a 14-hp saloon dating from 1924, and Rover would continue to favour the fabric body until 1932. Various points of Weymann construction are shown: *(1)* the window frame, *(2)* a door with the window mechanism, *(3)* a cross-section of the complete door with *(a)* the exterior fabric covering, *(b)* the cotton wadding used as insulation, *(c)* a waterproof fabric lining on both sides, *(d)* the interior trim, *(e)* the window glass, and *(f)* the cloth-covered rubber tubing into which the glass dropped.

The estate car/shooting brake/station wagon was a rare beast before the 1930s, but here are two examples showing its development. The 16-hp Napier of 1913 *(right)* offered no weather protection for the passengers, and was probably used to transport shooting parties who would have been amply provided with waterproof clothing. With its side-facing bench seats and rear door, it was closely related to the first estate cars made by Daimler in the 1890s. The Ford Model A station wagon *(below)* had forward-facing seats like a car, but a dropped tailgate as in a delivery truck. This example has an Australian-built body on a Canadian chassis, yet is very similar to the Detroit-built product.

saloon, used ordinary metal panels but covered the whole car in leathercloth, to save the time and expense of painting. As happened with the cyclecar, the poorer examples gave the whole movement a bad name, in addition to which the new cellulose bright-coloured paints made the dull black fabric seem drab. Weymann tried to give the fabric a metallic gloss, but this proved more expensive than aluminium, and it was difficult to work with.

Weymann closed his American factory in 1931, and the French one shortly afterwards. Only Weymann of Addlestone lived on, to manufacture bus bodies and, eventually, to be merged with the big engineering and shipbuilding group Metropolitan–Cammell. As Metro Cammell Weymann, they became the largest bus-body building firm in Britain. In 1971, they launched their own design of double-decker bus with a Scania engine and transmission, the Metro-Scania, later known as Metrobus and Metropolitan. Fabric bodies had long been forgotten.

The "Woodie"

The estate car, or station wagon, is a widely-used and popular vehicle today, but it is a comparative newcomer to the motoring scene. Station wagons were not offered by an American manufacturer until 1929, and did not reach the catalogues in Europe until after World War II. They originated in the shooting brake, built on Daimler and other chassis at the turn of the century. But they subsequently tended to be considered as a commercial vehicle. Indeed, in America, station wagons were catalogued as commercials, and sold along with vans and pick-ups, until about 1941.

The first station wagons on passenger-car chassis were built by the Stoughton Wagon Company of Stoughton, Wisconsin—on the Model T Ford from 1919, and from 1923 on the Star, which was W.C. Durant's cheap car. Inevitably, Ford attracted more station-wagon builders than did any other car, because it was beloved by farmers: and thus, they were among the first users of the new style. Early examples were also called "depot" wagons or hacks, referring to calls at the bus or train station. These had only a roof and a row of seats behind the driver. The all-enclosed wood-panelled body arrived on the scene in 1924.

Ford was the first to offer a "woodie" as part of their standard range, in 1929 on the Model A chassis. The bodies were assembled by Briggs in Detroit, from wood supplied by the Mengel Company of Louisville, Kentucky. Each car cost $695 as compared with $525 for a sedan, and only 5,251 out of the 1,507,132 Fords sold that year were woodies. Sales dropped even below this figure in the early 1930s, and Ford did not exceed their initial total before 1938.

Station wagons were built on Chevrolet chassis throughout the 1920s. But General Motors began to offer them as a regular line only in 1935, and then the car was a metal-panelled eight-seater called a Suburban. The Huntingdon, New York, firm of J.T. Cantrell produced wooden bodies on Chrysler Corporation chassis from 1929 to 1931, yet all these types were made in small numbers. While they appealed to farmers, explorers, film studios, and hotels, the station wagon would not be accepted as ordinary family transportation until the early 1950s, by which time it was no longer a woodie. Evidently the name and the natural material had done little for the success of this style of car, and it had to await an era of mass motoring when— perhaps not coincidentally—the hint of driving to "stations" was made more attractive by sheer nostalgia.

THE SPORTS CAR

6

The invention of automobiles gradually introduced people to a new and fascinating experience of moving themselves rapidly on land in a machine. A natural interest in competition led them to race cars almost as soon as there were any to race. The 1894 Paris–Rouen Trial had 21 starters, ranging from a steam tricycle to a ten-passenger steam bus. No specially designed racing cars existed for several years, but streamlining appeared on the Amédée Bollées by 1898. Before long, more powerful engines distinguished the racing car from the touring vehicle. These types interacted to create the sporting variety, which also allowed a wider public to enjoy the speed and glamour of cars. Converted Grand Prix racers, used on the road by adventurous souls until 1914 and later, were undoubtedly sporting as well. But they were not sports cars in the accepted sense: an automobile with above-average performance built for use on the road rather than the race-track.

Early racing in Europe

The origin of the sports car lies in a series of competitions held in Germany between 1905 and 1911. The Herkomer Tour—or, to give its full name, the International Touring Car Competition for the Herkomer Trophy—was a run of 500 miles (800 km), including a hill-climb and a speed trial. The 1905 event attracted only touring cars, but in the following year, when there were no awards for coach-work, the entrants reduced their weight by substituting canvas flaps for doors, and sketchy flared wings for the heavier type. The Trophy was won by Dr. Rudolf Stöss of the Horch company, in an 18/20PS four-cylinder Horch. At 2.7 litres, the engine was one of the smallest in the event, but it had a well-designed cylinder head with overhead inlet and side exhaust valves. This was a recurrent theme in the development of the sports car—the search for power through improved design, rather than by the brute force of an enormous engine.

In 1908, the Herkomer Trophy was replaced by the Prince Henry Trial, organized by Prince Henry of Prussia, younger brother of the Kaiser. The Horch cars were much more radical than they had been two years earlier: no doors, and a cowl between front and rear-seat passengers, in the style of the dual cowl phaeton of twenty years afterward. The front wings resembled surfboards, and there was no windscreen or any weather protection for the driver or passengers. British journalists were very scathing about these "freakish stream-lined cars", little realizing that the onlookers were being treated to a

glimpse of the future. What is interesting about the Prince Henry cars is that they were built to circumvent the rules of the competition to the limit. Had Prince Henry's regulations been strictly adhered to, his name would never have been perpetuated in connection with the history of the sports car.

The 1910 Prince Henry Trial saw the appearance of two machines which, more than any other, can be considered the first sports cars, although no car would be described as such until after World War I. They were the 20-hp Vauxhall from England and the 27/80PS Austro-Daimler from Austria. Neither was the largest car made by its company, yet both had superior performance, thanks to engine design and a judicious degree of weight-watching. The Vauxhall engine was derived from an L-head 38-bhp 3-litre touring unit of 1908, from which chief engineer Laurence Pomeroy extracted 60 bhp for the Prince Henry Trial cars. He did this mainly by using lighter pistons that allowed greater engine speed, and improved valve porting. The Vauxhall's body was very advanced for 1910, having a straight-through line from the handsome Vee-radiator to the scuttle, and a simple open four-seater body without doors. The relatively small Vauxhalls were not among the winners of the Trial, but two of the three entrants made non-stop runs, while the third was only slightly delayed. The Prince Henry Vauxhalls did well in Swedish and Russian trials over the next three years.

The Austro-Daimler was a larger car and, in some ways, of more advanced design. The work of Ferdinand Porsche, who drove the winning car, it had a 5.7-litre four-cylinder engine with inclined overhead valves, operated by a single overhead camshaft and forked rockers. Ignition was by two Bosch magnetos, and there was an elaborate lubrication system with a series of plunger pumps driven from the camshaft. The four-seater body tapered from top to bottom because, while Prince Henry's regulations stipulated a minimum width, this had only to be measured at the top. The only old-fashioned aspect of Porsche's design was its chain drive, and this was replaced by a shaft in 1912. A total of eleven Austro-Daimlers took part in the 1910 Prince Henry Trial, and the make took the first three places. As with the Vauxhall, the car was put on the market a year later. Though not the biggest, it was the most expensive of the Austro-Daimler range, costing more than the massive 50/60PS model, with a side-valve shaft-drive chassis. The company did well to sell 200 between 1911 and 1914, compared with 190 of the Vauxhall Prince Henry sold during the same period.

Austro-Daimler and Vauxhall set a fashion that was taken up by a

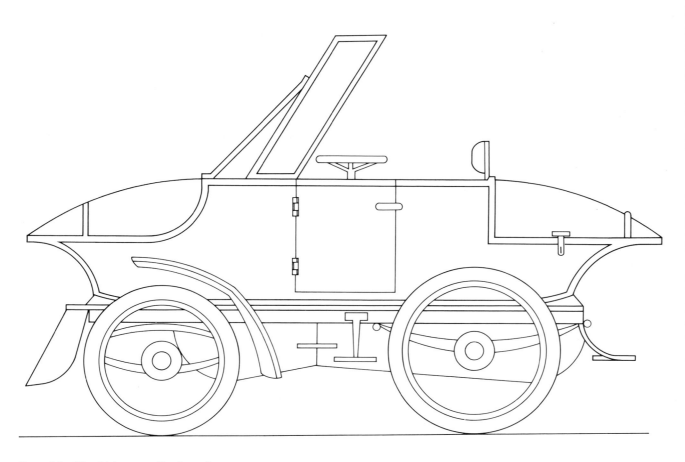

(Left) The first streamlined bodies, with some attention to the best shape for penetration through the air, were made by Amédée Bollée for the cars he entered in the Paris-Amsterdam-Paris Race of 1898. They were also remarkable for being built in aluminium. Orders from private customers followed, including this design of 1899, made for the Comte de Paiva by the coachbuilders Rheims & Auscher. As the Comte presumably used it for road work, it could be considered an embryo sports car. The sloping windscreen was the first example of its kind.

(Opposite) Probably the most desirable of the prewar sporting tourers, this 1914 Prince Henry Vauxhall is of the second series, with the engine enlarged from 3 litres to just under 4 litres, and with doors on the body which was built in the Vauxhall works. Having a top speed of 75 mph (120 km/h), and exceptionally sensitive handling, the Prince Henry was an attractive proposition at £580. But sales of less than 200 cars in four years indicated that the public was not yet ready for the sports car. This example was owned for many years by Laurence Pomeroy Jr., son of the designer.

One of the "freakish streamlined cars" which so displeased British journalists covering the 1908 Prince Henry Trials was the 2.7-litre 11/22PS Horch (below), with ultra-light four-seater body by Kathe und Sohn of Halle. The surf-board-like flared wings were featured on several other Prince Henry competitors, and were copied in the 1920s by a number of manufacturers.

number of manufacturers. No longer was the fastest car in the catalogue necessarily the largest. Tuned, high-speed engines and light bodies, rather than sheer size, were the key to performance. But a few of the old monsters survived: the 9,500-cc chain-driven Mercedes 90 was listed until 1914, as was the even bigger 10,618-cc Isotta-Fraschini Type KM, also chain-driven. The Mercedes had an L-head engine, yet the Isotta was quite advanced as well as enormous, with a single overhead camshaft and four valves per cylinder. This car also featured four-wheel brakes, the pedals acting on the rear wheels and transmission, and a big outside lever on the front wheels.

At the other end of the scale were the small sporting cars developed for competitions such as the French *Coupe de l'Auto*. Held between 1905 and 1914, this race was sponsored by the magazine *L'Auto* to encourage the sporting light car. Some freakish engines resulted from the regulations, which restricted only the cylinder bore, so that designers gained the greatest possible capacity by using very long strokes. The extreme was reached in the Lion Peugeot of 1910, with 80 × 280 mm twin cylinders in a narrow-angle V, and a bonnet so high that the driver and mechanic had to peer round it in order to see where they were going.

However, more practical cars were built for the *Coupe de l'Auto*, such as the single-cylinder Sizaire-Naudin with transverse-leaf independent front suspension. Likewise, the 10-hp Isotta-Fraschini had a 1,327-cc single overhead-camshaft engine which ran at 3,500 rpm, a very high figure for 1908. This was a jewel of a car and, with road equipment, it looked like a smaller version of the Mercer Raceabout. It was not unduly expensive, at £285 on the British market, although surprisingly few were sold during its four years of production. Nor was

Isotta-Fraschini the last manufacturer to discover that the quality light car yielded uncertain profits. Other attractive sporting cars with small four-cylinder engines included the Swiss Martini, and the Type 13 Bugatti with its single overhead-camshaft engine and curved, sliding tappets operating the overhead valves.

From 1910 to 1914, the *Coupe de l'Auto* was for larger cars of up to 3 litres capacity, and some fine sporting tourers resulted from these events. Sunbeam finished first, second, and third in the 1912 race, and marketed a handsome sporting two- or four-seater based on the winners. It had much lower lines than the regular Sunbeams, a "lipped" radiator inherited from the racers, and wire wheels. The competitions also gave rise to the long-stroke four-cylinder Hispano-Suizas, named "Alfonso XIII" after the Spanish king who owned several of them. A short-chassis two-seater Alfonso was good for 80 mph (130 km/h), and at £545 it was cheaper than a Vauxhall Prince Henry. In the same class was a sporting car produced by a British firm that took no part in racing—Crossley. Their Shelsley 15.9-hp model had an L-head monobloc engine, and was available with attractive torpedo bodies, similar to those mounted on the Sunbeam chassis.

Several other quality medium-size sporting cars existed in the immediate pre-war years. The French D.F.P., for example, was not particularly sporting until the English importers, H.M. and W.O. Bentley, got hold of it and fitted aluminium pistons to raise its output from 25 to 40 bhp. Many other cars of sporting shape were made between 1912 and 1915, usually on stock touring chassis. With a clean-lined torpedo body and wire wheels, quite staid cars like the 15.9-hp Belsize, 14-hp Hurtu, and 14/20-hp Spyker looked fairly daring. Some manufacturers did not pretend that the sporting qualities

A fine French approach to the sports car. Maurice Sizaire and Louis Naudin, in 1908 *(opposite)*, chose a horizontal single-cylinder engine in a light chassis—with a very early example of independent front suspension, by sliding pillars and transverse leaf springs. The Sizaire won fame in races such as the *Coupe de l'Auto* and the Sicilian Cup, and was reasonably priced at £178.

The Spanish-built Hispano-Suiza achieved international fame after victories in the 1910 *Coupe de l'Auto*, and the following year came a production car derived from the race winner. The Type 15T, or Alfonso XIII, shown here from 1912, had a long-stroke four-cylinder engine (80 × 180 mm) and, in short-chassis form, was good for 80 mph (130 km/h) at an unhurried 2,300 rpm. Thus it was not tiring to drive over long distances, and the Spanish monarch after whom it was named covered thousands of miles over the indifferent roads of his kingdom in a series of Alfonsos.

(Pages 100-101) A sporting road car could be made from a racing car, as happened with this 1911 *Coupe de l'Auto* Delage. Driven by Louis Bablot, the car won the race, also known as the *Coupe des Voitures Légères*, carrying the same road equipment as seen in this photograph. It is one of the few early racing cars to take part in road events today, another being the celebrated 1908 Grand Prix Itala. An unusual feature is its five-speed gearbox, with direct drive on fourth and an overdrive top gear.

One of the most enjoyable and comfortable to drive of any pre-1914 cars was the Rolls-Royce Silver Ghost, and the best of these was the Continental or Alpine Eagle tourer. This came about because of the failure of James Radley's privately entered car in the 1912 Austrian Alpine Trial. The company prepared four team cars for the following year, with four-speed gearboxes and, due to a higher compression ratio and larger carburettor, with a power increase of more than 10 bhp. They won the 1913 Trial by a considerable margin, and replicas went into production under the name Continental. However, Rolls-Royce engineer Ernest Hives always referred to them as Alpine Eagles, the name by which they are generally known today. Shown here is a 1913 example.

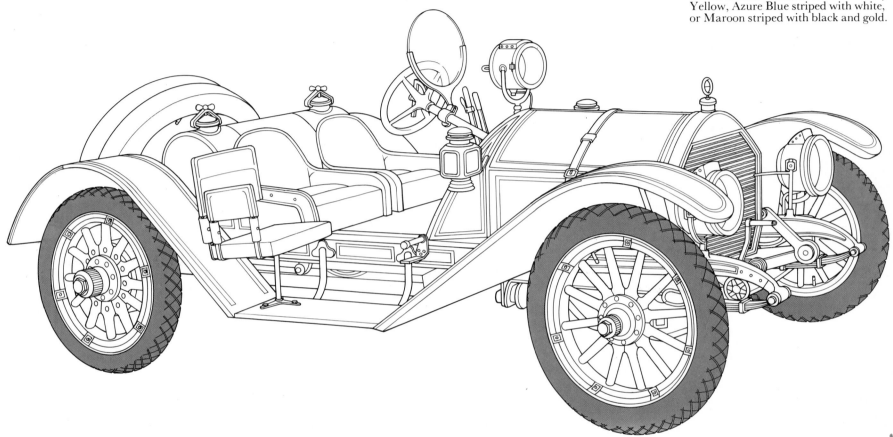

The Mercer Raceabout, seen here as in 1912-13, has come to symbolize the pre-World War I American speedster, with its spartan passenger accommodation, bolster fuel tank, and monocle wind-screen. Its 4.9-litre T-head engine developed 58 bhp and, thanks to light weight and a high rear-axle ratio, this gave the car a top speed of 75 mph (120 km/h). Early cars had three forward speeds, but later ones had four, of which top was an overdrive. The usual colours for the Mercer Raceabout were Canary Yellow, Azure Blue striped with white, or Maroon striped with black and gold.

were any more than skin-deep. Thus, the Briton sporting car was described as having "mechanical features almost identical to the standard model, but a greatly modified appearance. It is intended to meet the requirements of purchasers desiring a car of racy appearance."

The largest prewar sporting cars were inspired by another competitive event, the Austrian Alpine Trials of 1911 to 1914. Among the makers who entered sporting four-seaters were Austro-Daimler and Puch from Austria, besides Horch, Audi, and Benz from Germany. From England came Rolls-Royce, whose tuned 40/50, familiarly known as the Alpine Eagle, was about the best example one could find of a fast, silent touring car, able to hold its own with any car made at the time. It was developed from the standard 40/50, or Silver Ghost, as a result of the failure of a three-speed 40/50 to start on the steep incline of the Katschberg Pass in the 1912 event. The 1913 models were specially prepared for Alpine conditions, with four-speed gearboxes (standardized that year on all Rolls-Royces) and engine power increased from 60 to 75 bhp. Their larger radiator had an expansion chamber above the cap, nicknamed the "water tower". The team of four swept the board in the 1913 Trials, winning six awards which included the Archduke Leopold Cup.

The first American speedsters

Across the Atlantic, the sports car was developing in a very different way. There was little influence from Europe, and no American cars took part in the Prince Henry or Austrian Alpine Trials, although two Buicks ran in the 1913 *Coupe de l'Auto*. Nevertheless, many American companies put light two-seater bodies on their stock chassis, with no modification to the engine, while the rear-axle ratio might be raised. These cars went under diverse names such as the runabout, raceabout, roadster, or speedster.

Sometimes, a local dealer would strip and tune a car to take part in hill-climbs and races, thus boosting the sales of touring cars. Success might lead to a demand for replicas, which would be passed to the factory, and result in a roadster appearing in the catalogue for the following year. The number of American roadsters is too great to list, but certain makes achieved a reputation in this field. Among them were Apperson, Kissel, Marion, Marmon, Midland, National, Overland, Stoddard-Dayton, and Thomas. Head and shoulders above these were the makes regarded primarily as sporting—Chadwick, Mercer, Stutz, and Simplex.

Countless words have been written about the Mercer Raceabout and the Stutz Bearcat, indeed more than they deserve in terms of their production figures and importance at the time. Both companies made touring cars in bigger quantities, and the Mercer Type 35 limousine was used as a taxicab. A study of registrations reveals that one was three times as likely to see a Stutz Bearcat as a Mercer Raceabout. Both followed the recipe of a large four-cylinder T-head engine, a three-speed gearbox, and a high-ratio rear axle which gave a road speed of 75 mph (120 km/h) at only 1,500 rpm. Coachwork was limited to two bucket seats, with a bolster fuel tank behind them. In back of that were a small toolbox and, usually, two spare tyres. No windscreens were fitted, but a monocle could be attached to the steering column. This cannot have given much protection at high speeds, and goggles were essential for the driver and passenger. The Mercer in particular was weak in the braking department—it was said that, by the time the car had stopped, the emergency was twenty yards to the rear.

The Chadwick was a larger and more expensive car, costing $6,500 for a runabout, compared with $2,000 to $2,600 for a Mercer or Stutz. For his money, the Chadwick owner got an 11.2-litre six-cylinder engine with pushrod-operated overhead valves, and a three-seater body with a little "spyder" seat behind the driver. The make is best known for being the first in the world to use what would later be called a supercharger. This was apparently meant to compensate for the poor performance of the first Chadwick six-cylinder engine, which initially developed less power than the version with four cylinders of the same dimensions. At the outset, Chadwick's leading competition driver, Willy Haupt, tried three carburettors, but he found that the limited valve area was the main problem. The valves could not be enlarged because of the copper water-jackets surrounding each pair of cylinders, so Haupt devised a compressor that would force the fuel mixture into the cylinders at a pressure greater than atmospheric. He employed one, then three compressors, driven by a leather belt from the flywheel. This "blower" helped Haupt to win some hill-climbs, yet it did not work well for long periods. Contrary to some accounts, the blowers were never used on cars sold to the public.

After the War

The 1920s can justifiably be called the most important decade in the history of the sports car. The breed flourished in all price categories, and the small makes were not threatened until the Depression. Nor was there any concern about safety or pollution, which has emasculated the whole concept of the sports car in more recent times. Britain still had a nominal speed limit of 20 mph (32 km/h), abolished only in 1930—but the roads of France were open, straight, and inviting. The spirit of the age was summed up in a painting which graced a 1924 issue of *The Brooklands Gazette* (now *Motor Sport*). It showed two cars racing on a straight poplar-lined French road, with the caption: "A ten mile straight, foot hard down, dust for the other fellow—that's life!"

National characteristics emerged more clearly in the sports cars of the 1920s. Britain was typified by the large, relatively slow-revving engine in a sporting four-seater, of which the Bentleys, the Vauxhall 30/98, and the Sunbeam 3-litre were the best known. At the end of the decade, Cecil Kimber's M-type MG Midget showed what could be done with components from the mass-produced Morris Minor. France became famous for the small four-cylinder sports car—typified by Amilcar and Salmson—and for fast tourers such as the Delage 14/40, Ballot 2LTS, Hotchkiss, Chenard-Walcker, and many others. Germany produced a variety of sports cars for sale within her borders, but the only make which achieved international fame was Mercedes-Benz (the amalgamation in 1926 of those two pioneer firms), with their increasingly powerful and formidable SS and SSK six-cylinder supercharged models. Italian sports cars tended to be small, and even the immensely successful Alfa Romeo 6C was under 2 litres in capacity. America took an individual path, with the descendants of the prewar speedster.

Putting the valves upstairs

There was a general trend in the 1920s toward overhead valves, in the interests of better engine breathing and more efficient use of fuel. Sports cars tended to lead the way in this respect, although the Italian O.M. and German N.A.G. managed very well with side-valve units, more than holding their own in competitions. Three types of overhead-valve engine existed: the pushrod type with a single side-mounted camshaft, which operated the valves via pushrods and rockers, and the types with single or twin overhead camshaft. A variation on these was the Riley Nine, introduced in 1926. It used two camshafts mounted high in the block, but not over the valves. The latter were inclined at 45°, and the cylinder head had a hemispherical combustion chamber.

Three classic British sports cars of the 1920s—two Bentleys and a Vauxhall. As a result of their successes at Le Mans (with victories in 1924 and 1927-1930 inclusive) and their glamorous, wealthy drivers (such as Woolf Barnato, Sir Henry Birkin, and Bernard Rubin), Bentleys came to be regarded as the archetypal vintage sports cars. The 3-litre model *(opposite)* was announced in 1919, but the first was not delivered to a customer until September 1921. By 1925, when this one was made, it was well-established, and had been joined by the 6.5-litre six-cylinder model. The latter was a fast tourer rather than a sports car and, when the 3-litre became uncompetitive (although remaining in production until 1929, W. O. Bentley brought out a larger "four", the 4.5-litre. This 1929 Vanden Plas-bodied 4.5-litre tourer *(above)* has extra-wide running boards as requested by its first owner, a maharajah whose bodyguards rode on the running boards. However, many knowledgeable enthusiasts rate the 30/98 Vauxhall higher in terms of handling. Whereas Bentley used a single overhead camshaft on all his designs, Vauxhall made do with side valves on their E-type 30/98. This model, shown here as in 1920 *(right)*, was produced from 1919 to 1922, when it received pushrod-operated overhead valves as the OE-type. With a 3.09-to-1 axle ratio, the E-type could reach 80 mph (130 km/h). Braking, on the transmission and rear wheels only, was not much of a drawback, given the generally empty roads of the period.

(Below) The twin overhead-camshaft layout, as used on Vittorio Jano's 6C Alfa Romeo 1750 engine at the end of the 1920s. Jano's twin-ohc 1500 and 1750 Alfa Romeos were derived from the P2 Grand Prix engine, although they had six cylinders instead of eight, and plain instead of roller-bearing crankshafts. They set a trend for a new, lighter type of competition engine which made the Bentleys seem old-fashioned, and twin-cam Alfas dominated sports car racing in the early 1930s.

The Mercedes Benz S series has come to represent the German sports car in the same way as the Bentley does the British. In fact, far fewer of the Porsche-designed six-cylinder cars were made—less than 400, compared with 1,690 of the 3-litre Bentley alone. The SS, known in Britain as the 38/250, shared the wheelbase of 11 feet 2 inches (3.4 metres) with the S model, but had a higher bonnet which gave the cars a more imposing appearance. The SSK, with a shorter wheelbase of 9 feet 8 inches (2.95 metres), was made only

with two-seater coachwork, and not more than 45 were sold. *(Opposite)* This is a Model K of 1927, the touring predecessor of the sporting S models. With a smaller cylinder bore (94 mm, compared with 98 for the S), the K had a capacity of 6,240 cc. It also used a supercharger, which gave the engine a maximum output of 160 bhp. It was produced from 1926 to 1929, and 267 were made.

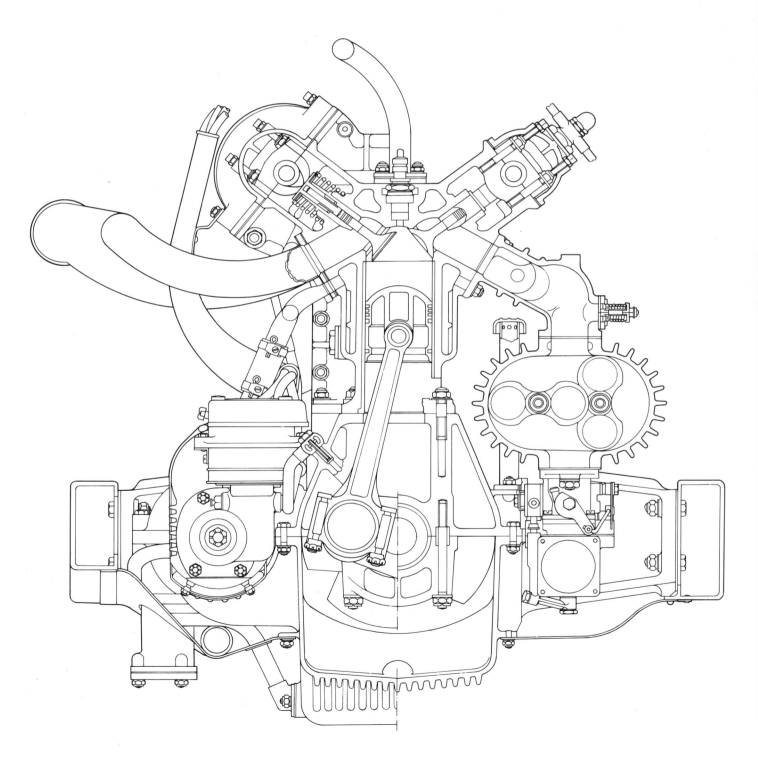

(Above) The most common form of supercharger, the Roots type, was derived from blowers used to supply air for blast furnaces. Its intermeshing two-lobe rotors do not quite touch, so no internal lubrication is needed. Roots blowers were used by Alfa Romeo, Bentley, and Mercedes-Benz, and also on the only modern car to employ supercharging rather than turbocharging, the Lancia.

Touring and sports versions of the Hillman Ten, dating from 1919. The two-seater tourer (opposite) followed closely on prewar practice, as one would expect of a car launched only a few months before the Armistice. Its 1,593-cc side-valve engine had a fixed cylinder head, although aluminium pistons were used, and electric lighting and starting was standardized from 1919 onward. The sporting model (left) has a totally different look, thanks to its Vee radiator, disc wheels, and copper exhaust pipe. Capacity was reduced to 1,496 cc so as to bring it into the 1.5-litre class, but power was raised by 10 bhp to 28 bhp with lightened and balanced pistons and con rods, and a high-lift camshaft.

The low-production specialized sports car was something that Britain excelled at, and this one attracted a keen following which has only increased until the present today. The 12/50 Alvis was made in the largest numbers, about 7,000 between 1923 and 1932, with a variety of touring and saloon bodies as well as sporting versions. It was one of those fortunate designs which combined reliability with useful performance, and about 650 are still running today.

Popularly priced sports cars based on mass-produced small cars (the Austin Seven and the Morris Minor). The 1927 Austin *(left)* carries a striking aluminium body by Burghley with the kind of flared wings which were pioneered in the Prince Henry Trial of 1908. Note the scuttle-mounted head-lamps which were features of all Austin Sevens until 1927. The Morris-based MG M-type Midget was cheaper at £175, although this example *(opposite)* is a Double Twelve Replica based on the cars which finished in places 3-7 of their class in the 1930 Brooklands Double Twelve Hour Race. With a high-profile camshaft which raised output from 20 to 27 bhp, these cost £245, and only 18 were sold to the public between August and December 1930. M-type buyers had the option of a four-speed gearbox in 1931, and a super-charger at an extra £65, but few of these were sold. A total of 3,235 M-type cars had been sold by the time production ended in June 1932.

So many sports cars used pushrod overhead valves that it is impossible to mention them all. Among the more prominent exponents were Vauxhall, who introduced them on the OE 30/98 of 1922; Straker-Squire, who made a big six-cylinder car with separately cast cylinders and exposed valve gear; and most of the French fast tourers, such as Delage, Hotchkiss, Georges Irat, and Cottin-Desgouttes. The last had three valves per cylinder, two inlet and one exhaust.

The overhead camshaft, driven by either a vertical shaft or a chain, had been pioneered in 1905 by Isotta-Fraschini's famous designer, Giustino Cattaneo, and was used on all their models from then onward. Porsche had put it on the Prinz Heinrich Austro-Daimler. It was also chosen by W.O. Bentley, when he brought out a car under his own name in 1919. Bentley used four valves per cylinder—as Ettore Bugatti had done, on the 1914 racing versions of the Type 13—and managed to extract 80 bhp from 2,996 cc at the relatively modest engine speed of 2,500 rpm. Bentley kept to the single overhead-camshaft layout until the time of his unsuccessful 4-litre model of 1931, by which point his company was on the verge of collapse and sale to Rolls-Royce. The only change was that, on the six-cylinder 6.5-litre and 8-litre cars, the camshaft was driven by a system of coupling rods, quieter than the shaft.

The 75-mph (120 km/h) Bentley from 1919 was considered a fast tourer rather than a sports car. Yet its series of victories at Le Mans in 1924 and 1927–30 placed it firmly in the ranks of the best competition machinery. In fact, the distinction between fast tourer and sports car was somewhat blurred. For the leading sports car races of the day, such as Le Mans and the Belgian 24 Hours, required all cars over 1,100 cc in capacity to have four seats. Thus, since most manufacturers entered these events, their sporting cars were four-seaters.

In 1921, Sunbeam announced sporting versions of their four-cylinder 16/40 and six-cylinder 24/60 cars. These had four inclined overhead valves per cylinder, operated by an overhead camshaft. Known as the OV models, they were theoretically available in 1922 and 1923, but very few were made. It was not until the advent of the twin-camshaft 3-litre model in 1925 that Sunbeam had a true sports car. Other firms were getting into the overhead act as well. AC had a 2-litre six, with steel liners in an aluminium cylinder block. In France, there were Ariès, Ballot, Bignan, and Hispano-Suiza. Bugatti, of course, had put his camshaft upstairs since his first car of 1909, and followed this tradition until the end of his production, using twin camshafts from 1930 onward.

In Italy, Alfa Romeo adopted an overhead camshaft on Vittorio Jano's 1.5-litre 6C, made since 1925. The rarely seen 3.5-litre Nazzaro also had a single overhead camshaft, operating one inlet and two exhaust valves per cylinder. Of the latter, one opened slightly before the other, but—whatever advantages this may have had—it did not popularize the car, which vanished in 1922 after quite a small run. Other continental makes to feature a single overhead camshaft were

Bugatti covered most sections of the sports-car market, apart from the very cheapest. The Brescia shown here was descended from the original Type 13 of 1910, with its single overhead-camshaft four-cylinder engine enlarged to 1,453 cc in 1921, and to 1,496 cc in 1923. Four valves per cylinder were featured on the postwar models, and front-wheel brakes arrived in 1925, the year of this model. They had, however, been fitted earlier by private owners. A touring Brescia could reach 75 mph (120 km/h), which was a remarkable speed for a 1.5-litre car in the early 1920s, but they were not cheap. A chassis cost £735 in 1920, although this had fallen to £385 five years later.

The two great rivals for the French light sports car market. The Amilcar *(above)* is a CGS, a development of the original Petit Sport, but with a redesigned cylinder head and front-wheel brakes. It provided 75 mph (120 km/h) for £220, and similar models were made in Italy by S.I.L.V.A. of Verona and in Germany by Pluto of Zella St. Blasii, Saxony. The Salmson Grand Sport *(opposite)* was similar in concept, but had a more advanced twin overhead-camshaft engine in place of the Amilcar's pushrods. For 1926, both companies brought out more up-to-date designs, with lower chassis and cycle-type wings. Both were made until the end of the 1920s, when the small French sports car all but disappeared.

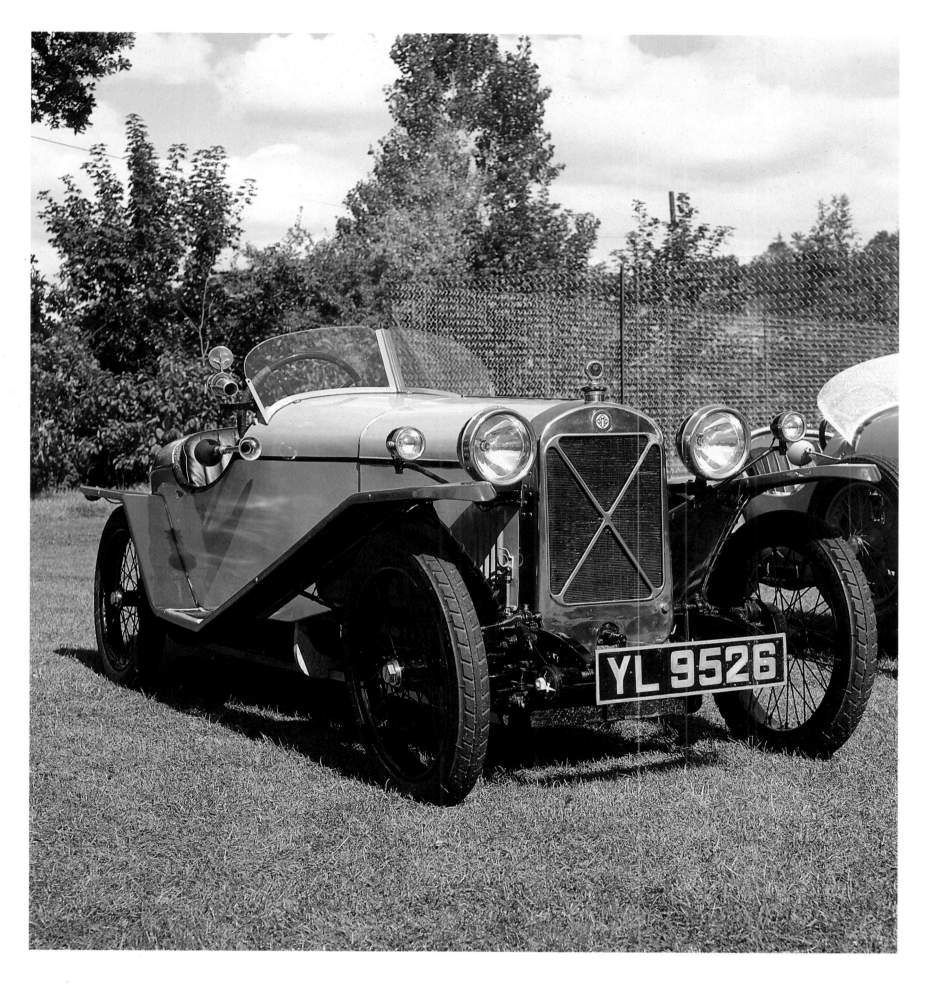

Frazer-Nashes, like this 1927 two-seater *(left)*, appealed to a limited public, and fewer than 400 were sold in the interwar years. They won and kept owners' loyalty by success in competitions, and a good proportion of those sold were entered in rallies, trials or races—as was also true of Aston Martins.

the German Stolle, a very neat 1.5-litre sports car with four-wheel brakes and Rudge wire wheels, and the Austro-Daimler and Steyr from Austria.

The Peugeot designer, Ernest Henry, produced a 4.5-litre four-cylinder engine in 1912 for the company's Grand Prix racing cars, with *two* overhead camshafts—one to operate the inlet valves, and the other for the exhausts. This permitted greater engine speeds, and soon became the accepted design for racing-car engines. After the war, Henry joined the Ballot firm, which had made rather ordinary proprietary engines and was about to launch a programme of Grand Prix and sports cars. There, his first designs were straight-eight racers with twin overhead camshafts, but in 1921 he brought out the 2LS. This 2-litre sports car was the first road-going car to have a twin-camshaft engine. It developed a remarkable 75 bhp, and had a top speed of 92 mph (150 km/h), but was very expensive. Not more than 100 were made in four years, after which Ballot adopted a single overhead-camshaft engine for their quite pleasant 2LT and 2LTS sporting tourers.

Racing cars such as Fiat, Rolland-Pilain, and Sunbeam were using twin camshafts by 1923. Yet the next make of road cars to adopt the twins was a small German company, Simson of Suhl in Thuringia, now part of East Germany. Its designer, Paul Henze, was responsible for the 1924 Simson-Supra Typ S, with a 2-litre four-cylinder engine and twin camshafts operating inclined overhead valves. With 60 bhp available, the tourer on a wheelbase of 9 feet 10 inches (3 metres) could do 75 mph (120 km/h), and the short-base two-seater with twin carburettors was good for 85 mph (135 km/h). Unfortunately, the

market for an expensive sports car in Germany was very limited, and Simsons were never exported. At most 30 of the Typ S were sold, compared with about 300 of their single overhead-camshaft model, and 750 of the pushrod-engine six-cylinder Typ R.

Sunbeam then put the twin-cam engine on the road by bringing out a 3-litre version of the successful 2-litre racing engine, which had given Britain her first Grand Prix victory at Tours in 1923 (and her last until 1955). It was mounted in a long-wheelbase chassis, but never made a great mark, because company politics starved Sunbeam of development money—which was channeled instead to Talbot, the French part of the Sunbeam-Talbot-Darracq empire. Nonetheless, about 250 twin-cam Sunbeams were made between 1926 and 1930. A chassis cost £950, compared with £895–925 for a 3-litre Bentley, and £950 for a Vauxhall 30/98 of the same period. It is surprising that the Sunbeam did not cost more, as a twin-cam engine is complicated to build, and early examples tended to be rather noisy in operation. For these reasons, few others were made, and—apart from Salmson—no manufacturer made them continuously for long, until after World War II when Jaguar produced a reliable and reasonably priced power unit for the XK120. The French Lombard company made some beautiful little sports/racing cars with 1,015-cc twin-cam engines and, in Italy, both Itala and S.P.A. used this layout for a while.

The rise of the supercharger

After the pioneer efforts of Willy Haupt on the Chadwick, no more was heard of forced induction until the end of World War I. Then, as they so often have done, Mercedes startled the world with a new develop-

ment: a two-lobe blower, driven from the camshaft, running at 10,000 rpm. The car to which this was fitted for the 1921 Coppa Florio in Sicily was not a new model, being a large four-cylinder 28/95PS, made since 1914. Still, Max Sailer won the race—and what is more, he drove all the way from Stuttgart to Sicily and back, as well as the 268 miles (430 km) of the race, on one set of tyres. Rubber was so scarce in Germany at the time that the combined resources of Mercedes and the Continental Tyre Company could not spare more than one set!

Production Mercedes with supercharged engines were advertised in 1921: a 6/25/40PS of 1,570 cc, and a 10/40/65PS of 2,600 cc. But they were not in evidence at the Berlin Motor Show in October 1921, and probably very few were made. The supercharger was available on the big 6.2-litre Typ K in 1925, yet it really became famous only when it was applied to the K's descendants, the Porsche-designed S, SS, and SSK. On these, it gave a boost of some 55 bhp over the output of the unblown engine. The Mercedes supercharger differed from others in that it forced air into the carburettor, instead of being placed between the carburettor and engine. Moreover, it was not permanently engaged, but could be cut in at will, by additional pressure on the accelerator. It worked well as long as a reasonably high engine speed had been attained. Otherwise, it simply absorbed power and did not work fast enough to exert any effective pressure. Using it in bottom gear, or keeping it applied for more than 20 seconds, led to blown gaskets, a common failure of the big Mercedes-Benz. In spite of that, the eerie wail of the blower gave a great boost to the driver's ego, and usually persuaded slower cars to move over.

Another German company, Dürkopp, offered a Zoller-blown version of their 2-litre sports car in 1924. Four years later, Alfa Romeo and O.M. were both selling supercharged cars to Italian sportsmen. The Alfa's Roots-type blower turned at 1.5 times the engine speed, or about 6,000 rpm. In England, the best-known supercharged car of the 1920s was the "blower 4.5" Bentley, which W.O. Bentley never had much faith in, since he feared that failures would damage the reputation of his cars. Only 55 blower Bentleys were made, from 1929 to 1930.

The small sports car

For all the glamour of the Bentleys and Mercedes, the real importance of the 1920s to the sporting motorist was the diverse supply of moderately priced sports cars. Hillman were first in the field, with a sporting version of their four-cylinder 11-hp light car ready for the market by May 1919. Their way of going about making a sports car was typical of many of their successors. Lightened pistons and con rods, together with larger valves, raised the power from 18 to 28 bhp—and in anticipation of increased fuel consumption, the tank capacity was doubled to 10 gallons (40 litres). The car's appearance was completely transformed by the V-radiator, polished aluminium body, disc wheels, and large copper exhaust-pipe. The choice of too high a top gear denied it a very good performance, and Hillman found that, while it could reach 60 mph (95 km/h) in second gear, it did not manage more than 56 mph (90 km/h) in top. Later models were improved, and the famous racing driver Raymond Mays had warm praise for his Hillman Speed Model.

Three American speedsters from the later 1920s, the years of the last flowering of the American sporting car, until the Corvette and Thunderbird appeared in the 1950s. The Auburn boat-tail speedster *(right)* was not only among the most striking-looking cars on the road, but fast as well, thanks to the straight-eight Lycoming engine. The speedster was made in two models, the 88 with a 4-litre 90-bhp engine, or the 115 with a 4.9-litre 115-bhp engine, the latter on a 130-inch (3.3-metre) wheelbase with 3.9 or 4.45:1 rear axle ratios. Priced at $1,695 and $2,195 respectively, they were very good value. The Stutz speedster *(page 121)* was in a different class, with the company's own make of 5.2-litre single overhead-camshaft straight-eight engine, four-speed gearbox, and vacuum servo brakes that were adopted first on Stutz cars at Le Mans. Prices ran to over $3,000, and even higher for the twin-ohc DV32 models with 32 valves, introduced in 1931. Packard's 734 speedster *(page 124)* was an unusual car for the normally staid Detroit firm, having a tuned 6.3-litre engine with larger inlet and exhaust manifolds, higher compression ratio, and a vacuum booster pump attached to the front of the camshaft to help breathing through the inlet when operating on full throttle. Each speedster carried a plaque on the dashboard, stating that racing driver Tommy Milton had driven it for 250 miles (400 km) on the Packard speedway.

Other British firms to make sports cars from their light touring models included Calthorpe, whose Sporting Four had drilled con rods and aluminium pistons. It thus had a 60 mph (95 km/h) top speed, and its polished aluminium body came from Mulliners, whose factory at Bordesley Green in Birmingham was conveniently located next door to Calthorpe's. AC, Bayliss-Thomas, Crouch, Deemster, Horstman, Rover, Singer, and Wolseley were some of the further makes who offered sporty-looking cars, usually with unpainted but polished aluminium bodies and aluminium discs over their artillery wheels. Two-cylinder sports cars were made by ABC and Douglas in the early 1920s, and G.N. kept the sporting cyclecar alive up to 1921.

By 1925, the sporting motorist was acquiring some sophistication, and demanded more than an aluminium body and a noisy exhaust. Most of the light-car manufacturers found that four-seater tourers were better for their balance sheets, and they left sports cars to the specialists. Foremost among these were Alvis, Aston Martin, and Frazer-Nash. The Alvis 12/50 shot to fame after Major C. M. Harvey's win in the 200-Mile Race for light cars at Brooklands in 1923. It was up-to-date but not especially advanced, with a pushrod overhead-valve engine of 1,496 cc having duralumin con rods. At £550 for a "ducksback" two-seater, it was not cheap, but very reliable. More than 7,000 were sold, including tourers and saloons, between 1923 and 1932.

Aston Martin and Frazer-Nash had quite a lot in common, besides the fact that in 1931 they would get a joint owner, H. J. Aldington. Both makes were specialist machines made on a shoestring, with a fanatical following that was out of proportion to the tiny numbers produced—about 350 Astons from 1921, and just 323 Frazer-Nashes from 1924, until 1939. Apart from a few early models powered by Coventry Simplex engines, Aston Martin made their own 1.5-litre four-cylinder engines. Yet Frazer-Nash almost always bought out: from Plus Power, Anzani, and in the 1930s Meadows and Blackburne. The only exception was a series of 26 single overhead-camshaft engines, designed by Gough and built by Frazer-Nash, between 1934 and 1938. The unique feature of the Frazer-Nash was its all-chain transmission, inherited from the G.N., in whose company Archie Frazer-Nash had been a partner.

Two cars that brought reliable sports motoring to a wider public than ever before were the Austin Seven and the MG Midget. Herbert Austin's small car emerged in 1922 (see Chapter 7), and the earliest sports models were on the market two years later. These were "more for show than go", since a perfectly standard Seven chassis and engine lay under the sporty pointed-tail body and raked steering column. More ambitious was the Brooklands Super Sports, based on the racing cars developed by E. C. Gordon England. For £265, the owner got a polished aluminium body with aluminium undershield, a high-compression engine having high-lift cams, and double valve-springs. The less sporty driver could have the Gordon England "Cup" model, with a more modest engine—and a domed back to the body, which contained the spare wheel.

By the later 1920s, at least a dozen firms were supplying sports bodies of various kinds for the Austin Seven. And while the factory did not offer a sports chassis until 1928, there was no shortage of tuning establishments to help out. Bassett & Dingle of Hammersmith in London, for example, would provide their standard "tune-up" for only £7.50. The 1928 factory-built Super Sports had a Cozette supercharger and offered 70 mph (115 km/h) for £225. A later, unblown version cost only £185, and the sports Seven became increasingly popular in the 1930s.

The MG Midget was launched in October 1928, as Cecil Kimber's first venture into the low-priced sports car market. He used the recently introduced 847-cc Morris Minor overhead-camshaft engine, and a chassis with lowered suspension and a raked steering column. The engine developed only 20 bhp, but with a very light fabric two-seater, which cost the makers only £6.50 each, a speed of 65 mph (105 km/h) was possible, and the car had a suitably sporty look. At £175, it could hardly fail to succeed. More M-type Midgets were sold in their first year of production than all previous MGs put together. This model would eventually account for 3,235 sales before it was replaced by the J-type. The tradition of a popularly priced MG using many components from Morris or Wolseley touring cars was continued until the 1950s.

The French popular sports car

Daring autos for the thrifty were even more numerous in France than in England. Almost every manufacturer of light cars felt obliged to include a *Type Sport* in his catalogue. Sometimes, this amounted to no more than a pointed-tail two-seater body and matching aluminium-disc wheel covers. But other makes lifted power output by 10 bhp or so, using lighter pistons and con rods, larger valves, and higher-profile camshafts. The majority of smaller manufacturers employed proprietary engines, and firms such as Chapuis-Dornier, Ruby, and S.C.A.P. were ready to supply pushrod overhead-valve units.

Two companies which made their own engines dominated the light sports-car scene, Amilcar and Salmson. The former was the epitome of the French sports car, with a two-seater body, flared wings, four-speed gearbox and, on early models, no differential. In 1926, it grew into the lower *Surbaissé* model, which had cycle-type wings, an 1,100-cc engine with full pressure lubrication, and a differential. At their peak, around 1926 to 1928, Amilcar had 1,200 men at their St. Denis factory in Paris, and were making 35 cars per day, mainly sporting models. The Salmson began as a French-built G.N., but in 1921 they brought out an 1,100-cc sports car with a four-cylinder engine. The design was unusual: a single pushrod operated both the inlet and exhaust valves, acting as a "pullrod" for the former. In 1923, this was replaced by a twin overhead-camshaft unit, the first to be seen in a light car. All subsequent Salmsons, both touring and sports cars, were to use twin-cam engines until the make's demise in 1956.

In 1926, Salmson met the challenge of the Amilcar *Surbaissé* with their own lowered model, the Grand Prix. This cost £265, compared with £285 for the Amilcar—and £250 for the Ruby-engined Sénéchal, which was the next most popular small sports car after Amilcar and Salmson. Other makes with more than passing fame included the air-cooled S.A.R.A. The 1925 Montlhéry from B.N.C. (Bollack, Netter & Cie.) was the first production French car to use a supercharger. The Rally began life with a V-twin Harley-Davidson motorcycle engine, but was later powered by Ruby, CIME, or Chapuis-Dornier, and followed the Amilcar/Salmson progress from a high narrow body to a low wide one.

More speed in the States

As in prewar days, the American sporting car went very much its own way during the 1920s. Unaffected by European developments, it was seldom exported. Oddities like the Noma were listed in Britain, but hardly anybody bought one. The usual recipe was the maker's stock engine and chassis with a rakish two-seater body, occasionally with staggered seating to give the driver more elbow-room for rapid manoeuvring of a low-geared steering wheel. Kissel and Paige featured a folding seat which could be pulled out like a drawer from a locker in the side of the body, just behind the doors. This must have been very uncomfortable at almost any speed, not to say dangerous—yet perhaps a passenger fortified by Prohibition hooch did not mind.

Mercer and Stutz made speedsters until the mid-1920s, although they lacked the charisma of the old Type 35 and Bearcat. They had acquired windscreens, doors, and running-boards in response to public demand, which was no longer happy with truly Spartan motoring. None of the 1920s speedsters were entered in competitions, since these did not exist in America for that class of car. Not until the end of the decade did firms such as Chrysler, Du Pont, and Stutz run cars at Le Mans. By 1927, most of the traditional speedsters had vanished.

Yet a striking newcomer was the Auburn, made by a company which was in the process of being revitalized by the dynamic young Errett Lobban Cord. His first step had been to do up about 700 unsaleable cars, by judicious repainting and nickel-plating. He featured dual colours on most of his cars from 1927 onward. The 8-90 speedster of 1928 was extraordinary in appearance, with a beautiful boat-tailed two-seater body and a Vee windscreen. The 4.5-litre straight-eight Lycoming engine had received attention, too, in contrast to most of their earlier speedsters. Its alloy pistons and con rods, high-lift cams, and larger valves raised the output from 68 to 90 bhp. At $1,895 to $2,195, the Auburn speedster was very good value.

In a loftier price-range was the Stutz SV16, with 5.2-litre single overhead-camshaft straight-eight engine, at $3,150. So was one of the few sports models ever made by Packard, the 734, with a 6.3-litre straight-eight engine, giving 145 bhp. A two-seater could reach 100 mph (160 km/h), but cost over $5,000. Only 150 of the 734s were made, and this figure included some two-door sedans and tourers as well as the speedster. At that velocity, however, one could finally expect to get a vicarious thrill which, in the age before automobiles, had only been possible by stealing a race-horse.

MASS PRODUCTION

7

In 1910, motoring was still very much a minority activity. The rich might argue about the relative merits of Rolls-Royce, Napier, or Mercedes, and young enthusiasts like Godfrey & Nash might build cheap cyclecars for the amusement of themselves and their friends—but the great majority of the world's population had never ridden in a motorcar, let alone owned one. Even in America, there was only one car per 330 of the population, while in Britain the figure was one per 600 and, in Italy, less than one per thousand. By 1925, however, America had a car for every 23 inhabitants, and although Europe took many years to catch up, the movement was on. America was the obvious place for an explosion in car ownership, as it alone possessed a working class sufficiently well paid to be able to afford a car. It was also the homeland of Henry Ford.

A lot of misconceptions have grown up around Ford, including those which suggest that he invented mass production, and that he alone put America on wheels. What he actually did was scarcely less remarkable, for he was the first to adapt mass-production methods to the motorcar. In so doing, he led the way where other ambitious manufacturers had to follow, if they were not to go out of business. Ford saw the advantages of quantity production during his first year as a car maker. In 1903, he said: "The way to make automobiles is to make them one like another, to make them all alike, to make them come through the factory just alike." Such a principle was to become fundamentally important in the development, not only of cars, but of industrial society in the entire modern world.

The Ford Model T

By the time of the appearance of the Model T in 1908, Ford was already the industry's leader, with a production of 10,202 cars. Yet he was still an assembler rather than a manufacturer, buying most of his components from outside, so that the labour force in his own plant was only 2,595 men. In contrast, Packard—which delivered only 1,803 cars in 1908—employed 4,640 men, making practically all of the car by themselves, including the body. With the Model T, which was launched in October of that year as a 1909 model, Ford adopted a one-model policy. And as he increased production, so he learned to rely less and less on external suppliers.

Eventually, Ford would operate his own woodlands and garnet mines (for grinding and polishing plate glass). Bodies, on the other hand, were bought from suppliers—notably O. J. Beaudette and Kelsey—until 1919. In 1910, he opened the Highland Park factory on

a 56-acre site between Dearborn and Detroit. It was here, in 1913, that he inaugurated the production line, in which the cars were moved on a power-driven line, the parts being assembled as the line passed each worker's station. This was not a new system: its first use was probably for the assembly of rifles during the American Civil War (1861–1865), and it had also been employed by the clock industry in Connecticut. Henry Ford is said to have obtained his inspiration from the Chicago meat-packing industry, where hog carcasses were brought on overhead trolleys past each worker who would take a cut.

The car chosen for this mass-production exercise was not particularly unusual by contemporary standards. It had a 2,894-cc four-cylinder L-head engine, in which the most advanced feature was the detachable cylinder head. This made maintenance easier, and undoubtedly helped sales to those who did their own decarbonizing and other jobs. Transmission was by a two-speed epicyclic gearbox, quite widely used in 1908, although abandoned by the rest of the industry within a few years. For this reason, and because there were so many people who had driven nothing but Model T's, some states in America of the 1920s issued two different classes of driving licence: one for Fords, and another for all other cars.

The Model T was the first Ford to have left-hand drive, for most American cars were steered from the right side, even though the rule of the road had always been to drive on the right. As in other matters, where Ford led, the rest followed—and within ten years, right-hand drive was practically extinct on American cars, limited to a few luxury makes such as Pierce-Arrow, who were said to retain it so that the chauffeur could leap out nimbly onto the pavement to open the passenger door.

The standard body on the 1909 Model T was a four-seater tourer, which cost $850. Within four years the price was down to $550, and in 1915 to $440. During this period, sales leapt from 69,762 to 170,211 between 1911 and 1912, and the rate of growth was even more remarkable once the moving assembly line was established. In 1913, no less than 202,667 Fords found buyers, and the 1914 figure was up by over one-half to 308,162, while 1915 saw an increase of nearly two-thirds to 501,462. In addition, it took 12.5 man-hours to build a Model T before the production line was installed, but only 1 hour and 33 minutes afterward. Thus, seven times as many cars were made in 1915 as in 1911, yet with less total manpower!

A drawback of such rapid production arose in painting the cars. Only one colour would dry quickly enough to keep up with the assembly line, and that was Japan black enamel—hence Henry's joke that you could

(Opposite) The car that revolutionized manufacture, setting a lead which other makers had to follow to stay in the sales race. By the time this 1914 Model T was built, Ford had made more than 492,000 others, and in 1915 alone over half a million were turned out at Highland Park, not counting those from the British factory at Manchester. Black was now the standard colour, but four different body styles were available, as well as commercial models.

(Above) By 1918, Buick was among the established American makes, with a 14-year history of building sound middle-class and middle-priced cars. For several years they had held third or fourth place in production, but they were more expensive than their rivals Ford, Willys, Dodge, or Chevrolet, and also offered more. This Model E-44 two-seater roadster had a six-cylinder 4.1-litre engine developing 60 bhp, and cost $1,265. In 1918, 10,666 were made, out of a total Buick production of 77,691.

have a Ford in any colour so long as it was black. A variety of colours had been available prior to 1914, and would be again in 1926 when the fast-drying Duco lacquer came into use. From 1923, Model T cars assembled in Copenhagen were painted light grey (with black wings) and were advertised in Scandinavia as "The Grey Beauty".

The number of buyers who flocked to the showrooms was reflected in the flood of workers that entered the factory. These were encouraged by a reduction in daily working hours from ten to eight, and by a doubling of the usual pay-rate to $5 per day. Ford also made a great effort to attract immigrant labour, establishing a school for those who could not speak English, and offering jobs to the physically handi-capped, whom most firms regarded as unemployable. He may have called the five-dollar wage "a plain act of social justice", but it also brought increased sales. For by 1914, a Ford worker could afford to buy a Model T on less than four months' wages.

The success of the Model T led to expansion into foreign countries. In 1911, Ford set up a British assembly plant at Manchester, followed by a French plant at Bordeaux. The former turned out 7,310 cars in 1913, more than any other European car manufacturer, and almost 29% of the total British production in that year. By 1919, two out of every five vehicles—including commercial ones—on British roads was a Ford, and the company had a thousand agents in the British Isles. Assembly in Germany and Australia began in 1925, and by 1930 ten countries outside the United States were making Fords. As yet, they were all of American design, and only during the Depression years of the 1930s would the European factories start to produce smaller cars tailored for local markets. No other American firm expanded inter-nationally so early, although General Motors took a different route by

Two rivals for the popular-priced four-cylinder market, the 1924 Willys Overland Four tourer *(opposite)* and the 1926 Chevrolet *(above)*. Both makes were riding high in the mid-Twenties, Chevrolet on a one-model policy, and Willys playing safe with two models of the cheap Overland, a four and a six, besides the more expensive sleeve-valve Willys-Knight also offered in four- or six-cylinder versions. The Overland four was their best seller, helping towards sales of 163,000 cars in 1924, when Willys-Overland provided 40% of employment in Toledo, Ohio. Chevrolet's 2.8-litre four-cylinder engine was largely unchanged until 1929, when it was replaced by the famous "Cast Iron Wonder" six-cylinder engine which lasted up to 1953. This Superior tourer cost $510, but open cars were giving way to sedans by then.

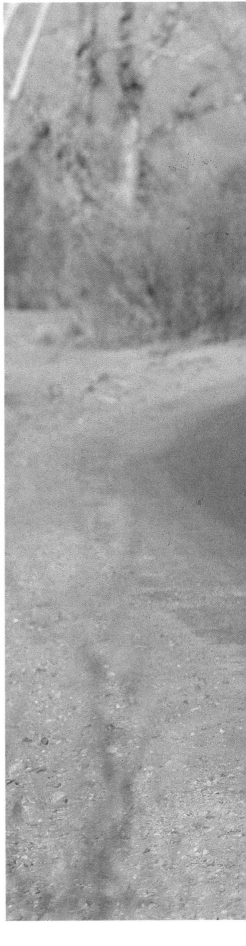

Three makes which suffered from competition with the American industry's big battalions. Apperson was a pioneer there, but never turned out more than 2,000 cars per year. Their 8-20 model *(opposite)*, advertised as "The Eight with Eighty Less Parts" (it was never made clear *which* parts), had a 72-bhp 5.4-litre side-valve straight-eight engine, and sold for around $2,600. This was good value for a well-made car, but sales dwindled from 1923 onward—and even though the maker tried to keep up to date with four-wheel brakes and balloon tyres, they were out of business by 1926.

Auburn was another make heading for extinction when this Beauty Six *(above)* was made in 1923. Cheaper than the Apperson, and powered by proprietary engines from Continental or Weidely, the Auburn had little going for it when the company was acquired by Errett Lobban Cord. He engaged J. M. Crawford to redesign the cars with striking dual-colour schemes, and so gave Auburn another eleven years of life. Kissel was one of the more successful makes of assembled cars, with fine lines enhanced by a high, rounded radiator and wire wheels on most models. They

made their own six-cylinder engines until 1925, then brought out a straight-eight which used a Lycoming block and Kissel's own head. By the time this 1927 coupe *(page 134)* was made, sales were sliding—from 2,124 in 1925 to 889 in 1928 (including 285 taxicabs and 200 funeral cars). Kissel collapsed totally in 1930, through involvement with the dubious Archie Andrews and the front-wheel-drive Ruxton car, but they would probably not have survived the Depression anyway.

(Above) Wills Sainte Claire was one of the more attractive small-production makes, and was unusual in its use of a V-8 engine with an overhead camshaft to each block. The 67-bhp 4.3-litre unit was designed by Childe Harold Wills, who had been one of Henry Ford's original partners, and it was built—like most of the rest of the cars—in Wills' factory at Marysville, Michigan. This roadster was made in 1922, Wills' best year, when 4,300 cars were sold. From 1924, the V-8 was replaced by a single overhead-camshaft six, which lasted until the end of production in 1927. All Wills cars had disc wheels.

acquiring suitable foreign companies, namely Vauxhall in Britain and Opel in Germany.

Ford's expansion was so meteoric that we tend to forget other manufacturers who followed in his wheeltracks. His closest rival between 1912 and 1918 was John North Willys (1873–1935), a successful car dealer from Elmira, New York. Willys took over the moribund Overland company in 1908, acquired a large factory in Toledo, Ohio, and made a profit of a million dollars within twelve months. His best-selling product was a conventional four-cylinder car, about the same size as the Model T, but with an ordinary three-speed gearbox. While it was never as cheap as the Ford, he got the price of a five-passenger tourer down to $615 by 1914, and was rewarded with sales of 91,904 the next year, then 140,111 in 1916. During the decade to come, Willys sales would rise even higher, reaching a peak of 315,000 in 1928, although by that time they had given up second place to Chevrolet. Willys, unlike Ford, also made more expensive cars, which were still of good value in their way. The 1914 Willys-Knight, at $1,095, was the cheapest sleeve-valve car in the world. And when Willys brought out a V-8 in 1917, this cost under $2,000.

The stimulus of the Great War

Between 1914 and 1921, several other American firms climbed into the mass-production league, with annual sales of well over 100,000 cars each. These included Buick, Dodge, and Chevrolet, the latter offering an overhead-valve four-cylinder model for only $490 in 1916. The economic advantages of mass production are shown by the fact that all of these makes are still in business today, while some 250 other American makes that existed at that time have vanished.

Whatever might be said in the long run about its qualitative or social disadvantages, there was soon no doubt that the assembly line presented a key to prosperity in the automobile industry. Before the Great War, few people had been accustomed to owning machines such as cars, or to using machines that made things in quantity. But the conflict drew much of the world into a process of technological modernization, democratization, and reconstruction. This was a new opportunity for car manufacture and sales.

America's involvement in World War I lasted for just twenty months (from April 1917 to November 1918), and caused only a temporary hiccup in car production. In 1919, most of the major manufacturers delivered more vehicles than ever before. The total output was about 7,000 cars per day, of which 3,000 were Fords, 700 were Chevrolets, and 300 were Buicks. The relatively expensive Cadillac V-8 was being made at a daily rate of 70–80. Compared with 1914, production had trebled, while capital investment and the work-force involved in the industry had multiplied by four and a half times. A car was now on the road for every 27 Americans, as against one for every 180 Britons, over 200 Frenchmen, and 1,000 Italians.

Exports, too, began to grow, particularly in directions such as Australia, South Africa, and Latin America. Their territory favoured a robust and fairly large car, like the Model T or the Chevrolet 490, rather than a smaller and higher-revving European vehicle. Admittedly, some British makers produced colonial models with high ground-clearance, but the price of a Colonial Argyll or Napier put it out of the question for an average sheep-farmer or *gaucho*. Indeed, American cars sold well even in Europe. Between 1908 and 1919, around 40,000 of them came into England (not counting the Manchester-assembled Fords), whereas a mere 881 went the other way across the Atlantic.

The mass-producers forged ahead during the 1920s and, by the middle of the decade, they had wrought havoc among the smaller

André Citroën and William Morris brought American mass production to Europe, and used American materials as well as ideas. Citroën's Model A of 1921 *(opposite)* used Bliss presses for body manufacture, while Morris bought not only engines but gearboxes, axles, and steering gears from America for his 1915 Cowley. By 1926—the last year for the famous Morris "bullnose" radiator— when this Cowley *(page 138)* was made, all its components were British-built, though the engine design still harked back to the Continental unit as in the first Cowley. Its central gear lever, resulting from the American transmission, had also featured on Citroën's Model A of 1919, together with left-hand drive, full electrical equipment, and disc wheels.

The chief British-built rival to the Morris Cowley was Frank Smith's 10.8-hp Clyno. The 1926 tourer matched Morris prices exactly, at £135 for a chassis and £162.50 for the four-seater tourer. It offered four-wheel brakes as standard, which Morris did not do on all models until 1928. But Clyno's price-cutting was dictated only by the need to keep up with Morris, and quality suffered accordingly in the late Twenties. This 1926 tourer is a Royal, the top-of-the-line model, with such delights as adjustable seats, carpets, leather upholstery, electric horn, and luggage grid.

In 1921, André Citroën entered the market with a smaller car than his 10CV, the 856-cc four-cylinder 5CV *(opposite)*. Like the larger car, this was a Jules Salomon design, featuring a detachable cylinder head, coil ignition, quarter-elliptic springing all round, and a pedal-operated transmission brake. It never received front-wheel brakes, and only on the final models of 1926 was the foot-brake coupled to the rear wheels as well. The little side-valve engine developed only 11 bhp, and it was unkindly said that the 5CV neither went

nor stopped—but it sold about 80,000 units in six years, and was the inspiration for the Opel *Laubfrosch*. In 1923, when this car was made, magneto ignition was replaced by the coil, and the wheelbase was lengthened to accommodate a three-seater cloverleaf body.

Peugeot's answer to the 5CV was the 667-cc Quadrilette, with a fixed cylinder head, three-speed gearbox in unit with the differential-less rear axle, a narrow punt-type frame which required

staggered seating, and hand- and foot-brakes working on separate rear wheels. The first Quadrilette of 1921 had acetylene lighting and no starter, but by 1926 it had grown up into the 172, with a conventional frame, larger 695-cc engine, and closed as well as open bodies with side-by-side seating. The final development was the 190S of 1929 *(above)*, which had front-wheel brakes and four-seater open or closed bodies. Total production of the Quadrilette/172/190 series was 94,948 cars.

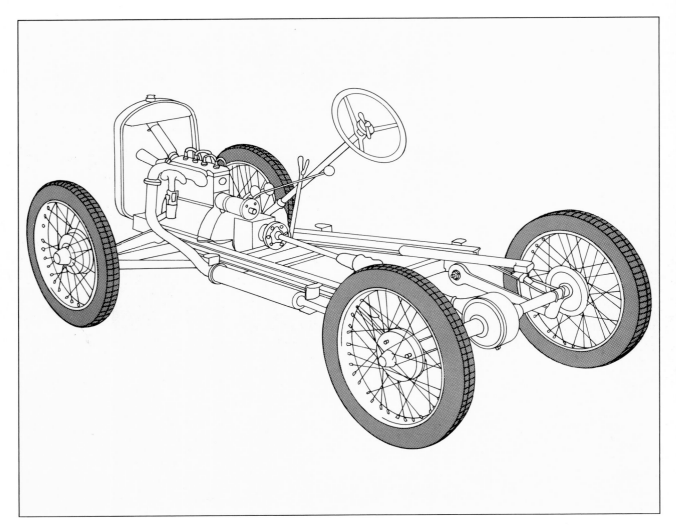

Herbert Austin's evergreen Seven was said to have been inspired by the Peugeot Quadrilette, but all they had in common was a small side-valve engine and their suspension by transverse front spring and quarter-elliptic rears. The Austin Seven never needed staggered seating, and indeed it offered four seats from its inception in August 1922. It had four-wheel brakes, though uncoupled until 1930. The 747-cc engine gave 13 bhp and a top speed of 45 mph (72 km/h). This example is a four-seater tourer, known as the "Chummy", but saloons were also available from 1926, and the chassis was the basis for numerous sporting models (*see Chapter Six*). Improved brakes appeared in 1927, and magneto ignition gave way to coil in 1929, by which date licences had been sold for manufacture of the Seven, in France by Rosengart, and in Germany by Dixi (later BMW). The American Austin followed in 1930, made at Butler, Pennsylvania. A four-speed gearbox was to come in 1933, with synchromesh on the top two ratios a year later. The Seven was not phased out until the spring of 1939, when more than 375,000 had been made.

Despite the attractions of the four-cylinder Austin Seven, several British makers offered twins in the mid-1920s. Rover's Eight *(below)* lasted from 1920 to 1925, selling a very respectable 17,000 units. Its engine was a 998-cc air-cooled flat twin, in unit with a three-speed gearbox, having shaft drive to a worm rear axle. It hardly surpassed 40 mph (65 km/h), but gave 40 mpg (7 litres/100 km), and was more smooth and reliable than most two-cylinder cars. First priced at £300, it could be had for £145 four years later. Saloon and delivery-van bodies were available, and it was made under licence in Germany by Peter und Moritz, of Zeitz and Naumberg.

The B.S.A. light car *(opposite)* used a 10-hp V-twin of 1,080 cc, made by the British Hotchkiss factory who also supplied fours to Morris. It featured overhead valves and coil ignition, but did not offer such good values as the Rover. Plenty of four-cylinder light cars matched its price (£215-225 in 1924), and the V-twin was noisy, though it pulled well. About 1,000 were sold between 1921 and 1924.

The 1924 Trojan Utility *(page 147)* was not a twin, but a four of a most unusual kind. The horizontal engine had a combustion chamber for each pair of cylinders, which were arranged side by side to make a square four in a single cast-iron block. The pistons were connected by a V-shaped rod to a common crankpin so that, as the crankshaft turned, one piston of each pair gained a varying lead over its partner throughout the cycle, though both reached the top and bottom centre together. The rods had to bend slightly at each turn, but this did not seem to matter at a maximum engine speed of 1,500 rpm, and the Trojan engine ran happily year after year without protest. The transmission was epicyclic, and final drive by duplex chain to a sprocket near the offside rear wheel. With only 10 bhp—and weighing 1,400 pounds (635 kg), compared with 800 pounds (363 kg) for the Austin Seven—the Trojan drove leisurely, barely exceeding 30 mph (50 km/h), yet it could slog up steep hills at very low revs. Its enthusiastic following bought about 15,000 between 1923 and 1932.

companies who tried in vain to compete. Many of these were more or less assembled cars, buying their components from specialist suppliers. The parts included Continental, Lycoming, and Herschell-Spillman engines, Borg & Beck clutches, Brown-Lipe transmissions, Gemmer steering, Parrish & Bingham chassis frames, and Hayes or Kelsey bodies. The resulting cars might be very worthy, but often the most individual thing about them was the assembler's badge on the radiator. Some makers of assembled cars were rather coy about the origin of their components, preferring to let the buyer think that they made most of the car by themselves—yet others relied on the reputation of the component suppliers to sell the cars. The Sayers & Scovill Company of Cincinnati, Ohio, actually listed its suppliers when advertising: "The mechanical parts bear names that stand for quality and service—Continental, Delco, Borg & Beck, Willard, Stewart, Hotchkiss, Fedders, and a host of others."

Such cars had been viable in the previous decade, when every manufacturer had lower production runs, and when a make could sell on local fame and pride. "A Little Higher in Price BUT Made in Dixie", proclaimed the creators of the Anderson, from Rock Hill in South Carolina. But as the 1920s proceeded, fewer people were sufficiently impressed to pay the little extra. By 1925, the Anderson was gone, and with it the motor industry in the American South, which had never been a flourishing one anyway. As the smaller regional makes died, so the industry began to concentrate on Detroit and its environs. The only important companies outside the Detroit area by 1930 were Willys-Overland at Toledo, Nash at Kenosha in Wisconsin, and Studebaker at South Bend in Indiana.

Another factor which led to the dominance of the "big battalions" was the rapid technical change that took place in the mid-1920s. Within two or three years, front-wheel brakes, balloon tyres, cellulose painting, all-steel bodies, and higher-compression engines became essential, if one was to compete in any market but that of rock-bottom prices (Ford and Chevrolet did not adopt front-wheel brakes until 1927 and 1928 respectively). It was enough of a drain on the resources of the major manufacturers to cope with these innovations. Buick and Cadillac, backed by General Motors' millions, could afford the changes—yet many firms, such as Apperson, Cole, Dorris, Haynes, and Premier could not. The latter were not fly-by-night concerns, but established companies with twenty or more years of car-making behind them. Some of them introduced the majority of the new features, and spent their entire reserves in doing so. As a result, from around 200 makes in the American industry in 1920, the number dwindled to 43 in 1930. The Depression brought still more hardship, and by 1940 only 17 remained.

Mass production in Europe

The story in Europe was much the same as in America, but took place later and on a smaller scale altogether. In 1913, the biggest European manufacturer was Ford of Manchester, with 7,310 cars built. The largest purely European company was Peugeot, which turned out about 5,000 cars, followed by Renault with 4,704, Benz with 4,500, and Darracq with 3,500. By contrast, in the United States, not only did Ford produce 202,667 cars, but ten other firms made more than 6,000 in that year. Nothing approaching Henry Ford's moving production line was set up in Europe until 1919, when André Citroën installed one at his new Paris factory on the Quai de Javel. In Britain, William Morris founded a production line at Cowley in 1924, and soon

overtook Ford to become the nation's biggest car maker.

It was appropriate that Morris should have brought American practices to Britain, as he had been an admirer of transatlantic methods almost from the start. His first Oxford two-seater of 1913 used a Coventry-built White & Poppe engine of 1,018 cc, which cost him £50 per unit. He wanted to bring out a four-seater car, but needed a larger engine. Sketching out a design for a side-valve unit with the classic dimensions of 69 × 100 mm, giving 1,496 cc capacity, he took it to White & Poppe, but they could not charge much less than the price of the smaller engine. Morris then turned to Continental in Detroit, who quoted only £18 for a similar unit. To be sure, this firm already had such an engine in production, although too small for the average American car and, therefore, finding very few buyers. Morris obviously went for the Continental unit, ordering 3,000, and buying his gearboxes, axles, and steering in Detroit as well. One result, in addition to lower car prices, was that the 1915 Morris Cowley had several features in advance of contemporary British practice, including a central gear lever and, on the rear axle, helically cut teeth.

In 1919, Continental discontinued their small engine, having no other customers. But Morris was fortunate in locating a new supplier. Hotchkiss, the Coventry branch of a famous French armaments and car manufacturer, made a copy of the Continental with the slightly larger dimensions of 69.5 × 102 mm. Postwar inflation brought the price of this engine up to nearly £100, and only after he had ordered a considerable number was Morris able to get it down to £50. At first, the cars were hard to sell. Nonetheless, in February 1921, Morris took the radical step of cutting the price of a Cowley four-seater from £525 to £425. This was rewarded by an increase in sales from 1,932 to 3,077, and from then on he never looked back. Here was a clear example of the benefit of lowering prices to stimulate demand, instead of raising them to cover costs.

Morris went on in 1922 to sell 6,937 of the Cowley and its better-equipped sister the Oxford. In 1923, sales soared to 20,024. He was now in a position to reduce prices further, not as a desperate bid to stay in business—as had been the case in 1921—but because profits allowed it. Like Ford, he began to buy up his component suppliers, such as Hotchkiss for engines, Wrigley for gearboxes, the coachbuilders Hollick and Pratt, and Osberton for radiators. Later, in 1927, he would also acquire another car maker, Wolseley. His sales of 54,141 cars in 1925 represented 41% of the total British car production.

Morris' chief rival, Ford, became less of a menace when the tax of £1 per horsepower was introduced in 1921. Under this law, a Ford owner paid £22 each year, compared with £12 for the Morris, and the difference was worth well over £100 in today's money. The Ford Model T was also heavier on fuel, while its epicyclic gearbox was increasingly anachronistic. From about 1923, however, a new rival appeared in the shape of the Clyno, product of a Wolverhampton firm whose name derived from the inclined belt drive on motorcycles which they originally made. Their cars, manufactured from 1922 until 1929, were assembled machines, since the little motorcycle works did not permit a large scale operation. They used a 10.8-hp Coventry-Climax engine, Moss gearbox, Willenhall radiator, and bodies by Taylor and, later, Haywards. Clyno's boss, Frank Smith, tried to keep up with Morris, matching every price-cut by the Cowley giant with prices just a bit lower. He managed to sell 50,000 cars in six years, which was not bad going, and the best figure among all the British assemblers. Yet the firm was always undercapitalized. An attempt to beat Morris' £125 Minor saloon with a Clyno Nine at £112.50 was a disaster, and Clyno fell silent in March 1929.

The Hanomag *Kommissbrot* was in a way the German equivalent of the Trojan, although very different in design and appearance. For it had an unconventional design which worked well and pleased many customers. The 500-cc overhead-valve single-cylinder engine yielded only 10 bhp at 2,500 rpm, but the car reached a creditable 40 mph (65 km/h), no doubt helped by its light plywood body. The front suspension was independent, by swing axles. A total of 15,775 were sold between 1925 and 1928, in both open and closed versions.

The Morris Minor itself was a reply to a car made by Herbert Austin, the Seven. This had established a niche in a class smaller than any Morris. At 8 feet 10 inches (2.7 metres) overall length, and weighing only 800 pounds (365 kg), the 1922 Austin Seven was in the cyclecar class for size. Yet it offered four seats, a four-cylinder engine, and even four-wheel brakes, although the latter were uncoupled until 1930. By mid-1923, it was selling at the rate of 200 per week, and it killed the British cyclecar as effectively as the Ford Model T had eliminated the American ones.

Further up the scale, would-be mass-producers such as Bean and Cubitt lost their markets to Morris and the Austin Twelve. Most of the assemblers of small cars—Autocrat, Bayliss-Thomas, Eric Campbell, Horstman, McKenzie, Marseal, Meteorite, N.P., Seabrook, and countless others—also succumbed to the big firms capable of lowering prices. The situation differed from America in that a maker who catered to the sports car market, like Alvis, Aston Martin, or Frazer-Nash, could survive on a production of less than 100 cars per year, since these appealed to an elite that would pay high prices. For makers of family cars, small or medium-sized, the outlook was much less hopeful, and respected names such as Crossley, Star, and Swift barely made it into the 1930s. Two of Britain's pioneer names, Lanchester and Wolseley, survived only through takeovers, by Daimler and Morris

respectively, and at the cost of individuality.

In France, the industry was badly shaken by André Citroën. Although new to car manufacture in 1919, he had gained experience of mass production in the gear-cutting business. Citroën installed a production line in a factory once occupied by Mors, a company which he had acquired. There he turned out a conventional tourer with a side-valve engine, central gear-change, and left-hand drive (by no means general in France at the time). In 1921, production reached 10,000 cars, and manufacture of the 10CV Type A and its baby sister the 5CV was running at 250 per day by the end of 1924. In the latter year, Citroën took up Budd patents for making an all-steel four-door saloon on the 10CV B-12 chassis. As in America, mass production enabled this car to sell for no more than £100 higher than the tourer.

The established French makers, such as Peugeot and Renault, replied with their own small cars. In 1925, the combined forces of that country produced 550,000 cars, ranking them as the second largest automobile industry in the world. Here again, however, success for a few spelt disaster for many smaller firms. By the end of the decade, time-honoured names like Hurtu, Mors, Rochet-Schneider, Turcat-Méry, and Vermorel were moribund or defunct. Yet a brighter note was that the 5CV Citroën became the basis for the first mass-produced car in Germany.

Fiat was Italy's universal provider in the 1920s, as in every decade since then—making 87% of all Italian-built cars in 1925, and a high proportion of commercial vehicles as well. Their two best-selling models were the Tipo 501 *(opposite)*, made from 1919 to 1926, and the Tipo 509 produced from 1925 to 1929. The former's 1,460-cc side-valve engine gave 25 bhp, propelling its 2,000 pounds (907 kg) at no more than 45 mph (72 km/h). But the more efficient single overhead-camshaft 509 engine, with just 995 cc, produced 22 bhp and a top speed of at least 50 mph (80 km/h), while sports versions went up to 36 bhp and 70 mph (115 km/h). The 501 gained front-wheel brakes only in 1924, yet the 509 had them on all models.

The open touring car came in many sizes and models during the 1920s. Less celebrated than Bentley, Vauxhall, or Sunbeam, the Crossley company of Manchester made a number of attractive sports tourers in the 1920s. At the end of the decade came *(below)* the overhead-valve six-cylinder 2-litre model: the sporting version, for which the name Shelsley was revived, cost £625, which was £130 more than the saloon. The engine was subsequently used by Lagonda for their 16/80. This 1930 Shelsley has covered 191,000 miles (307,000 km) in the hands of the same owner since 1961.

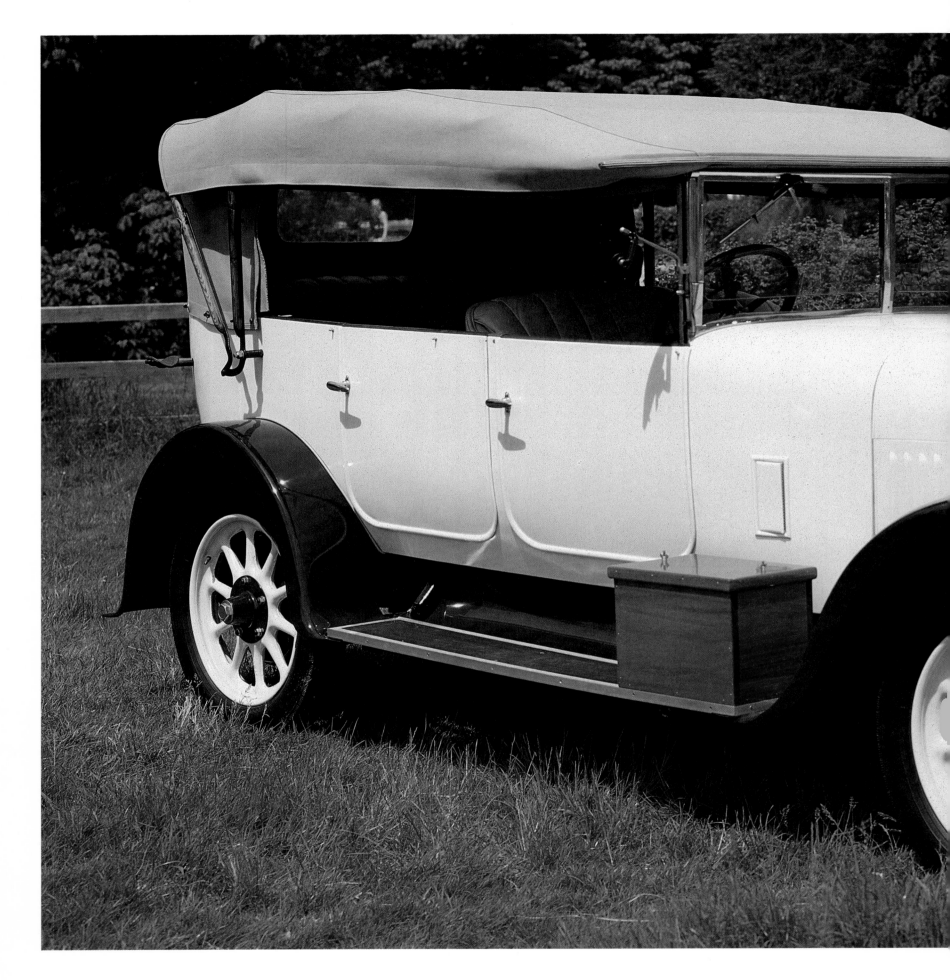

Medium-sized family tourers were solidly international, though not mass-produced in the Morris or Citroen manner. Built in respectable numbers, they provided sound, unexciting transport for the middle-class family. Humber had been one of Europe's larger makers before the War, and sold around 3,000 cars per year in the mid-1920s. The 14/40 of 1927 *(left)* came in the middle of a four-model range, and cost £460 for a tourer or £575 for a saloon. This difference, no greater than for most European cars, explains why closed car sales were still in a minority. The 1925 Bean and 1926 Standard *(page 155 top)*, both Fourteens, were cheaper at £395 and £365 respectively. Their engines had 75-mm bores, but the Bean's stroke of 135 mm gave a capacity of 2,386 cc, and the Standard's 110 mm only 1,944 cc. Standard was the first British manufacture to adopt cellulose finish, such as the American Duco, and in 1927 they pioneered the sliding roof on a closed car for the British market.

Austin's Twelve Four was one of the most successful British designs of the 1920s, despite the drawback of the fuel filler being located under the front seat! Introduced in 1921 with a 1,661-cc (72 × 102 mm) four-cylinder side-valve engine, it was increased to 1,861 cc (72 × 114 mm) for 1927, and remained in the catalogue until 1935, always with magneto ignition. This 1928 tourer *(opposite)* cost only £255, with a saloon available at £325.

When Assar Gabrielsson and Gustaf Larson launched the Volvo in 1927, they too followed the middle-sized family road. Their ÖV4 tourer *(right)* had a 25-bhp side-valve four-cylinder engine of 1.9 litres, three-speed gearbox, and semi-elliptic springs all round. Top speed was under 45 mph (70 km/h), but the car was rugged and well-equipped, and started the company on a most successful career.

This car, the Opel 4PS *Laubfrosch* (tree-frog), began to hop off the line at Rüsselsheim in 1924. Within a twelvemonth, 125 of the two-seaters were being made every day, and number 50,000 was turned out by the spring of 1927. Initially, they were near-replicas of the French car, with the same pointed tail and two-seater or cloverleaf three-seater bodies, but a three-seater saloon soon joined the range. André Citroën dropped the 5CV after 1926, whereas Opel continued the 4PS—with a slightly larger engine of 1,018 cc—until June 1931, by which time 119,484 had been made. The 4PS and its larger sisters helped Opel to be Germany's biggest manufacturer of cars in the later 1920s, with 37.5% of the market. This success was doubtless an important factor in leading General Motors to acquire a majority holding in the company in 1929.

If the Opel 4PS was conventional, its chief rival on the popular market was just the opposite. The Hannoverische Machinenbau AG had been a maker of railway locomotives since 1835, and subsequently of agricultural tractors. In 1925, to take up spare capacity in the factory, they entered the car business with a curious little machine, powered by a rear-mounted single-cylinder engine of 500 cc, in unit with a three-speed gearbox driving a single chain. Designed by Fidelis Bohler, it was made as a roadster, or as a square two-seater coupé which the makers dignified with the description *Zweisitzer Limousine*. The Hanomag body resembled an army bread-loaf, thus earning the nickname of *"Kommissbrot"*.

With many of the characteristics of a cyclecar, this was the type of vehicle for which one would have predicted a limited success, if any. But it caught on, and sold 15,775 units in four seasons. Its price certainly helped, at 2,650 Reichsmarks for an open two-seater, and 3,200 RM for the "limousine". These tags were reduced to 1,975 and 2,450 RM respectively in 1927, while a 4/12PS Opel cost 2,980 to 3,980 RM. The *Kommissbrot* was made in sports form, sometimes with wickerwork bodies, and as a single-passenger taxicab. It launched the Hanomag company on a successful career of manufacturing ordinary four-cylinder cars, although only one later model, the Rekord of 1934–38, was made in larger numbers than the *Kommissbrot*.

In Italy, there was only one mass-producer between the wars, and that—inevitably—was Fiat. They dominated the industry to such an extent that, in 1925, a full 87% of all Italian-built cars were Fiats. The best-selling models were the 1,460-cc L-head Tipo 501 (1919–26) and the 995-cc single overhead-camshaft Tipo 509 (1925–29), which sold 80,000 and 92,214 cars respectively.

By the dawn of the Thirties, some degree of mass production was the norm for any medium- or large-scale car maker, even if it amounted to nothing more than a track of parallel runners along which the bodies were pushed by hand on wooden sleds, as in the Singer factory. It encouraged the adoption of the all-steel body, and eliminated the fabric body. The principle of heavy investment, in capital equipment for a long production run, was to become even more important with one of the major automotive developments of the next decade—the integral construction of chassis and body.

THE GREAT BOOM ON WHEELS

8

Cars for everyone and from almost everywhere became a dominant theme of the 1920s. This decade saw a larger variety of automobiles than did any time before or since. At its beginning, they ranged from cyclecars even cheaper and more rudimentary than those of prewar days, up to luxury vehicles like the Rolls-Royce Silver Ghost and the Hispano-Suiza. For the price of one of the latter, around £3,000 in 1919, you could have bought thirty-six Cambro monocars, quite possibly more than the company ever made. Such extremes of cost and character suited the social climate of that period, in the many countries which were still coming to terms with the new technology and tastes involved in automobile life.

National trends in Europe

The initial years of peaceful intercourse among European car designers were now gone forever. More optimistically, it was being realized that not only individuals, but also whole peoples, could take advantage of their means of transportation in defining their special identity, both as users and as producers of cars. Local traits of style and engineering became increasingly clear, often due to equally regional factors of economics and imagination, as a brief survey in each area will indicate.

Britain

The Cambro, built at Kilburn in London, resembled a child's pedal-car, and was scarcely any faster. Being powered by a 192-cc single-cylinder engine, driving the rear wheel directly by chain and with no gearbox, it weighed 165 pounds (365 kg) and had a claimed fuel consumption of 100 miles per gallon (2.8 litres/100 km). This was at the very bottom of the country's cyclecar market, where a host of machines in the higher £120–200 class still fell below the standard offered by the Austin Seven. By 1925, the cyclecar was virtually dead in Britain, except for a few three-wheelers which benefitted from a £5 annual tax, compared with a sliding scale of £1 per horsepower for four-wheel vehicles.

The British tax system encouraged small-bore and long-stroke engines, for the horsepower was calculated only on the bore. Thus the 3-litre Bentley, with cylinders of 80 × 149 mm, was rated at a modest 15.9 hp for its 2,996 cc, whereas the Crossley with 80 × 120 mm had the same rating and tax for only 2,410 cc. Admittedly, the Bentley had been planned two years before the horsepower tax was introduced, and long-stroke engines were favoured by many manufacturers for other reasons. But the habit was perpetuated until after World War II, when a flat-rate tax came into use.

An example of the lengthening in strokes is provided by Rolls-Royce. The 40/50 Silver Ghost began in 1907 with square dimensions of 114 × 114 mm (7,036 cc), and in 1909 the stroke was extended to 121 mm, giving a capacity of 7,428 cc. Once hit by the horsepower tax, this cost £49 per year, equivalent to more than £600 in today's money. In 1925, Henry Royce and his design team brought out the Phantom I, on which the bore was reduced to 108 mm and the stroke grew to 140 mm. As a result, the capacity was raised to 7,668 cc, while the annual tax was lowered to £44.

France

Continental countries did not suffer under a tax based on cylinder bore. Yet the effect of this freedom was not really felt until the 1930s, when cars like the Peugeot 402 (at 83 × 92 mm) and the Opel Super 6 (at 80 × 82 mm) paved the way for higher piston speeds and more efficient engines in the postwar era. Nevertheless, France did breed some characteristic types, of which the small four-cylinder sports car (see Chapter 6) and the *Grand Routier* tourer were the best known.

The latter were fast touring cars, normally four-seaters, with a comfortable cruising speed of 60 mph (100 km/h) and probably a maximum of 70–75 mph (120 km/h). They were ideal for covering distances on the *routes nationales* and, as the surfaces of these roads improved, high cruising speeds became more feasible. At the same time, four-speed gearboxes with well-spaced ratios made the cars suitable for mountainous country. Nearly all of them had overhead-valve engines, some including overhead camshafts, although Peugeot and Voisin used large four-cylinder sleeve-valve designs. Notable models were the Ballot 2LT and 2LTS, milder versions of the twin overhead-camshaft 2LS (see Chapter 6); the Bignan, ranging in sizes from 1.7 to 3 litres; the 3.5-litre Lorraine-Dietrich, which won at Le Mans in 1925 and 1926; the Delage 14/40, Chenard-Walcker, Cottin-Desgouttes, and numerous others. Ettore Bugatti's contribution to this breed was the 3-litre straight-eight Type 44.

Germany

The cars of the 1920s in Germany were instantly recognizable due to several distinctive features. This was because defeat in the war had cut them off from the rest of the world until at least the middle of the decade. They were not allowed to exhibit at foreign motor shows, while the British and French press barely acknowledged the existence of a motor industry to the east of the Rhine. Having no markets abroad, the German makers went their own way, producing heavy touring cars with high solid bodies, disappearing hoods in heavy overhanging tails and Vee radiators.

The Ballot 2LT, seen here from 1924, was one of the most popular French fast tourers. Like the Delage 14/40DIS, it was in the 2-litre class but had a top speed of around 75 mph (120 km/h), and could cruise comfortably at 60 mph (95 km/h) for long periods. Ballot used a single overhead camshaft to produce its 40 bhp, with inclined valves in the 2LTS which joined the range in 1924, while Delage relied on pushrods. Both makes later offered six- and eight-cylinder cars, yet the fours were preferred at that time, and have remained so with vintage-car enthusiasts until today.

Gabriel Voisin followed his idiosyncratic style throughout the eighteen years of his car-making career. His first car was the 3,970-cc four-cylinder C1, with Knight sleeve-valve engine and aluminium pistons. With a reasonably light body, the C1 could reach 80 mph (130 km/h), and it was made with only slight modifications and changes of name until 1927. This is a C3 of 1924, with boat-deck tourer body.

The last characteristic was most common, and probably not a single German or Austrian car made between 1918 and 1924 had a flat radiator. Some front ends were just slightly pointed, as on the Maybach, but most had a sharp aggressive prow. This was expensive to produce, as it really held a V-shaped radiator—not simply a Vee grille over a flat radiator, which later became popular in the 1930s. Such a cooling system was not the most efficient, and this is why Vauxhall abandoned the V-shape of the Prince Henry in 1913 to adopt the flat radiator of the 30/98. One can only explain the Vee phenomenon as a slavish following of fashion, which indeed left it behind from 1925 onward, so that it became almost totally obsolete within a single season. The sole firms to continue it were Mercedes-Benz, on the big S and SS sports cars, and Steyr on some models.

German import duties were halved in 1925, leading to an influx of foreign cars, particularly from America. These influenced native design considerably, and brought about a number of straight-eights from Adler, Audi, Mercedes-Benz, and Stoewer, among others. Smaller cars, such as the Adler sixes and the Dixi 9/40PS, also had quite American lines, with all-steel saloon bodies that were supplied by the American-owned Ambi-Budd company of Berlin.

At the other end of the scale, the cyclecar survived in Germany longer than elsewhere—partly thanks to the law, which exempted owners of cars under 200 cc in capacity from both a road tax and a driving license. One of the most primitive cyclecars was the Slaby-Beringer, a tiny single-seater resembling a crate on pram wheels, powered by an electric motor that drove via a single chain to the solid rear axle. Steering was by a tiller, and the contraption was so antique-looking that a 1920s specimen of it was entered in an early postwar London to Brighton Run, bearing the date 1902! A later version was a tandem two-seater powered by a 3PS DKW motorcycle engine.

Another peculiar machine was the Mauser Einspur-Auto, a two-wheeled car with two small outrigger wheels, which came into use only when the vehicle was stationary. Powered by a 498-cc single-cylinder engine, the Mauser was made from 1923 to 1925, and was even built in France under the name Monotrace until 1930. Other cyclecars included the Hanomag Kommissbrot (see Chapter 7), the tandem-seated Mollmobil with an engine of 164 or 198 cc, the electric Hawa and Omnobil, and the Goliath 198-cc three-wheeler which survived into the 1930s.

Italy

Although Fiat dominated the Italian scene, the more typical Italian car of the 1920s was to be found in the high-quality sporting tourer made by Alfa Romeo, Ceirano, Diatto, O.M., and SPA. Somewhat smaller than their French equivalents (with the exception of the 4.5–litre SPA), these cars were characterized by modern engines with single or twin overhead camshafts, and by excellent road-holding. However, the O.M. managed to do very well with a side-valve engine.

The Lancia Lambda was never thought of as a sports car in its homeland, but it was a pioneering design: sliding-pillar independent front suspension, integral construction of chassis and the lower half of the body, and narrow-angle V-4 engine. Italian designers were, on the other hand, almost as slavish as Germans in their attitude to radiator design. After a period when the pear-shaped front ends favoured by Fiat, Bianchi, and O.M., and the German Vee of the Alfa Romeo 22/90 prevailed, a fashion for angular Rolls-Royce patterns of bonnet and radiator took over. Virtually every Italian car followed this trend until the late 1920s. Then a vogue of American-type ribbon radiator shells began, exemplified by the Fiat Tipo 514 and 522 or the O.M. 667.

Riley was a sound, but not particularly notable, car until the introduction in 1926 of the 1,087-cc Nine, with twin camshafts mounted in the block and not overhead. This engine, designed by Percy and Stanley Riley, had inclined overhead valves, and was the basis of all Riley power units up to 1957. The Monaco fabric saloon shown here, made from 1927, was one of the leading models of the Nine, with good brakes and road-holding, as well as a 60 mph (95 km/h) top speed, for just £285.

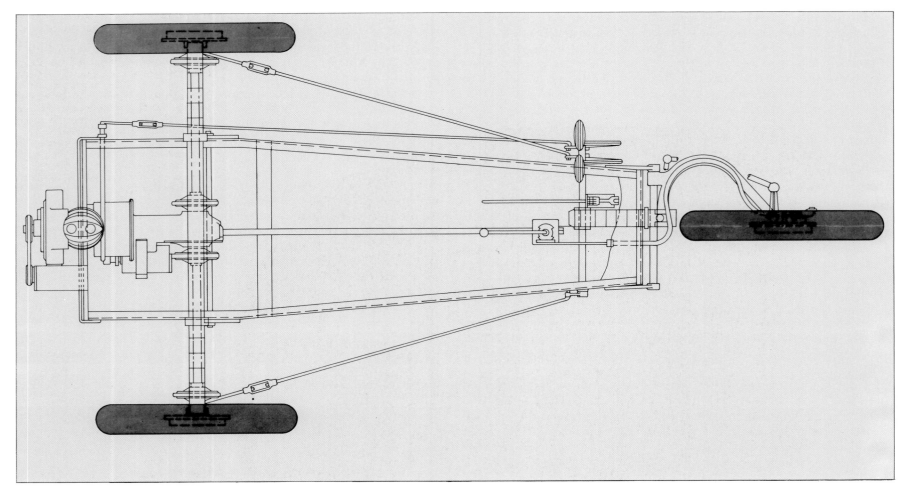

The Dutch car industry was never very large, and the only company to create an impression internationally was Spyker, who had begun as coachbuilders in 1880 and made vehicles from 1900 to 1925. Their six-cylinder racing car of 1903 was rather sensational: not only a pioneer six, it also offered four-wheel drive and braking. Hardly any were sold, and their regular offerings were more conventional, though known as the "Dustless Spyker" for the undertray shielding engine and transmission. This is a 12/18-hp four-cylinder shaft-drive tourer of 1905, like one which "starred" in the film *Genevieve*.

Most of the German cyclecars had died by 1930. But Karl Borgward made three-wheeled delivery vans from 1926, and in 1931 he launched a passenger-car version, the Goliath Pionier *(opposite)*. It was powered by a 198-cc single-cylinder engine which exempted the owner from car tax and the need of a driving licence. For those who had a licence and wanted more power, a 247-cc engine was available. Top speed was 32 mph (51 km/h) and an electric starter was standard equipment. About 4,000 Goliaths were made from 1931 to 1934, more than any of their contemporaries such as the Framo Stromer, the Hercules, or the four-wheeled Bungartz Butz.

Among the most significant cars of the 1920s was the Lancia Lambda. The Turin company pioneered the narrow-angle Vee engine, whose four cylinders were inclined at 13° in a single block, rather than the more usual 90° favoured by Cadillac or Ford. This made the engine very compact, shorter than an in-line four and narrower than a conventional Vee. Also, a single overhead camshaft sufficed, whereas later V-8 engines needed one camshaft per bank, or had to put the camshaft in the neck of the Vee operating the valves by pushrods. The Lambda's chassis was equally unusual: the lower half of the body was integral with the frame, being made of hollow steel pressings, and the seat squabs acted as cross-members of the frame. The Lambda was lighter than contemporary cars of the same size in both its frame, at 2,532 pounds (1,150 kg), and its body. Another advanced aspect was its front suspension, which was independent by sliding pillars and vertical coils. About 13,500 Lambdas were made, in nine series, from 1923 to 1931. Later models had the option of a separate chassis for custom coachbuilders. Four-wheel brakes existed from the start, as did pump cooling and full pressure lubrication.

Developments in other countries

The 1920s witnessed the final flowering of motor industries in a number of smaller European lands. Conspicuous was Belgium, which boasted a dozen makes at the beginning of the decade but, ten years later, had only three. Minerva and Excelsior were cars in the luxury bracket, the former being quite popular on the British and American markets. Minervas used sleeve-valve engines exclusively in this period, and their 6.6-litre Model AL was one of the very few straight-eight sleeve-valve cars ever made. At a lower price level, Metallurgique, Nagant, F.N., and Imperia all made cars of good quality, but in insufficient quantity to compete with imports. The Belgian tariffs against imported vehicles were the lowest in Europe, with the result that in 1921 the French sold 1,653 cars in Belgium, whereas only 12 went the other way. American cars poured into this little country, and assembly plants were set up after the tariffs rose in 1926. General Motors SA of Antwerp delivered 24,000 cars in 1929, more than the total production of the Belgian industry.

Switzerland suffered an even greater decline, and only two makes were produced in fair numbers. The Maximag, a four-cylinder light car with front-wheel brakes, was built by the Motosacoche company, better known for motorcycles. Several hundred came out between 1923 and 1928. The other Swiss manufacturer had a longer history. Martini was an armaments firm which had made its first car in 1898, and had acquired a sound reputation for reliable cars and trucks. These were continued at a decreasing rate until 1934, but few Swiss were patriotic enough to buy one when they had the world's markets to choose from. The appearance and design of vintage Martinis showed Germanic influence, and this was reinforced when the company was taken over by the Steiger brothers from Burgrieden, later to make German Wanderers under licence.

Austria and her former province of Czechoslovakia were in a happier position, and developed some interesting cars to cope with the generally poor roads of central Europe. Austro-Daimler had a single overhead-camshaft engine in 1921, and in 1927 they brought out the 3-litre ADR, whose tubular backbone frame was given independent suspension at the rear. Swing-axle rear suspension was also taken up by Austria's other major vehicle producer, Steyr, although they kept to a conventional frame.

On the other hand, the Czech Tatra—as made from 1923 onward—had a tubular frame, swing-axle suspension, and flat-twin air-cooled engine. Designed by Hans Ledwinka, the Tatras were later made in larger models with four- and six-cylinder engines, and in 1931 a 6-litre overhead-camshaft V-12 was offered briefly. Vintage Skodas and Pragas were conventional and rather American in looks, but during the 1930s these, too, would go over to tubular frames and all-independent suspension. Unlike the industries of Belgium and Switzerland, the Czech industry flourished behind very high tariff barriers. At the beginning of the 1930s, only eight percent of the cars on the road were of foreign origin. There were no foreign assembly

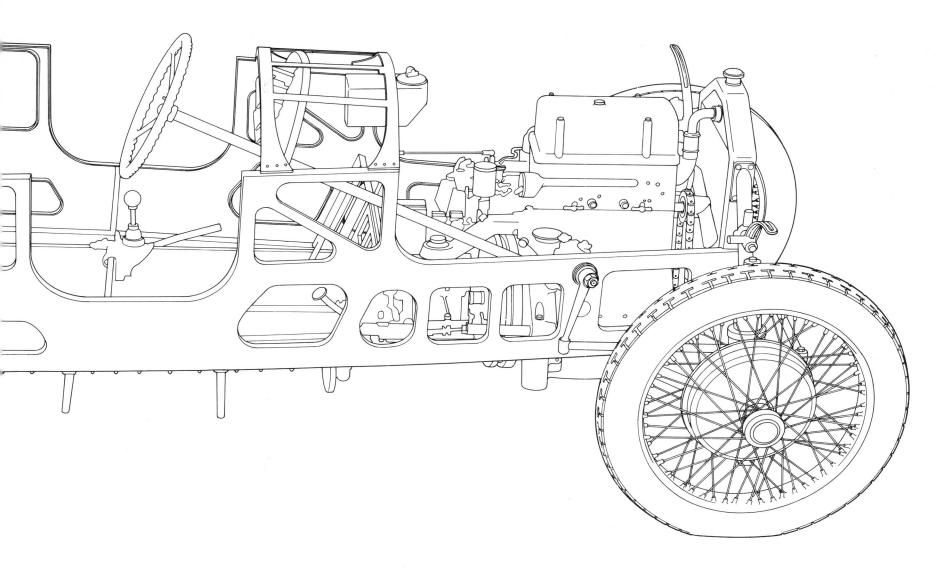

plants in Czechoslovakia, although some Fiat designs were made by Walter.

Further east, Hungary produced only one car in any numbers, the Magomobil (Magosix from 1927). This was a very conventional side-valve four or six, with rectangular Fiat-like radiator and artillery wheels. Hydraulic brakes were featured on the Magosix, and engine sizes were 1,638 cc (for taxicabs), 1,991 cc, 2,112 cc, or 2,443 cc. Manufacture ran at no more than 1,500 cars per year, and ceased in 1935. In the Soviet Union, apart from a few prototypes of the NAMI two-cylinder light car, no passenger cars were made until the appearance of the Ford-based GAZ-A in 1932.

The only Scandinavian country which established a motor industry of its own was Sweden. The two old established companies, Maskinfabriks AB Scania of Malmö, and Vagnfabrik AB of Södertälje (Vabis), merged to form Scania-Vabis in 1911. Large, solid cars with Germanic Vee radiators were made under this name until 1924, after which they concentrated on commercial vehicles. More important was Volvo, set up by Assar Gabrielsson and Gustaf Larson, with finance from the SKF ball-bearing company. In 1927, these partners launched a sturdy, simple touring car powered by a 1.9-litre four-cylinder side-valve engine. Only 297 were made during the first year of production—but by 1929, a 3-litre six joined the range, and 639 Volvos were made in 1930. From then on, it was a growing success story, even if the make did not become well-known outside Sweden until after

World War II.

In Norway, the bus-body building firm AS Geijer & Co. of Oslo assembled a few saloons, powered by straight-eight Lycoming engines and with hydraulic four-wheel brakes, but they were not commercially significant. Nor was the moribund Dutch car industry, which consisted of the long-established Spyker company, making a few large and expensive vehicles with 5.7-litre six-cylinder Maybach engines.

As for Japan, which today makes more passenger cars than any other country in the world, the 1920s industry was represented by two small makes, Otomo and Gorham. The latter was backed by an American aircraft engineer, William R. Gorham, who settled in Japan. His first car was a three-wheeler, built in 1919 for his crippled works manager. Later, he progressed to small four-wheelers with air-cooled four-cylinder engines, sold under the name Lila. These were made until 1926, when Gorham's company merged with another to concentrate on trucks, sold under the initials D.A.T. This led to the Datsun car in the 1930s.

The United States

Many of the American trends of the 1920s have been described in regard to mass production and closed bodies (see Chapters 5 and 7). Generally speaking, the American cars were larger than their European equivalents, and nothing under 2.8 litres stood a chance for long. There were a few light cars in the early part of the decade, such as

(Opposite) By 1930, Alfa Romeo was well-established as the leading Italian sporting make, a position they held until the arrival of Ferrari after World War II. The 6C 1750, introduced in 1929 as an enlarged version of Vittorio Jano's successful 6C 1500, was made in three models: the single overhead-camshaft Turismo with 10-ft 2-in wheelbase (3.1 m), the twin-ohc Gran Turismo with 9-ft or 9-ft 6-in wheelbase (2.75 or 2.9 m), and the Super Sport—a supercharged Gran Turismo having 85 bhp and a top speed of 95 mph (155 km/h). Shown here is a 1930 Gran Turismo with Zagato body.

The Belgian industry made a valuable contribution to European manufacture before World War I, and built some fine cars in the interwar period, though signs of decline were seen in the early 1920s. The 1912 Linon (above) came from a small firm in Ensival-Verviers who made ordinary cars from 1900 to 1914, with their own engines as well as other units—De Dion Bouton in earlier days, then Ballot, Fafnir, Fondu, and Vautour. Production seldom exceeded 200-300 per year, barely viable in Edwardian days but not in the Twenties. Wisely, the Linon brothers did not re-enter the car market after the War.

Minerva was in a much stronger position, making commercial vehicles as well as high-quality cars with Knight sleeve-valve engines. In 1927, Minerva sold 2,500 cars, the top of the line being the 6-litre AK, with Dewandre servo assistance for its four-wheel brakes. Builder of this two-seater's coachwork *(opposite)* was Erdmann & Rossi of Berlin, while most main coachbuilders in Belgium, France and Britain also worked on Minerva chassis.

F.N. made more popularly priced Belgian cars, backed up by a good small-arms and motorcycle business. Their conventional small four-cylinder vehicles had pushrod overhead-valve engines and, from 1924, front-wheel brakes. They began with a light two-cylinder voiturette in 1900, and by 1910 *(page 171 top)* were making ordinary four-cylinder cars at the rate of four or five per day. This 1925 F.N. 1300 tourer *(above)* was an example of their best-known model, made from 1924 to 1933. The engine was enlarged from 1,327 to 1,450 cc in 1928, when coil ignition replaced the magneto, and again to 1,628 cc in 1930. During its nine-year life, the small four-cylinder F.N. sold 7,302 cars.

Imperia was also in the popular price range, but less conventional. The 1,100-cc model had a slide-valve engine, whose slides were recessed into the cylinder walls on opposite sides, being opened and closed by double cams with no springs. Introduced in 1923, it was made until 1934 with the expected gradual improvements. Front-wheel brakes, optional at first, were standardized from 1926, and hydraulic brakes came in 1933. Coil ignition replaced magneto in 1928, and chassis lubrication became automatic in 1929. But the little Imperia was often burdened by too-heavy bodies, and never had very many customers. The best year was 1927 for the 6CV, with 504 cars sold—and it was 1930 for all Imperias, with 492 of the 6CV and 233 of the 10CV six-cylinder version sold. Seen here is a 6CV of 1930 with modified roadster body *(above)*.

Austria and Czechoslovakia produced some of the most interesting designs of the interwar years, thanks to men of the calibre of Ferdinand Porsche and Hans Ledwinka. The latter's Tatras ranged from the little flat-twin Type 11 and its successors, up to a massive 6-litre V-12 of which only 25 were made from 1931 to 1935. All these cars had a tubular backbone frame, with all four wheels suspended independently by transverse springs. The Type 11 got 11 bhp at 2,800 rpm from a 1,056-cc air-cooled overhead-valve flat-twin engine. It was amazingly reliable and durable, and of the 11,000 made between 1923 and 1930, many were still to be seen on Czechoslovakia's roads until the end of the 1950s. Also using a tubular frame, but a much more expensive car, was the Austro-Daimler, made in six- and eight-cylinder form from 1927 to 1934. This

chassis *(opposite bottom)* is the 4.6-litre straight-eight Alpine Eight of 1931, but similar to the more common 3.6-litre six-cylinder ADR Bergmeister model. These engines, with single overhead camshafts, were descended from Porsche's design of 1923, while the frame was the work of his successor, Karl Rabe. Rear suspension was like the Tatra's, yet the front axle was suspended by conventional longitudinal semi-elliptic springs.

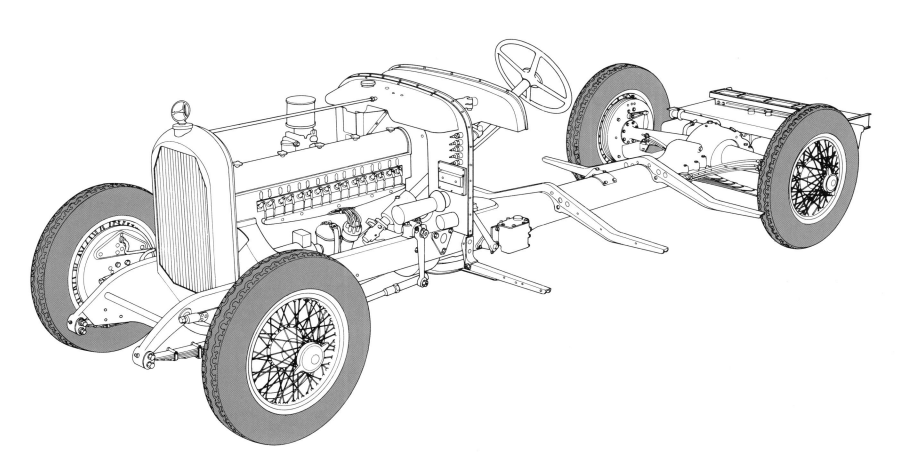

Not all Czech cars were as unusual as the Tatra. At the end of the 1920s, Skoda and Praga were making a rather similar range of conventional cars with four, six, and eight cylinders. These two small saloons, the 995-cc 18-bhp Praga Piccolo *(left)* and the 1,122-cc 22-bhp Skoda 442 *(above)*, both had slide-valve fours, though the Skoda boasted a five-bearing crankshaft, three-speed gearboxes, and semi-elliptic suspensions. Yet by 1934, both makes would go over to backbone frames and independent suspension all round. Right-hand drive does not indicate export models—Czechoslovakia, like Hungary, drove on the left until 1939.

the two-cylinder Brook-Spacke. Yet they, like all the unusual designs, soon faded before the onslaught of mass-produced orthodoxy. Steam and electricity were effectively dead by 1930 (as seen in Chapter 2), and the only surviving air-cooled car was the Franklin.

Multi-cylinderism became increasingly popular. In 1924, the major mass-producers, Ford, Chevrolet, Dodge, and Willys, made only four-cylinder cars, which accounted for more than 70% of all manufacture. By 1929, the latter three companies were turning out sixes, and no fours were left in large-scale production except the Ford Model A, the Plymouth newly introduced by the Chrysler Corporation, and the Willys Whippet. The lure of the eight-cylinder engine was very strong, and the straight-eight was particularly favoured for the long, handsome bonnet needed to accommodate it. This applied to expensive makes like Packard, Pierce-Arrow, and Stutz, as well as to several of the medium-sized and medium-quality cars which were to suffer

badly from the Depression, such as Chandler, Kissel, and Moon. The V-8, so popular in wartime and the early 1920s, was temporarily out of fashion, although used on the small-production luxury Cunningham. At the end of the period and in the early 1930s came a sudden enthusiasm for multi-cylinder power, with V-12s from Cadillac, Packard, Lincoln, and Pierce-Arrow, and even V-16s from Cadillac and Marmon.

Financially, the mid-1920s saw numerous makers of assembled cars go to the wall. Within only a few years, quite well-established companies were also driven out of business. An annual production of 12,000 to 20,000 cars was more than enough to keep a firm solvent until 1926, but thereafter the pressure on makes like Chandler, Moon, Hupmobile, and Reo grew ever more severe. The first two were gone by 1930, while Hupmobile staggered on until 1940, and Reo gave up cars in favour of trucks in 1936.

Although virtually no cars were made in the Soviet Union in the 1920s, pre-Revolutionary Russia supported a few makes, the best-known being Russo-Baltic and Lessner. Based at St. Petersburg (now Leningrad), the G.A. Lessner works, which specialized in machine tools and boilers, built a number of cars with two, four, or six cylinders, between 1904 and 1910. Designed by Boris Loutsky, they included this 8-hp two-cylinder two-seater, with a box at the rear for carrying mail. Fourteen of these were ordered by the St. Petersburg Post Office in 1905.

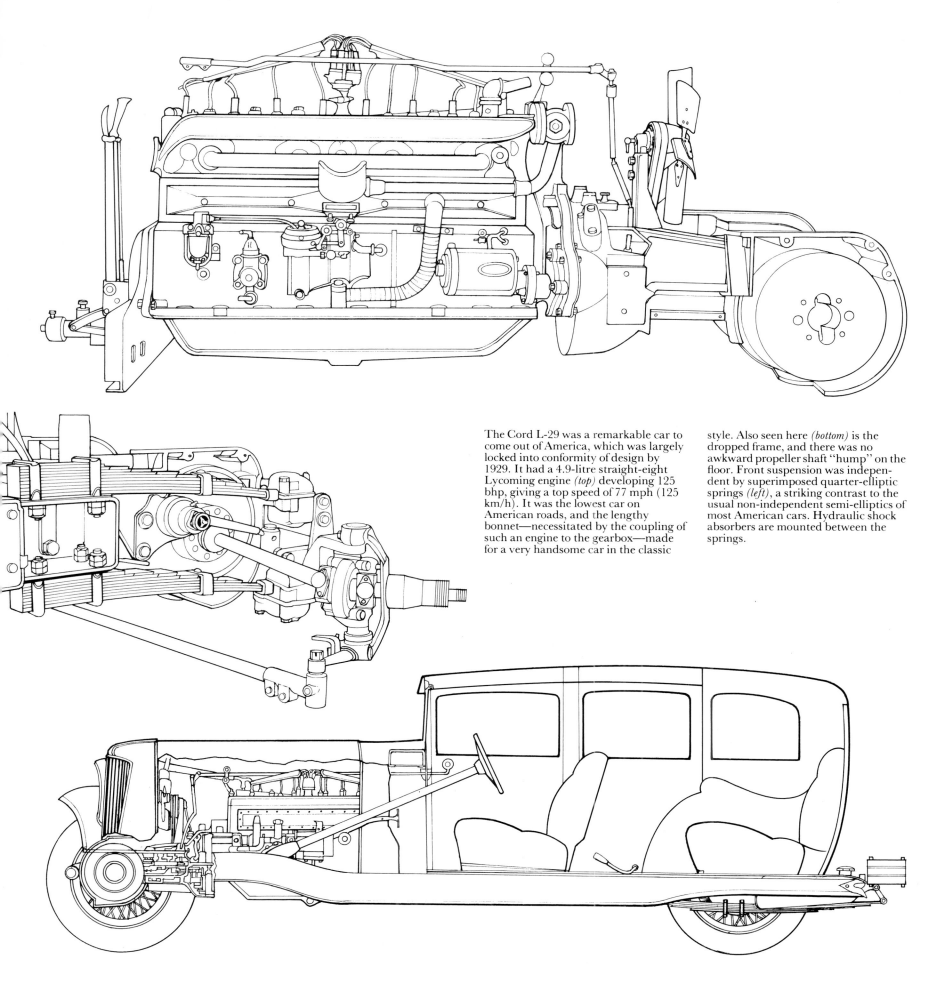

The Cord L-29 was a remarkable car to come out of America, which was largely locked into conformity of design by 1929. It had a 4.9-litre straight-eight Lycoming engine *(top)* developing 125 bhp, giving a top speed of 77 mph (125 km/h). It was the lowest car on American roads, and the lengthy bonnet—necessitated by the coupling of such an engine to the gearbox—made for a very handsome car in the classic style. Also seen here *(bottom)* is the dropped frame, and there was no awkward propeller shaft "hump" on the floor. Front suspension was independent by superimposed quarter-elliptic springs *(left)*, a striking contrast to the usual non-independent semi-elliptics of most American cars. Hydraulic shock absorbers are mounted between the springs.

Front-wheel drive was a relatively untried principle before 1930, but here is a pioneer in the field. In 1925, the Alvis company produced a front-wheel-drive racing car, and three years later they marketed a production sports car, whose modified 12/50 engine was turned round in the chassis to drive the front wheels. Suspension was independent, at the front by eight transverse quarter-elliptic springs, two upper and two lower on each side—and at the rear by longitudinal torque arms and reversed quarter-elliptic springs. About 150 of these cars were made, mostly two-seaters as shown here from 1928, and some four-seaters and saloons. But they were noisy and temperamental, and vanished from the Alvis catalogue after 1931.

Electric starters were on all but seven of the 228 models exhibited at the London Motor Show. The prewar compressed-air starter was not revived, and the few alternatives to the conventional starting-handle were confined to light cars and cyclecars. The Horstmann, built in Bath, was set in action by a kick-starter from the driving seat, while some cyclecars had a cord pull-starter like a modern lawnmower.

Another change in the electric department was the steady adoption of coil ignition, at the expense of the magneto. In 1923, only one-sixth of the cars on the British market had coils, which were associated with mass-produced American practice. When Henry Royce adopted coil ignition on his 20-hp model of 1922, he was widely criticized, and there were some who said that the car was not a proper Rolls-Royce at all. But as batteries improved, and held their charge for longer, the coil gained in popularity. It was cheap to manufacture and simple to maintain. Further, it provided a stronger spark for starting. By 1928, coils were seen on nearly half of the cars on the United Kingdom market. Over the next decade, they became almost universal, apart from some high-performance machines like Alfa Romeo and Maserati.

The gearbox received very little attention until the end of the 1920s. The traditional sliding-pinion system, evolved by Emile Levassor back in 1891, still prevailed. Ford's loyalty to the epicyclic two-speed transmission was regarded as the eccentricity of an ageing autocrat. Curiously, the only other make to feature the epicyclic gearbox was the luxury German Maybach, which offered a two-speeder on its six-cylinder 5.7-litre and 6.9-litre models W3 and W5, from 1921 to 1928. Maybach followed this change with the enormously complicated *Doppelschnellgang*, whose four forward speeds were each operable on two ratios, giving eight forward speeds and, if anyone wanted them,

four in reverse. Such was the gearbox on the V-12 Maybach Zeppelin, but it seems a needless elaboration for an engine which delivered 200 bhp with turbine-like smoothness.

Friction drive was employed on a few cyclecars in the early 1920s. This survived on the French Lafitte until 1928, and on the British GWK until 1931. The Lafitte system was unusual in that the whole engine swung, to give varying ratios. When the friction discs met face to face, a clutch was formed and gave a direct-drive top gear.

The major development in transmissions came in 1929, when General Motors launched the synchromesh gearbox on that year's Cadillac—and on its companion cheaper line, the La Salle. In this invention, the engine and gearbox speeds were automatically synchronized, so that there was no need for double declutching, and the "prolonged side-grubbing of teeth" became a thing of the past. At first, it was confined to the upper two ratios, American gearboxes normally being three-speeders. By 1932, synchromesh had become virtually ubiquitous on American cars, and then it arrived in Europe on the Vauxhall Cadet. Two years later, the Alvis Speed Twenty had synchromesh on all ratios, something which many manufacturers would not offer until well after World War II.

Developments such as synchromesh had a radical effect on motoring. The 1930s were the first decade when driving ceased to be regarded by most people as a skilled art, or as a pastime indulged in for its own sake. More and more, the car was simply a useful aid to personal mobility. Unfortunately, as cars became easier to drive, there were also more of them, and the motorist passed—from coping with a sometimes tricky car on open roads—to keeping an obedient car on crowded highways.

THE LUXURY CAR

9

Advanced technology and old-fashioned craftsmanship became keynotes of the 1920s. For people with enough money to buy the finest cars available, these were golden years. Engineering had progressed sufficiently to allow speeds of 80 mph (130 km/h) in reasonable silence, while the dedicated sportsman did not find 90–100 mph (145–160 km/h) impossible. Four-wheel brakes, assisted by servos, rendered such exciting trips safer than they would have been in prewar days, and there was still relatively litle traffic about. Coachwork continued to be built by the handcrafted methods of the Edwardian era, yet it looked much lighter.

Engines and chassis

Eager to get back into car production as quickly as they could, many manufacturers revived their prewar designs for the 1919 Motor Shows. Two firms, however, brought out brand-new models which set the pace for development over the next ten years and more: Hispano-Suiza in France, and Isotta-Fraschini in Italy.

The Spanish company of Hispano-Suiza had set up a French factory in 1911, but until the outbreak of war they made Spanish designs, notably the famous Alfonso XIII. During the war, they produced V-8 airplane engines with an overhead camshaft in each bank, and this experience was evident in the very advanced H6 model, which appeared at the 1919 Paris Salon. It had a 6.6-litre engine with single overhead camshaft, and other features that were derived from the airplane engines included fully-enclosed valve gear and screwed-in steel cylinder liners. Dual coil ignition was a surprise—for although the designer, Marc Birkigt, had used dual ignition on his prewar cars, this had consisted of a magneto and coil.

If the multi-plate clutch and three-speed gearbox were perhaps not up to the rest of the car, the four-wheel brakes assisted by a mechanical servo driven from the gearbox were superb. The engine developed 135 bhp at 3,000 rpm, giving a top speed of over 90 mph (145 km/h) with a light, open body. The H6 Hispano quickly became one of the most glamorous cars of the 1920s, associated with the wealthy and slightly raffish postwar world of Mayfair and Monte Carlo. Iris March, the doomed heroine of one of the most popular novels of the day, *The Green Hat* by Michael Arlen, drove—and eventually killed herself in—a Hispano. Novels and gossip columns made the name familiar to many people who had never seen a Hispano-Suiza, let alone owned one. At £2,600, it was more expensive than a Rolls-Royce on the British market.

The Isotta-Fraschini never quite acquired the *panache* of the Hispano, and was certainly less pleasant to drive, having very heavy steering. However, it was advanced in its straight-eight engine, a 5.9-litre unit whose cylinder block was a single aluminium casting. The pistons were also aluminium. The single overhead camshaft of prewar Isottas had been abandoned in favour of pushrods, and the engine developed only 80 bhp at 2,600 rpm. As Italy was a poor country, most Isotta-Fraschinis went for export, America being the best customer. Owners there included the film star Rudolf Valentino, who had two, as well as the boxer Jack Dempsey and the press baron William Randolph Hearst.

The immediate postwar years were good ones for the luxury market, as many fortunes had been made during the conflict. Numerous car makers brought out new models, or entered the field for the first time. Among the latter was the French Farman aircraft company, which launched a single overhead-camshaft six-cylinder car of 6.6-litre capacity, with a four-speed gearbox. Leyland, the British commercial vehicle makers, had the 7-litre Eight with a detachable cylinder head, a single overhead camshaft operating inclined valves, and hemispherical combustion chambers. Designed by Parry Thomas, the Leyland Eight also featured a four-speed gearbox which incorporated the starter motor. This was actuated by moving the gear lever. Output was 145 bhp, and top speed around 90 mph (145 km/h). But the Leyland was ferociously expensive, at £2,500 for the chassis alone, when it was introduced in 1920. The following year, the price was reduced to £1,875, but the Leyland never caught on—perhaps because their trucks and buses were so well known that wealthy customers did not want to be associated with a common omnibus or coal truck. Not more than 18 Leyland Eights were made.

Other luxury cars on the British market in the early 1920s included the old-fashioned, and short-lived, Sheffield-Simplex with six separately cast cylinders. The British Ensign was equally ephemeral, but up-to-date with a single overhead camshaft and aluminium cylinders having steel liners. The Lanchester Forty and Napier 40/50 both had six-cylinder overhead-camshaft engines. Alongside these new models were two survivors from before the war, which in fact did better in sales than any of the newcomers: the sleeve-valve Daimler and the Rolls-Royce Silver Ghost. These were still braked only on their rear wheels, and the side-valve Rolls engine did not deliver more than 80 bhp from its 7,428 cc. However, they acquired front brakes in 1924, and Rolls-Royce went over to pushrod overhead valves on the New Phantom—later known as the Phantom I—in 1925.

The H6 Hispano-Suiza was one of the most glamorous cars of the Twenties, embodying the spirit of the age in the same way as the Lamborghini Miura was to do in the Swinging Sixties. This is one of the later models, an H6B of 1929 with two-seater coupé body by the American coachbuilders Hibbard & Darrin. The H6 was made from 1919 to 1933, production from the French factory alone amounting to 2,660, far more than any other Hispano-Suiza. They were also made in Spain (1919 to about 1938), and by the Skoda company in Czechoslovakia (1924-27).

By the end of the 1920s, a luxury car needed to have eight or more cylinders, although Rolls-Royce made do with six for five years longer. Isotta-Fraschini was the first company to make straight-eight engines in series, their Tipo 8 appearing in 1919 and lasting through three series to the early 1930s. Designed by Giustino Cattaneo, chief engineer at Isotta from 1905 to 1935, it began as a 5.9-litre unit developing 80 bhp, but in its final Tipo 8B form *(right)* it had 7.4 litres and 160 bhp. Alas, the company had severe financial difficulties, and only thirty 8Bs were completed in 1931-32. Numerous cars and components went unsold, to be scrapped just after World War II. Shown here is a 1931 Tipo 8B, with landaulette *de ville* coachwork by Castagna of Milan.

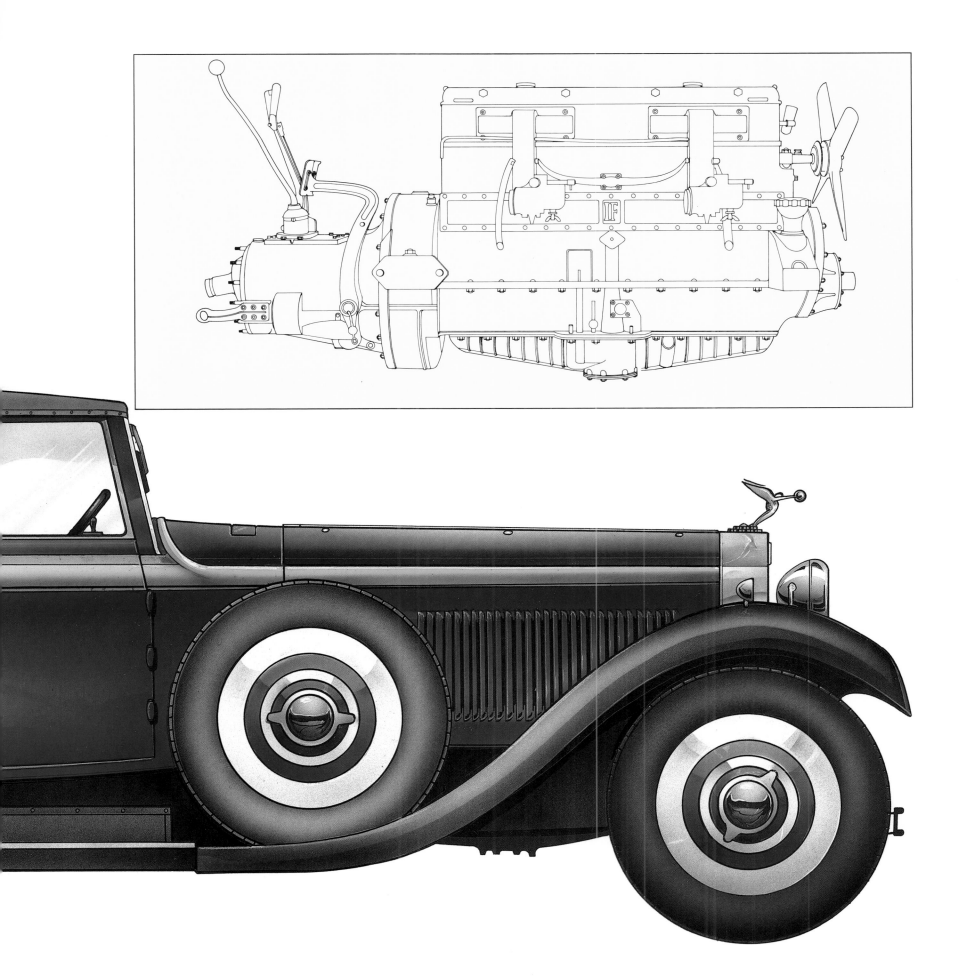

Leyland Eight

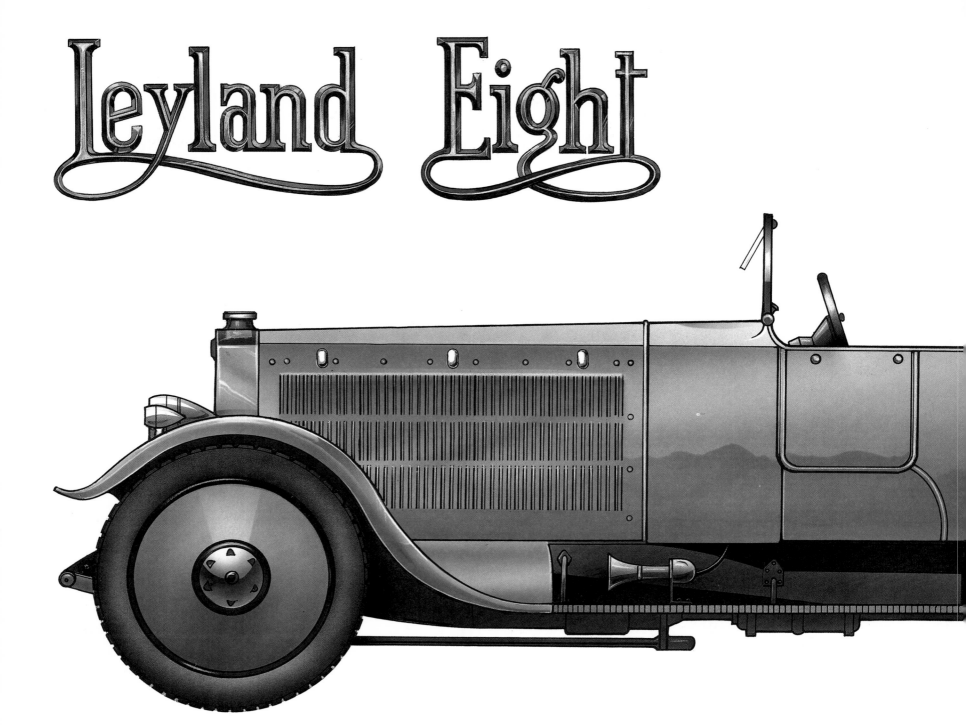

Wheels on Wall Street

American luxury cars were, on the whole, less innovative than their European equivalents. An exception was the Packard Twin Six, with its 6.9-litre V-12 engine, which had aluminium pistons and full pressure lubrication. The straight-eight Duesenberg, with overhead camshaft and hydraulic-servo four-wheel brakes, made the latter feature a "world first" on a production car. But the 8.5-litre Locomobile "48", one of America's most expensive cars at $12,000 for a sedan, and a favourite with the conservative East Coast rich, still had a T-head engine with two side-mounted camshafts, and continued with this archaic layout until the company closed down in 1929. When they

introduced a model in 1923, the 6.1-litre "90", it was only modernized to the extent of having side valves in an L-head. Overhead valves did not reach Locomobile until 1925, when they were adopted on the more modestly priced Junior Eight. Front-wheel brakes appeared as an option in 1923, at $350 on a new car, or at $450 as a conversion.

Pierce-Arrow was another company which clung to the T-head engine (until 1928). Their massive "66" had the largest engine of any production car, at 13.5 litres, and was made from 1912 to 1918. Still a big car was its "small sister", the 8.6-litre "48" which lasted up to 1920, when the staple offering became the 6.8-litre "38". This soldiered on until 1928, although the bulk of Pierce-Arrow production from 1924 onward was taken up by the 4.7-litre L-head "80". Here, in

Leyland Motors, after 23 years' experience in making commercial vehicles, introduced their expensive and advanced Eight at the 1920 London Motor Show. Designed by the company's chief engineer, J.G. Parry Thomas, who was later to break the World Land Speed Record at 171 mph (275 km/h) in 1927, it was Britain's first straight-eight, and the first British car to have vacuum servo-assisted brakes. As originally shown, the engine's capacity was 6,967 cc (89 × 140 mm), but in 1921 the stroke was lengthened to 146 mm, giving 7,266 cc. The inclined overhead

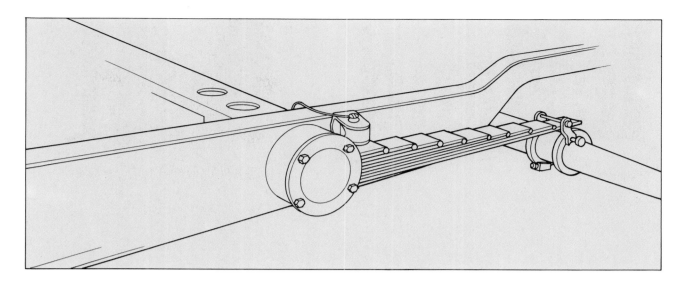

valves were actuated by a single overhead camshaft, and closed by leaf springs rather than the usual coils. Front suspension was by semi-elliptic springs, but at the rear were quarter-elliptics combined with a torsion bar *(above)*. The twisting of the bar absorbed the initial shock, before the leaves came into operation. Three wheelbases were offered: 10 ft 6 in (3.1 m) for open sporting models, and 11 ft 9 in (3.58 m) or 12 ft 6 in (3.8 m) for touring and limousine bodywork. The original model *(left)*, built in 1920 and used by Parry Thomas for testing, was a close-coupled open four-seater on the 11-ft 9-in chassis. The 1922 London Motor Show was the Leyland Eight's last public appearance, and the model was dropped after about eighteen cars had been made.

particular, one can see that it had begun to require a stock-exchange mathematician to make sense of the various model numbers and engine specifications on the super-car market.

Other heavy, conservative vehicles were manufactured by McFarlan and Stevens-Duryea. The Cunningham and the Daniels were somewhat more advanced in having L-head V-8 engines, but they were both small-production cars with annual figures of no more than 300 to 400. Cadillac continued its V-8 throughout the 1920s, yet this was in the upper middle-class price bracket, not the luxury car that it would eventually become.

In 1923, Packard dropped the Twin Six in favour of a straight-eight engine. For a few years, it seemed as if the V-12 was an anachronism

whose complexity and expense could no longer be justified. However, Daimler introduced the first of a series of Double Sixes in 1927, and sparked off a new wave of multi-cylinderism. Not all were particularly expensive, and Auburn managed to get the price of their 6.4-litre V-12 down to $975 in 1932. Other companies to make V-12s, mainly in the 1930s, were Cadillac, Franklin, Hispano-Suiza, Horch, Lagonda, Maybach, Packard, Pierce-Arrow, Rolls-Royce, Tatra, Voisin, and Walter. Indeed, the ultimate in turbine-like smoothness was provided by the V-16 engine. If one excludes the Bucciali Double Huit, which may never have run under its own power, the V-16 was a purely American speciality, being offered by Cadillac from 1930 to 1940, and by Marmon from 1931 to 1933.

(*Above*) Rolls-Royce were seldom in the technical vanguard, and have often preferred to adopt and improve a ready-tried system—whether it be the mechanical servo brakes which they took from Hispano-Suiza, or more recently General Motors' Hydramatic automatic transmission. Yet they have always been in the lead for quality. Parry Thomas said that the Rolls-Royce was the only car which he would consider a match for his Leyland Eight. The New Phantom introduced in 1925 had a new, longer-stroke engine with overhead valves, but the chassis was virtually identical to that of the Silver Ghost. The main improvement came in 1928, when the cast-iron cylinder head was replaced by an aluminium one. The coachwork on this 1929 *sedanca de ville* is by Kellner of Paris. In September 1929

came the Phantom II, leaving the New Phantom to be called the Phantom I. This time the innovations were in the chassis, with a lower frame and semi-elliptic springs all round, while the 7,668-cc engine was little changed. This reflects Rolls-Royce policy, which tends to make changes in stages, not introducing a totally new engine and chassis at the same time.

(*Opposite*) The final flowering of the overhead-camshaft Bentley was the 8-litre, announced at the 1930 London Motor Show and made until the summer of 1931, when the original Bentley company was dissolved. The 7,982-cc 230-bhp engine was an enlarged version of the 6.5-litre, but the 8-litre had a lower chassis frame and a new gearbox. Chassis price was £1,850, the same as a Rolls-Royce Phantom II, and two wheelbases were available, 12 and 13 ft (3.65 and 3.95 m). Bodies varied from rather light tourers to limousines giving a total weight of over 2.5 tons. One fortunate family acquired two new 8-litres at the same time, a 12-ft wheelbase sports saloon at £2,680 and a 13-ft wheelbase limousine at £3,055: in all, more than £115,000 in today's money. This is a sports saloon by Mulliner.

Ettore Bugatti first hinted in 1913 that he would like to build a "supercar" to outdo all others, but it was another thirteen years before the Type 41, *La Royale*, saw the light of day *(left)*. The prototype had an enormous straight-eight engine of 14,726 cc and a quoted wheelbase of 15 ft (4.6 m). But the latter was probably an error of W.F. Bradley, correspondent of *The Autocar*, as later models had 12,763 cc and 14 ft 2 in (4.3 m). The chassis price was fixed at £5,250, but only three of the six cars ever built were sold, the others being kept by the Bugatti family.

Two generations of Pierce-Arrow, a "48" tourer of 1915 *(left)* and a series 133 convertible coupé of 1929 *(opposite)*. When the former was made, the firm was riding the crest of a wave, often selling a year's output before it began. Between 1914 and 1916, about 1,350 of the 8.6-litre "48" were built, compared with 1,650 of the smaller "38" and only 100 of the huge 13.5-litre "66". The characteristic fender-mounted headlights, seen on practically all Pierces from 1912 to the end of production in 1938, were designed by Herbert M. Dawley, head of the Art Department, who later became a famous Broadway actor and director. Prices of the "48" ran from $4,900 to $6,250. The Series 133 used the same 6-litre side-valve straight-eight engine as the 143, their model numbers referring to the wheelbase. In 1929 they gave Pierce-Arrow its best year ever for sales, with 9,840 cars. There was a wide price range, from $2,875 for a 133 roadster to $8,200 for a 143 French Brougham.

Among the unostentatious expensive cars made in small numbers in America, the Cunningham was unusual in using a V-8 in every model from 1915 onward. Designed by Volney Lacey, this was a large side-valve unit of 7.2 litres and 90 bhp. The cars were built at Rochester, New York, and sold to a few discriminating motorists, mainly on the East Coast. At around $5,500 to $7,000, they were some of the most costly cars in the country. Annual production seldom exceeded 400 during the 1920s, and more than half of these were funeral cars, which had been a specialty of James Cunningham & Sons since their horse-carriage days. Shown *(above)* is a 1926 sport tourer.

No American-made car has more charisma than the Model J Duesenberg, which plays a much larger role in the classic-car world than it ever did when new. With only 470 built between 1929 and 1937, many American motorists never saw one, although the make was greatly admired in Hollywood and other centres of wealth. The twin-cam straight-eight engine of 6,882 cc gave ample power to propel the 2.3-ton car, even if the often-quoted figure of 265 bhp is thought to be exaggerated. Introduced in December 1928 as the prestige car of Errett Lobban Cord's automotive empire, the Model J was available with various recommended bodies. These were built, at least partly to Duesenberg's design, by such well-known names as Derham, Murphy, Bohman & Schwartz, Brunn and Rollston. This 1929 Model J carries a dual phaeton body by Murphy *(opposite)*.

Coachbuilding

In the 1920s, the best motor bodies were built in the traditional manner whose ancestry could be traced back to the horse-drawn days of Samuel Pepys. The main difference—and this had come about well before 1914—was that the panelling was in metal rather than wood. As a result of the war, aluminium and other light alloys had been developed, and these were generally used over a wooden frame. The wrought-iron strengthening plates were replaced by sheet-steel plates, contributing to the reduction in weight, which was such a feature of coachwork in the 1920s. Lightest of all were the Weymann and other fabric bodies (see Chapter Five).

The construction of the wooden frame began with the preparation of full-size drawings, made on vertically hung paper. Next, the paper was laid out on thin, soft wood, which was cut to shape. These templates were patterns for the ash timber that would be used for the actual frame. The main timbers, to take the greatest strain, were reinforced with iron stays. Roofs were generally made of leather, and this was put on wet, so that it shrank as it dried, giving a really snug fit. The favourite wood for the interior of the body—with the dashboard, window surrounds, division housings, refreshment cabinets, and so on—was figured walnut, generally with a high gloss finish.

Seat covering was usually of leather, although the rear seats might well be upholstered in Bedford cord, or West of England cloth. The chauffeur's seat was nearly always leather, as this was easier to clean. Truly exotic coachwork, such as that favoured by some Maharajahs, might include silk-covered upholstery, silk-brocade loose covers, and mahogany interior panelling with a satin veneer inlaid by mother-of-pearl, not to mention fittings in solid gold or silver. This kind of body could cost up to £4,000, bringing the total cost of the car to £6,000, while a more normal price for a custom body was between £700 and £1,000. Not all of the exotic examples went to the East. The Clark body on a Rolls-Royce Phantom I commissioned by a director of Woolworth's had a Louis XIV interior, with hand-painted door panels and ceiling, and Aubusson *petit point* upholstery. The latter alone cost £600.

The viability of the coachbuilding trade depended on a dedicated and highly skilled work-force, many of whom had learned their crafts in the days of horse carriages. Until 1930 or so, they could not command more than £3–4 per week. As wages rose in the next decade, the coachbuilding firms would resort to mechanical substitutes as far as was possible. But in the "golden age", quality had to be human, and there were fourteen crafts which a coachbuilder needed to know before he could call himself a master craftsman. These were as follows:

pattern making and setting out
wood machining
body making
panel beating
coach smithing
brass working
fitting and vicing
brushing
varnishing

coach joining (with
  interior cabinet
  work, distinct from
  body making)
French polishing
trimming (upholstery,
  leatherwork)
electrical work
heraldic painting

(Opposite) The only company to make a continuing success of the V-16 engine was Cadillac, who introduced their 7.4-litre 185-bhp overhead-valve unit for the 1930 season, and sold an average of 500 per year for eight years. Later, they brought out a new shorter-stroke V-16 with cylinders banked at 135°, which was made until 1940. This is a 1931 Series 452, with town car body designed by its British owner, Peter Hampton.

(Above) The first series of "factory-recommended" bodies on any Rolls-Royce were those designed by Ivan Evernden, to be built by Barker on the Twenty chassis from 1923 onward. They included a tourer, limousine, and coupé, and were made in series of about twenty per year. This is a drophead coupé of 1925.

Heraldic painting was a very specialized craft, and it would have been possible to be a master coachbuilder without acquiring this skill.

The genuine one-off custom body, built to the purchaser's own demands, was always a fairly rare beast. However, details of the interior fittings, dashboard, and so forth, could be varied to the owner's wishes. Most customers needed some guidance in the design of their coachwork, so the coachbuilders would have pattern books with a great variety of suggested designs. When the Rolls-Royce Twenty appeared in 1923, a number of standard or recommended bodies were made by Barker, to the design of Ivan Evernden of Rolls-Royce. This was the first time that a series of almost identical bodies was made by a major coachbuilder, but it did keep the cost down. A touring body cost only £490 and a limousine £600. Added to the Twenty's chassis price of £1,100, this meant that one could have a complete Rolls-Royce for under £1,600, compared with nearly £3,000 for a Silver Ghost with a more individual body. The "recommended" body was adopted by several other coachbuilders, including Vanden Plas on touring Bentleys in the 1920s, and Park Ward on saloon Bentleys and Rolls-Royces in the 1930s.

Many coachbuilders were at work in the 1920s, from the leading firms with an international reputation, down to small provincial companies which also built bodies for trucks, buses, and horse-drawn carrier's carts, although the latter very seldom worked on the top-class chassis. Of the major houses, Britain had three undisputed leaders: Barker, Hooper, and H. J. Mulliner, followed closely by Park Ward, Rippon, and James Young.

In France, the top coachbuilding firms were Binder, Chapron, Kellner, Labourdette, and Letourneur et Marchand. Germany had her own masters with Erdmann & Rossi, Gläser, Neuss, and Papler. The principal American makes were Brewster, Brunn, Derham, Locke, and Willoughby. Many of these, both in Britain and abroad, were quite old-established companies. Rippon dated back to the days of Queen Elizabeth I, and Barker to 1710 when it was founded by an officer of Queen Anne's Guards. The oldest coachbuilder in America, Brewster, opened its doors in 1810, and was later acquired by Rolls-Royce of America.

Yet few of the automotive artists survived World War II, and not one is in business today as a builder of motorcar bodies. This might show either that their tradition is lost, or that others have taken it over, according to one's faith in the future of cars!

ADVERTISING 10

The advertising industry and the automobile grew up side by side, and each was a major stimulus to the other, certainly from the 1920s onwards. Both were made possible by modern trends in technology, ranging from mass communications to engine design—and both were to serve a new consumer society, by satisfying more than the plain necessities of life that had concerned older forms of propaganda and transportation. When motorcars first appeared towards the end of the nineteenth century, advertising was in a very elementary and unsophisticated state, and was largely concerned with presenting facts in a basic, though often wordy, fashion. This had to change radically when such a strange, yet potentially popular, invention as the automobile arrived.

Early car advertising developed mainly in the United States. Several themes run through it, particularly the reassurance that the car was easy to handle, would not explode or rush away, and could be compared favourably to a horse. Some typical early claims were:

"A woman can operate it conveniently and with perfect safety."
   (Toledo Steam Carriage, 1901)
"Ladies and children can readily understand its mechanism."
   (Oldsmobile, 1903)
"Our car is so simple that a child can operate it."
   (Monarch, 1905)
"All of the Mechanism is so simple that the boy of the family can operate it." (Rambler, 1905)

A patronizing tone towards women merely reflected general attitudes, but manufacturers soon understood the wife's important role in the final choice about a car. She may not have had the purchasing power, but she had plenty of persuasive influence.

The superiority of the car over the horse was an obvious keynote, and was laboured in countless advertisements. Oldsmobile announced:

"This graceful and practical automobile will do the work of six horses at an average cost of thirty-five dollars a year (10,000 miles). Board alone for one horse costs $180 a year, so the economy is very evident. The Oldsmobilist has the satisfaction of knowing his machine is always ready."

Some of the "Passing of the Horse" advertisements seem rather to arouse sympathy for the horse: one showed a young lady stepping into her Rauch & Lang electric car, watched by a sorrowful steed, and was entitled "Jilted". Perhaps the horse had the last laugh, for the country road winding away in the background would not have been very suitable for that most urban of vehicles, the electric brougham. The horse definitely survived the steam car, despite the Grout Steam Wagon advertisement which displayed an equine skeleton with the words: "These animals were used until about the year 1901." Grout themselves stopped making steamers four years later!

Before long, advertising was aimed not so much at the horse owner, as at the man who had no personal transport whatever. Thus, in 1910: "Can you afford to be without Everyman's Car—the Brush Runabout?" However, customers were thought to be sufficiently versed in technicalities to appreciate the detailed advertisement by 1910: "There are 112 parts of the Cadillac 30 which are accurate to one thousandth of an inch." Unconventional designs such as the two-stroke engine were explained thoroughly even in 1908: "The Car That Has No Valves—let us tell you the vital points about the Elmore valveless two-cycle engine."

Some advertisements were oriented to dealers rather than retail purchasers, and were necessarily more technical. In 1912, Marion preceded its detailed specifications by an encouragement: "Here is a car you can sell with the confidence and certainty that the sale does not entail a burden of attention and subsequent cost." Many early advertisements, although addressed primarily to the customer, carried a message on the lines of "Good Dealer Agents Wanted in a Few Localities" (Lambert, 1907), or the more general "Agents Needed Everywhere" (Buick, 1905).

The impact of sport

Another favourite theme which emerged quite early was that of sporting successes. In 1906, Buick listed not only their triumphs in hill-climbs, but the names and prices of cars they had defeated. A few years later, this would have seemed a dubious practice, which was not to be revived until the 1970s, and then only with such items as fuel consumption and luggage space. Marmon, in 1910, cited their own victories in racing and record-breaking, a win being added the next year in the first Indianapolis 500-Mile Race. Stutz adopted the slogan "The Car That Made Good in a Day" after their performance in this 1911 race. Trumpeting "500 Miles in 442 Minutes—The Amazing Record of a Model Car", they neglected to mention the actual position of Stutz in the race, an unremarkable 11th out of 22.

By the 1920s, advertising tended to concentrate more on long-distance runs by production cars than on racing. "Seven Days Without a Stop", crowed Packard in 1925, referring to the 3,965-mile (6,380-

Patentirt in allen Industriestaaten!

Neu!   **Praktisch!**

Patent-Motorwagen

mit Gasbetrieb durch Petroleum, Benzin, Naphta etc.

Immer sogleich betriebsfähig! — Bequem und absolut gefahrlos!

Vollständiger Ersatz für Wagen mit Pferden.
Erspart den Kutscher, die theuere Ausstattung, Wartung und Unterhaltung der Pferde.

Lenken, Halten und Bremsen leichter und sicherer, als bei gewöhnlichen Fuhrwerken. — Keine besondere Bedienung nöthig. Sehr geringe Betriebskosten.

Patent-Motorwagen mit abnehmbarem Halbverdeck und Spritzleder.

von

BENZ & Co.

Rheinische Gasmotoren-Fabrik

MANNHEIM.

Neue Fabrik: **Waldhofstrasse.**

(Opposite) This advertisement for the Benz three-wheeler dates from 1888 or 1889, and is probably the world's earliest attempt to address a market for a motor vehicle. The announcement at the top, that the design was patented in all industrialized countries, was a warning to imitators rather than an attraction to purchasers.

Apparently the first advertisement for a British car was given by this proud announcement (above) from the Great Horseless Carriage Company Ltd, in May 1896. The nobility and gentry would have been disappointed if they had responded at once, for no British-built Daimler was available until 1897. Still, the drawing is a pretty accurate rendering of what an 1897 Daimler would look like, with its tiller steering and dos-à-dos body. The graphics, and particularly the hands pointing out the illustration, are typical of late nineteenth-century advertising.

DISPENSE WITH A HORSE

and save the expense, care and anxiety of keeping it. To run a motor carriage costs about ½ cent a mile.

THE WINTON MOTOR CARRIAGE

is the best vehicle of its kind that is made. It is handsomely, strongly and yet lightly constructed and elegantly finished. Easily managed. Speed from 3 to 20 miles an hour. The hydrocarbon motor is simple and powerful. No odor, no vibration. Suspension Wire Wheels. Pneumatic Tires. Ball Bearings. ☞ *Send for Catalogue.*

Price $1,000. No Agents.

THE WINTON MOTOR CARRIAGE CO., Cleveland, Ohio.

The Winton Motor Carriage Company of Cleveland, Ohio, was among the first in America to build cars in series for sale, and by 1898 they were running regular advertisements in magazines such as *Scientific American*. Their car *(above)* is still described as a motor carriage, although by this date Alexander Winton had already introduced the word "automobile" to the American language.

In contrast to the wordiness of the Daimler advertisement, manufacturers on the Continent often preferred to let the picture speak for itself. Some very fine art had been produced for advertising bicycles, and the tradition passed on to the motorcar. F.I.A.T. made only eight cars in 1899, the year of this ad *(opposite)*, so it was more of an attention-grabber than a proper sales effort.

km) nonstop Los Angeles–New York drive by a flying ace, Linton Wade. A year later, Studebaker announced "Another victory in the conquest of time and space" when a racing driver, Ab Jenkins, crossed the continent in 86 hours and 20 minutes.

Sometimes the record-journey angle was backed up by a personal testimonial, usually from a famous racing driver. "My Marmon Surely Stands the Gaff", says Barney Oldfield in 1923, as he "Crosses Continent Eight Times" according to a headline. In England, record-breakers like Malcolm Campbell and George Eyston frequently endorsed cars and accessories. However, this was to be more a feature of the 1930s, when the Land Speed Record fever was at its height.

Manufacturers had an ambivalent attitude to large-scale production. On the other hand, it implied an important, solid firm, and not a fly-by-night concern. There was also the suggestion that 100,000 buyers couldn't be wrong. But exclusiveness had its charm as well, particularly when aiming at a wealthy market. "Only 15 cars of this type will be built for 1907", said Apperson of their Jackrabbit roadster, although these were perhaps all they could sell at $5,000 each. Similarly, one heard "Only two Ohio cars a day", and "Springfield—the Made to Order Car for 300 Exacting People."

Away from nuts and bolts

Edward S. (Ned) Jordan is often credited with initiating the movement away from technicalities and specifications, toward "atmospheric" advertising. Yet in fact, this trend emerged a good six years before the first Jordan car was built. Pierce-Arrow were probably the first to leave behind all wordy paragraphs, letting the picture speak for itself. They, or rather their agency Calkins & Holden, employed a variety of well-known artists—including Edward Borein, Louis Fancher, the brothers Joseph and Frank Leyendecker, Adolph Treidler, and Newell Conyers Wyeth. The ads showed Pierce-Arrow cars in elegant settings: at the opera, at the aviation meet, or in foreign cities such as Nuremberg.

One of the most famous of these, by Treidler, displayed a lady pulling on her gloves in an elegant hall. A footman held open the front door, through which just a small portion of the car was visible. Such understatement, which is possible only for a company already well-established, reached its peak in the 1929 Duesenberg advertisements. They showed traditional figures of power and wealth—the yachtsman at the helm of his own craft, the lady giving instructions to her gardener—with the caption "He/She Drives a Duesenberg", and not a car in sight.

The rise of the copy-writer

The other route away from nuts and bolts was pursued by companies which elevated the copy-writer in the same manner as Pierce-Arrow exalted the artist. In 1915, Cadillac produced their philosophical piece "The Penalty of Leadership". Packard, in similar vein, offered a quotation from the English art-critic John Ruskin. Then came Ned Jordan, of whom it would not be unfair to say that his advertising copy is more famous than his cars. These were always assembled machines, not really much better than countless other makes fighting for a share of the market in the 1920s, although their bodies had more style than many.

But the ads were something else. Jordan had been writing his own copy since he founded his company in 1916, but he really came to the public's attention with his advertisements for the Playboy model. The most famous of these was "Somewhere West of Laramie", which appeared in the *Saturday Evening Post* in June 1923. Others which have

THE MICHIGAN

SOME POINTERS
ABOUT THE
Michigan Automobile.

A Finished Product.

A Strong Hill Climber.

Air cooled motor —nothing to freeze.

Easily Controlled.

New Tires very cheap compared to larger cars. Carries two persons easily —plenty of room.

Easy to learn to handle.
Costs but little to run it.
Cheaper than horses.
Runs easily twice as fast.
Never gets tired.

Perfectly practical on ordinary roads.
Goes and comes back.
Frequently called "a beauty."
Made of the best materials.
Highest mechanical skill.

And the Price, only $475

Manufactured by

Michigan Automobile Company, Ltd.
Kalamazoo, Mich., U. S. A.

In complete contrast to the artistry of F.I.A.T. is the down-to-earth piece put out by Michigan, far across the Atlantic, in 1903. The listing of its qualities and superiority to the horse was typical of early American car advertising. There is perhaps a hint of its limitations in "Perfectly practical on ordinary roads." The phrase "Goes and comes back" is not so naive as one might think, for one could not take it for granted that every car would make a return journey, even if it had worked faultlessly on the way out. The Michigan Automobile Company made about 100 of these light 3.5-hp cars in 1903, its first year. Production ended in 1908, but a descendant of the firm makes the well-known Fuller transmissions for heavy trucks.

passed into history include "The Port of Missing Men", "A Golden Girl from Somewhere", "A Million Miles from Dull Care", and "I Think She Came From a Land of Fire". They were very short indeed on nuts and bolts, while "Missing Men" did mention 24.1 miles per gallon (11.6 litres/100 km). The emphasis was fully on romance, outdoor boys and girls, and—above all—escapism. One ad ran:

"I am sick of four walls and a ceiling. I have business with the sunshine and the summer wind. I am weary of dishes and doctors—I am tired of going to stores and helping with meals. I am going somewhere if it is the last thing I ever do in my life. Give me a Blue Silhouette Jordan—summer days—uncluttered hours—mountains—landscape—far silhouette plains—freedom—relaxation—moonlight on the open road. . ."

Jordan's advertisements also gave promise of pleasures that were frowned upon in a highly puritanical America. "After the dance—when tiresome chaperones have gone to bed—and youth will have its fling—let's wander away." This one got by, but then a Jordan illustration for "The Port of Missing Men" showed a Playboy parked outside a house, in which the only light was a pale red spot of colour behind a bedroom curtain. It brought down the wrath of the powerful Society for the Prevention of Vice, and the ad appeared with no lights at all in the house.

Practically every one of Jordan's advertisements displayed his cars against a romantic or exotic background, and this belonged to a general trend from about 1915 onward. Previously, apart from the pioneering work of Pierce-Arrow, cars were shown as photographs against a plain, cut-out background. But suddenly the cars began to be seen in settings of parkland, stately homes, polo clubs, yacht marinas, or dreamy foreign locations such as the Taj Mahal. Bore and stroke, prices and wheel-bases were out, replaced by elitist copy on such lines as:

"Those who are distinguished for their Owen Magnetic Motor Cars are strict individualists, though not bizarre. Their town and country houses, their gardens, all their possessions are far from the commonplace. And so, when it comes to a car, they insist on getting away from the monotonous. Up and down the Avenue, or at the Opera, or at the Country Club—wherever the world of fashion congregates—certain cars distinguish the vivid personalities from the drab." (Owen Magnetic, 1919)

Or:

"While the great mass of automobile users still employ the motorcar merely as a means of getting about, there are those who seek to express in the equipages they own, something of the finer impulses and of the finer ideals that guide them in the choosing of their friends and of their homes." (Premier, 1920)

Women and advertising

The earliest references to women in car advertisements were of the patronizing variety mentioned above. Even as late as 1916, these were being used to boost sales to men. Liberty, after listing the many ways in which a Six suited a woman's sensitivity and lack of muscle, went on: "If a woman can drive the Liberty without effort—all day and every day—think how the Liberty must respond to a man's control."

This Lyons-Knight advertisement from April 1914 continues the theme of wordy argument, treating the customer as someone who needs to be persuaded by reason rather than swayed by emotion, as Ned Jordan was to do a few years later. In fact, this one is aimed more at the prospective dealer than the retail customer, although doubtless Lyons-Atlas would have been happy to pick up a few buyers as well.

Lyons-Knight
"The Car of Silence"

Just Three Reasons

Here are three out of hundreds of reasons that are influencing dealers in securing the Lyons-Knight agency:—

(1) The makers have one of the world's greatest automobile plants—are backed by unlimited capital and are leaving nothing undone to make this proposition a success.

(2) The car itself, with finest Knight motor, worm drive and many other distinctive features, offers the greatest of values at any price. The line also includes a smaller four-cylinder Knight car, a six-cylinder Knight car and commercial cars, meeting every class of trade.

(3) The dealer's proposition is by far the most liberal offered by any reliable manufacturer. It includes substantial profits for every Lyons-Knight dealer.

Already many of the most important cities are taken by prominent and well-established dealers. They are without exception men of years of experience, who have quickly realized the opportunities of this great proposition.

Your territory will be closed just as soon as we find the right dealer. There are going to be good profits for the Lyons-Knight dealer right in your town. If you will write us for particulars we will gladly show you hundreds of other reasons why this is true.

Lyons-Knight Features

50 horse power silent Knight engine—the finest power plant ever made.

Silent, smooth, efficient worm drive.

130 inch wheel base with 37 x 5 inch tires, non-skid in rear, on quick-detachable, demountable rims.

Full-floating rear axle, strong, flexible springs, ample brakes.

Left-hand drive, center control.

Extra complete equipment, with electric starting and lighting system, patent one-man top with drop side curtains and every other refinement.

Price—Five-Passenger Touring Car—$2900; Seven-Passenger Touring Car—$2980.

Value unequaled.

Ask for our Advance Catalog and "Proofs of the Lyons-Knight" today

Lyons-Atlas Company
Indianapolis : Indiana

Dealers

HERE'S a real opportunity! A four—with beauty, finish, speed, power, endurance—everything a car should have,

—built in one of the finest factories in Michigan, and backed by a wide-awake, progressive organization with real money and lots of it.

The Olympian has handsome double cowl lines, 114-inch wheel base, cantilever rear springs, full floating rear axle, and factory equipment that includes a spot-light, bumper, motometer and ignition lock.

The Olympian is second to no four-cylinder car within hundreds of dollars of its price class.

We want good wide-awake dealers to handle this car in every city and town of the United States. They must be men capable of handling a big business and handling it well.

Such men should make big money in the Olympian. The car wins immediate and lasting popularity the day it is introduced.

Listen—*We furnish more sales prospects to our dealers than any other automobile manufacturer in the business.* We help you right from the word GO.

OLYMPIAN

Let us explain our proposition and our plans—present and future. They will surely interest you.

Communicate with us today. We advise immediate action. Territory will go quickly. This chance is too good to lose. Better wire!

OLYMPIAN MOTORS COMPANY
PONTIAC, MICHIGAN

PRICE
$965
F·O·B·FACTORY

214

(*Opposite*) More blatantly dealer-oriented is this effort from Olympian Motors in 1917. No modesty here, false or otherwise, from a company which built a very ordinary assembled car that lasted only four years. It is unlikely that territory went as quickly as Olympian hoped. Most of the country probably never had an Olympian dealer at all.

Pierce-Arrow placed advertisements of high quality in exclusive magazines such as *Country Life in America*. This one (*right*), which appeared in the December 1912 issue, is by Frank X. Leyendecker (1877-1924). The domed roof, a favourite Pierce-Arrow design at the time, was known as a vestibule suburban.

The PIERCE-ARROW differs from other cars in three ways—in its engine, in its body and in the way the two are combined to make the most thoroughly artistic, comfortable, and dependable car ever built.—The Pierce-Arrow Motor Car Co. Buffalo

The Penalty of Leadership

IN EVERY field of human endeavor, he that is first must perpetually live in the white light of publicity.

Whether the leadership be vested in a man or in a manufactured product, emulation and envy are ever at work.

In art, in literature, in music, in industry, the reward and the punishment are always the same.

The reward is widespread recognition; the punishment, fierce denial and detraction.

When a man's work becomes a standard for the whole world, it also becomes a target for the shafts of the envious few.

If his work be merely mediocre, he will be left severely alone—if he achieves a masterpiece, it will set a million tongues a-wagging.

Jealousy does not protrude its forked tongue at the artist who produces a commonplace painting.

Whatsoever you write, or paint, or play, or sing, or build, no one will strive to surpass or to slander you unless your work be stamped with the seal of genius.

Long, long after a great work or a good work has been done, those who are disappointed or envious, continue to cry out that it cannot be done.

Spiteful little voices in the domain of art were raised against our own Whistler as a mountebank, long after the big world had acclaimed him its greatest artistic genius.

Multitudes flocked to Bayreuth to worship at the musical shrine of Wagner, while the little group of those whom he had dethroned and displaced argued angrily that he was no musician at all.

The little world continued to protest that Fulton could never build a steamboat, while the big world flocked to the river banks to see his boat steam by.

The leader is assailed because he is a leader, and the effort to equal him is merely added proof of that leadership.

Failing to equal or to excel, the follower seeks to depreciate and to destroy—but only confirms once more the superiority of that which he strives to supplant.

There is nothing new in this.

It is as old as the world and as old as the human passions—envy, fear, greed, ambition, and the desire to surpass.

And it all avails nothing.

If the leader truly leads, he remains—the leader.

Master-poet, master-painter, master-workman, each in his turn is assailed, and each holds his laurels through the ages.

That which is good or great makes itself known, no matter how loud the clamor of denial.

That which deserves to live—lives.

After "Somewhere West of Laramie", the most famous car advertisement ever created was surely Cadillac's "The Penalty of Leadership"—a complete breakaway from nuts-and-bolts advertising, with its wordy philosophy and its assumption that the reader would be familiar with the names of Whistler, Wagner, and Fulton. Packard's 1914 ad also follows a philosophical theme, but the reader gets a picture as well.

ALL works of taste must bear a price in proportion to the skill, time, expense and risk attending their invention and manufacture. Those things called dear are, when justly estimated, the cheapest. They are attended with much less profit to the artist than those which everybody calls cheap. A disposition for cheapness and not for excellence of workmanship is the most frequent and certain cause of the decay and destruction of arts and manufactures. —RUSKIN

Packard 2-38 Coupe

Ask the man who owns one
PACKARD · MOTOR · CAR · COMPANY · DETROIT

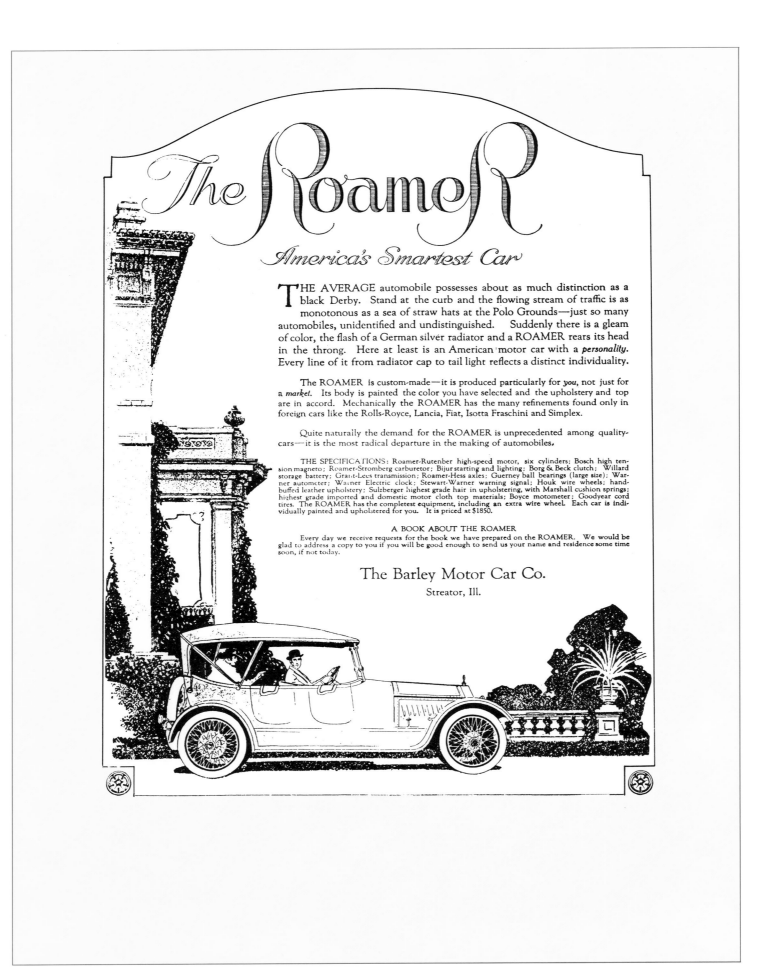

The Roamer

America's Smartest Car

THE AVERAGE automobile possesses about as much distinction as a black Derby. Stand at the curb and the flowing stream of traffic is as monotonous as a sea of straw hats at the Polo Grounds—just so many automobiles, unidentified and undistinguished. Suddenly there is a gleam of color, the flash of a German silver radiator and a ROAMER rears its head in the throng. Here at least is an American motor car with a *personality*. Every line of it from radiator cap to tail light reflects a distinct individuality.

The ROAMER is custom-made—it is produced particularly for *you*, not just for a *market*. Its body is painted the color you have selected and the upholstery and top are in accord. Mechanically the ROAMER has the many refinements found only in foreign cars like the Rolls-Royce, Lancia, Fiat, Isotta Fraschini and Simplex.

Quite naturally the demand for the ROAMER is unprecedented among quality-cars—it is the most radical departure in the making of automobiles.

THE SPECIFICATIONS: Roamer-Rutenber high-speed motor, six cylinders; Bosch high tension magneto; Roamer-Stromberg carburetor; Bijur starting and lighting; Borg & Beck clutch; Willard storage battery; Grant-Lees transmission; Roamer-Hess axles; Guerney ball bearings (large size); Warner autometer; Warner Electric clock; Stewart-Warner warning signal; Houk wire wheels; hand-buffed leather upholstery; Sulzberger highest grade hair in upholstering, with Marshall cushion springs; highest grade imported and domestic motor cloth top materials; Boyce motometer; Goodyear cord tires. The ROAMER has the completest equipment, including an extra wire wheel. Each car is individually painted and upholstered for you. It is priced at $1850.

A BOOK ABOUT THE ROAMER

Every day we receive requests for the book we have prepared on the ROAMER. We would be glad to address a copy to you if you will be good enough to send us your name and residence some time soon, if not today.

The Barley Motor Car Co.

Streator, Ill.

From around 1915 onward, there arose a fashion for advertising the exclusiveness of a car. This Roamer ad from 1916 *(opposite)* is fairly typical—the customer is asked for "name and residence" rather than the everyday "name and address" of lesser mortals. In fact the Roamer was not an especially remarkable car, and the closest it came to a Rolls-Royce was the shape of its radiator, which was a direct copy. However, the Barley Motor Car Company were not ashamed to admit that they made an assembled product, listing the origins of their engines, transmissions, axles, and so on.

One day in June 1923, Ned Jordan was travelling with a lawyer friend in his private railroad car across the plains of Wyoming. As the train pulled out of a small station, a beautiful girl on a spirited stallion rode up alongside the carriage and gave chase. Jordan, who was no mean horseman himself, was fascinated. "Where are we now?" he asked his friend. "Oh, somewhere west of Laramie," came the yawning reply. These words, and the view from the window, were music to Jordan, who pulled out a piece of paper and took a few minutes to write down the most famous advertising copy in automotive history. It was published in *The Saturday Evening Post* for June 23, 1923—but as late as the 1950s, Jock Ogilvy, of the prominent advertising firm Ogilvy & Mather, asked every junior copywriter to learn it by heart *(right)*.

With a radiator closely modelled on the Minerva from Belgium, it was logical for the Moon company in St. Louis, Missouri, to choose the name of another ancient goddess when they launched the Diana in 1925 *(page 220)*. Even more appropriate was the fact that Diana was a goddess of the moon itself, as well as of hunting. This ad is aimed particularly at women, although other Diana ads did not always feature women in their copy or illustrations.

Somewhere West of Laramie

SOMEWHERE west of Laramie there's a broncho-busting, steer-roping girl who knows what I'm talking about. She can tell what a sassy pony, that's a cross between greased lightning and the place where it hits, can do with eleven hundred pounds of steel and action when he's going high, wide and handsome.

The truth is—the Playboy was built for her.

Built for the lass whose face is brown with the sun when the day is done of revel and romp and race.

She loves the cross of the wild and the tame.

There's a savor of links about that car—of laughter and lilt and light—a hint of old loves—and saddle and quirt. It's a brawny thing—yet a graceful thing for the sweep o' the Avenue.

Step into the Playboy when the hour grows dull with things gone dead and stale.

Then start for the land of real living with the spirit of the lass who rides, lean and rangy, into the red horizon of a Wyoming twilight.

JORDAN MOTOR CAR COMPANY, Inc., Cleveland, Ohio

DIANA

THE·LIGHT·STRAIGHT·EIGHT

POWER

BALANCE

ENDURANCE

SPEED

EASY TO START
EASY TO STEER
EASY TO STOP

Tamed, harnessed, *under the thumb* —easy to start, steer, park and stop —Diana Eight's appeal to women is irresistible. They can't shut their eyes to it, can't disregard it. Diana was *engineered* for women to drive. And here are results they sense, see, feel and want. ¶ *Diana engineers won't go back.* They have burnt their bridges behind them, have definitely committed themselves to a design that fits the needs of the greatest potential market — women—and in pleasing women, they cater to all. ¶ Diana is the *Light* Straight Eight for 1926, sturdy, enduring, dependable—a pioneer of daring ideas and new-day performance. Its sensational sweep has stumped the industry. A great engine with every power advantage, eager to go, alive,

WOMEN BUYERS
OUTNUMBER MEN
15 TO 4

alert—73 horsepower with a flexibility of from 2 to 77 miles an hour. Acceleration, 5 to 25 miles an hour in 6½ seconds. The Lanchester Dampener positively eliminates vibration, blots it out. And the torque is the *smoothest*. The lighter and more frequent explosions stop the jerking at low speeds, stop the complaints from the rear seat. The entire chassis is designed and built for balloon tires. The brakes are 4-wheel hydraulic. But more than a new-day engineering achievement, Diana is the outstanding *coup d'état* since the self-starter came into use. ¶ Come, now, get into this great car, try it out. Make the hills and the rough your proving ground. That's where the Diana *Light* Eight shows her heels, takes the lead and holds it.

"THE EASIEST·STEERING CAR IN AMERICA"

Roadster $1895   *Phaeton* $1895   *Standard Four-Door Sedan* $1995   *Cabriolet Roadster* $2095   *Two-Door Brougham DeLuxe* $2095   *Four-Door Sedan DeLuxe* $2195   *F. O. B. St. Louis*
Built by the MOON MOTOR CAR COMPANY for the DIANA MOTORS COMPANY · Stewart McDonald, *Pres.*, St. Louis, U. S. A.

ON NE DÉPASSE PAS
LA 12 CH.
HOTCHKISS
USⁱⁿᵉˢ & Bᵉᵃᵘˣ 6 ROUTE DE GONESSE
Sᵀ DENIS.
MAGASINS D'EXPOSITION
CHAMPS ÉLYSÉES 154.

Three French advertisements with the stylized drawings which were popular between the wars, especially for the better-known makes of car whose manufacturers did not need to use hard-sell tactics. The Egyptian theme in the 1924 Voisin ad *(page 221)* reflects the interest shown in the recent discovery of Tutankhamen's tomb. The 1924 Hotchkiss *(left)* and 1931 Panhard *(opposite)* drawings are by the well-known artist Alexis Kow. The car being left behind by the Hotchkiss is not a Rolls-Royce, but looks very like a Sizaire Frères.

SUPÉRIEURES PAR LA SOUPLESSE DE
LEUR MOTEUR INDÉRÉGLABLE SANS SOU-
PAPES-SURBAISSÉES DONC PLUS STABLES
D'UNE SILHOUETTE PLUS SÉDUISANTE
SPACIEUSES-SEULES MUNIES DE 4 VITES-
-SES SILENCIEUSES: 6 CS-6 DS-8 DS

PANHARD

PARIS

(*Opposite*) Ansaldo was a medium-sized quality car from Italy in much the same class as the Ballot or Delage. This colourful advertisement from 1924 hints at the mountaineering qualities associated with many Italian cars, which were bred within easy reach of the Alps. The drawing is more realistic than those of Alexis Kow, but the driver and passengers seem to be the usual midgets beloved of advertising artists.

(*Right*) From midgets to giants—this advertisement for Bosch magnetos typifies some German marketing of the period shortly before, and after, World War I. The international use of the Bosch magneto is clearly depicted in the car radiators: from left to right, France, United States, Italy, Great Britain, and Germany.

Much car advertising before World War II was aimed at encouraging the man to buy a car for the little woman, rather than directly at the ladies. An anxious Chevrolet company inquired in 1921:

"Is Your Wife Marooned During the Day? The Chevrolet Utility makes an ideal extra car. The wife finds it of everyday utility for shopping, calling, taking the children to school in bad weather, etc."

Shopping and calling were activities particularly associated with the electric car, and this was very much the province of the woman driver. "Make this the Happiest Christmas—Give Your Wife an Electric", urged the Electric Vehicle Association of America in 1912. But the Waverley company thought that she might just as well give herself one: "A party of friends in your electric carriage adds much to the pleasure of your calling or shopping excursions." Not that Waverley wanted the public to believe there was anything unmanly about electric cars. In another advertisement, also of 1912, they stated that "Men and women—and *more* men than women—are buying this car."

A further theme often stressed was the role which women's intuition, and unerring sense of taste, played in the selection of a car. In 1913, the Cole Motor Company of Indianapolis advised: "Leave comfort, convenience and beauty lines to *her*—she is leaving the price and mechanical correctness to *you*." Cole even prepared two catalogues, the Technical Bulletin for him and the Blue Book for her. Other variations on this theme were provided by Pullman and Columbia. The former captioned the photo of their 1915 De Luxe Coupe: "Tailored for Her Majesty the American Woman". And what was more:

"The De Luxe Coupe instantly appeals to a woman. She realizes the personal touch that has been given it. Its interior comfort may only be equalled in her own home."

Columbia, in 1919, were claiming that women liked their Six because it was ". . .beautiful in lines, finish and in those niceties of equipment and furnishings which mean so much to the feminine mind." The ad went on, rather ingenuously:

"Because women, in so many cases, have the final say in the purchase of a car, Columbia dealers find the warm friendship between women and the Columbia Six a big sales asset."

In the 1920s, women were wooed from all sides of the price range. Ford was predictably down to earth in 1924:

"Through her dealings as business manager of the home, the modern woman brings sound commercial sense to bear on her judgement of a Ford closed car."

On the other hand, Rolls-Royce of America appealed to fashion consciousness in 1929:

"Little nothings, the French call them—but they're everything to a motorcar. Your gloves, your bag, your scarf, *ces petits riens*. But what big 'little nothings' they are. They can make or mar a costume. They simply must be right. Years ago, Rolls-Royce learnt this lesson from women and applied it to motorcars."

Yet women's lack of mechanical ability or interest was still stressed by some advertisers: "She knows little, nor need she, of the lifetime care and conscience engineers have dedicated to the nice simplicities of mechanism about her" (Paige, 1923). "If You *Really* Want Your Wife to Drive, telephone your Chandler dealer" (1924). Ned Jordan, who claimed to know Eve as well as any man, observed: "Engineer's language is fine and dandy if you're selling locknuts . . . but Eve doesn't give a hoot about locknuts."

The European flair

Fewer trends were set by advertising in Europe, much of which was pretty verbose and uninspired. However, in France, the Art Nouveau movement was seen in advertisements for cycles and motorcars from the 1890s onward. During the 1920s and 1930s, artists such as Geo Ham and Alexis Kow were hired to produce stylized drawings of cars. These did not even pretend to be accurate renderings, but were very strong on atmosphere. This was in contrast to the "stretched" cars, occupied by miniature people, which were found in many American ads and catalogues in the Thirties.

In Germany, advertising often carried Wagnerian overtones, with giants in seven-league boots looming over the automobiles in an alarming fashion, or towering mountains and apparently bottomless gorges above which a car made its way along a narrow ledge. These were in the nature of dramatic attention-grabbers, rather than providers of information, and the practical-minded customer was persuaded to write for a catalogue or to visit his dealer.

"When in doubt, list your maharajahs" was the automotive historian Michael Sedgwick's phrase for the custom of listing prominent owners. This was favoured by makers of luxury cars such as Napier, which mentioned customers ranging from dukes, earls, and Oriental magnates, down to plain "Misters" who happened to be very rich. The fashion had largely passed by the 1920s, although the British agent for Packard offered an impressive list in the 1939 catalogue. The custom was to be revived by Rolls-Royce in the 1980s with a roster of hundreds of well-known owners, past and present, in a series of advertisements in *The Times* of London.

The closest European equivalent to Ned Jordan's type of prose came, surprisingly, from the little Jowett company, which built utilitarian two-cylinder light cars in Bradford, Yorkshire. These were barely sold at all in the south of England until the mid-1920s. Yet, in 1925, the firm came up with the following:

"Step on the pedal, my master; the town's behind, the steep hill ahead. We've broken bounds, we're free. Ahead the dale and the stream, pinewood and hill. For us the zest of the wind on the heights, the gleam on the placid lake. . . So step on the pedal; gently—for I shall respond to your lightest wish, almost to your very thoughts. And so—softly over the hill in the sunset glow—home with the stars tonight."

Such lyricism had few imitators in the Old World. The Thirties were to break further away from the traditional nuts-and-bolts advertising, yet it was not with carefully written text, but toward greater stylization in graphics. And what else but the "picture worth a thousand words" could show the contemporary public that a car had at last become, in many ways, worth a thousand horses?

This must be one of the first Volvo advertisements to appear, published in the Swedish *Motorjournalen* during 1927. The conversion of the seats into a double bed was a feature which Nash, in America, would boast as an innovation ten years later. The "System Ström" mentioned in the first paragraph—named after the chief of Volvo's coachbuilding department—was a type of Weymann body construction, with leather on a padded wooden frame.

DEN SVENSKA BILEN

Volvos täckta vagn

har utförts enligt "System Ström" d. v. s. den är utvändigt klädd med konstläder på vadderad trästomme.

Därigenom uppnås låg vikt, låg tyngdpunkt samt frihet från resonans. Vagnen blir därigenom utomordentligt tystgående och behaglig att köra.

Framsätena äro förskjutbara i förhållande till ratt och pedaler samt nedfällbara bakåt, varigenom 1 eller 2 liggplatser kunna anordnas. Därigenom blir den synnerligen lämplig till långfärds- och campingvagn samt alldeles särskilt som läkarevagn.

VOLVO

Koffert ingår i standardutrustningen och priset är endast kr. 5,800:— fritt Göteborg

BIBLIOGRAPHY

As the Veteran, Edwardian, and Vintage periods have been respectable subjects among automotive historians for some time, we have more material than was available to Michael Sedgwick for his masterly volumes covering the years from 1930 onward.

Of the general books with a technical slant and highly readable style, there is nothing to beat the late Anthony Bird's *Early Motorcars*, originally published by Allen & Unwin, London (1967), and reissued by Treasure Press of London under the title *Antique Automobiles* (1984). The inimitable Mr. Bird took the story no further than 1914, but the vintage period has been comprehensively surveyed by Tim Nicholson in *The Vintage Car* (Batsford, London, 1966). This same author was responsible for most of the little colour books published by Blandford Press beween 1970 and 1975. In seven volumes (the last by Michael Sedgwick), these cover touring, sports, and racing cars from 1863 to 1942, with short entries on no fewer than 648 cars in all.

There are many useful national surveys and, for the early history of the motorcar in Britain, Tim Nicholson's monumental three-volume *The Birth of the British Motor Car* (Macmillan, London, 1982) cannot be faulted. A most helpful general book on the American industry is *The American Car Since 1775* (Dutton, New York, 1971), with its various chapters on the pioneers, on coachbuilding, and on the growth of the industry with production figures of the leading makes from 1896 to 1970. Would that similar figures were available for European cars!

A little-known but invaluable survey of the American car in the 1920s is *The Cars of 1923*, by Keith Marvin and Arthur Lee Homan, published privately in 1957. John Bentley's two volumes on American cars, *The Old Time Automobile* (to 1915) and *Antique Automobiles* (1915 to 1925), published by Fawcett Books, Greenwich, Connecticut, in 1952, provide much useful information on companies, as does the same author's *Old Time Steam Cars* (Fawcett, 1953). A series of books which did much to arouse nostalgia about the American automobile were Floyd Clymer's Motor Scrapbooks, published in Los Angeles between 1944 and 1955. These compilations of period advertisements contain a vast amount of useful information. Two books devoted specifically to advertising are *Advertising and the Motor Car*, by Michael Frostick and Ashley Havinden (Lund Humphries, London, 1970), and *Any Colour So Long As It's Black* by Peter Roberts (David & Charles, Newton Abbot, 1976).

Good histories of European national industries include *Les Automobiles Suisses des Origines à nos Jours* by Ernest Schmid (Editions des Château de Grandson, 1967) and *Histoire de l'Automobile Belge* by Jacques and Yvette Kupelian (Paul Legrain, Brussels, 1982). Werner Oswald's *Deutsche Autos 1920-1945* (Motorbuch Verlag, Stuttgart, 1981) is a marvellously thorough and comprehensively illustrated work.

The progress of coachbuilding, from horse-drawn days onward, is well covered in *Cars and Coachbuilding* by George Oliver (Sotheby Park Bernet, London, 1981). There is an enlightening chapter on the subject in *The Thoroughbred Motor Car* by David Scott-Moncrieff (Batsford, London, 1963). For a beautifully produced account of one man's life in coachbuilding, there is nothing to rival *Un Siécle de Carrosserie Française* by Jean-Henri Labourdette (Edita, Lausanne, 1972).

The social history of motoring had been largely neglected before the appearance of *Automania*, the book of the television series by Julian Pettifer and Nigel Turner (Collins, London, 1984). Although much of the book is inevitably devoted to the period after 1930, it contains plenty of interest on the early days as well.

Finally, there are the numerous one-make histories. Besides providing a great deal of detail which is inaccessible elsewhere, the better historians offer important perspectives on their periods as a whole. Among the one-make books that I have found particularly valuable are the following:

Bird, Anthony and Hutton-Stott, Francis. *Lanchester Motor Cars* (Cassell, London, 1965)

Dumont, Pierre. *Peugeot—Sous le Signe du Lion* (EPA, Paris 1976)

Langworth, Richard M. and Robson, Graham. *Triumph Cars* (Motor Racing Publications, London 1979)

Oswald, Werner. *Mercedes-Benz Personenwagen 1886-1984* (Motorbuch Verlag, Stuttgart, 1984)

Robson, Graham. *Magnificent Mercedes* (Haynes, Yeovil, 1981)

Sedgwick, Michael. *Fiat* (Batsford, London, 1974)

Sedgwick, Michael. *Vauxhall, a Pictorial History* (Dalton Watson, London, 1981)

Weernink, Wim Oude. *La Lancia* (Motor Racing Publications, London, 1979)

Many other works have been consulted for this book, including contemporary magazines such as *The Autocar, Automotor Journal*, and *Motor Car Journal*. Among the more recent publications, there are many excellent articles to be found in L. Scott Bailey's superb *Automobile Quarterly*.

INDEX

Page numbers in italics indicate illustrations.